Riding the Wave

WORLD BANK EAST ASIA AND PACIFIC REGIONAL REPORTS

Known for their economic success and dynamism, countries in the East Asia and Pacific region must tackle an increasingly complex set of challenges to continue on a path of sustainable development. Learning from others within the region and beyond can help identify what works, what doesn't, and why, in the search for practical solutions to these challenges. This regional flagship series presents analyses of issues relevant to the region, drawing on the global knowledge and experience of the World Bank and its partners. The series aims to inform public discussion, policy formulation, and development practitioners' actions to turn challenges into opportunities.

TITLES IN THE SERIES

Riding the Wave: An East Asian Miracle for the 21st Century

Live Long and Prosper: Aging in East Asia and Pacific

East Asia Pacific at Work: Employment, Enterprise, and Well-Being

Toward Gender Equality in East Asia and the Pacific: A Companion to the World Development Report

Putting Higher Education to Work: Skills and Research for Growth in East Asia

All books in this series are available for free at https://openknowledge.worldbank.org /handle/10986/2147

World Bank East Asia and Pacific Regional Report

Riding the Wave

An East Asian Miracle for the 21st Century

WORLD BANK GROUP

Contents

Boxes

Figures

Tables

Foreword

Developing East Asia and Pacific has led the way in showing how rapid and broadly shared growth can lift millions out of poverty. Over the past quarter century, the wave of prosperity that has spread across the region has meant that almost a billion people are no longer mired in extreme poverty. Sixty percent of its citizens are now economically secure in that they do not face the risk of falling back into poverty. In most countries, a sizable middle class has emerged and is growing rapidly.

However, there is no guarantee that inclusive growth—growth that reduces extreme poverty while delivering upward mobility and economic security for all—is assured, even for the countries of this successful region. While the region is now composed entirely of middle-income countries, its diversity has increased. Progress in reducing poverty and vulnerability and in promoting mobility has varied across countries. Extreme poverty, although limited, is now increasingly concentrated among specific groups, such as ethnic minorities and those in remote locations. Roughly one-fifth of the region's population remains at risk of falling into poverty, with this proportion especially high in Indonesia and the Philippines. Prospects for upward mobility are seen as increasingly elusive across

the income distribution, reflecting the growing concentration of income and wealth at the top, as well as limited access to basic services, often of poor quality, even among the middle class. Newer challenges—such as rapid aging in countries such as China, Thailand, and Vietnam—and uncertain growth prospects, especially among the region's lower-middle-income countries, are making it more difficult to ensure economic security for all.

Riding the Wave discusses how countries across the region can effectively confront these challenges to inclusive growth. In doing so, it looks at those who live in the region through the lens of economic class, ranging from the extreme poor at the bottom of the distribution to the middle class (which includes the rich) at the top. This partition, in turn, helps provide a nuanced view of how the income distribution has evolved in various countries so as to highlight their policy priorities in ensuring inclusive growth.

Riding the Wave underscores how, beyond reducing poverty, upward economic mobility (improving one's lot in life) and economic security (being able to hold on to the gains made) are key features of inclusive growth. The report illustrates how the constraints to securing upward mobility differ across economic classes. For some segments, such as the remaining extreme poor, the key challenge is very much about achieving mobility or moving up the distribution. For other classes, such as the vulnerable, the constraint that needs to be addressed is about enhancing economic security so that they do not fall back into poverty. For those who are economically secure or part of the middle class in these countries, enhancing their access to quality public services is the key.

The report outlines how policy makers in countries across East Asia need to approach these challenges in a selective and prioritized manner. The three pillars it highlights for policy are fostering economic mobility, enhancing economic security across economic classes, and strengthening the capacity of the state to deliver.

Although the relative emphasis across pillars and the policy details will differ across countries, many elements will be common. To promote economic mobility, addressing gaps in access to jobs and services, improving the quality of jobs, and deepening financial inclusion are important. To provide

more economic security will require a focus on strengthening social assistance systems, expanding social insurance, and increasing resilience to systemic shocks. For the state to be better able to deliver on this agenda for inclusive growth will require relying more on progressive taxation to raise public resources, promoting fairer competition, making inclusive spending programs more effective, adapting to the pressures of rapid aging, and fostering efficient urbanization.

This policy agenda, while ambitious, could form the basis for a new social contract that will allow governments in this region to address the needs of all groups in their populations while remaining fiscally responsible in the face of an uncertain global environment. Success in ensuring inclusion will mean that developing East Asia and Pacific can lay claim to another miracle well into the 21st century.

Victoria Kwakwa
Regional Vice President
East Asia and Pacific Region
The World Bank

Acknowledgments

This report is a joint product of the Office of the Chief Economist, East Asia and Pacific Region and the Poverty and Equity Global Practice. It was authored by Caterina Ruggeri Laderchi, Nikola Spatafora, Sudhir Shetty, and Salman Zaidi, with the guidance of Axel van Trotsenburg and Victoria Kwakwa, Regional Vice Presidents, East Asia and Pacific, and Ana Revenga and Carolina Sanchez-Paramo, Senior Directors of the Poverty and Equity Global Practice at the time of the report preparation.

The report synthesizes the work of a larger World Bank team that included Andrew Beath, Wendy Cunningham, Reno Dewina, Carolina Diaz-Bonilla, Samuel Freije-Rodriguez, Christoph Lakner, Nancy Lozano-Gracia, Ririn Salwa Purnamasari, Matthew Grant Wai-Poi, and Andrea Woodhouse. In addition, major contributions to the background work were made by Sarah E. Antos, Brendan Brian Brady, Dorothee Buhler, Imogen Cara Halstead, Leander Heldring, Yumeka Hirano, Alejandro Huertas, Taufik Indrakesuma, La-Bhus Fah Jirasavetakul, Vera Kehayova, Jae Kyun Kim, Chun Kuan, Barbara Parker, Obert Pimhidzai, Manohar Sharma, Yan Sun, Pham Thu Trang, Michele Tuccio, Ikuko Uochi, Daniel Walker, Darendhra Wardhana, Laura Wijaya, and Judy Yang.

Additional background notes were produced by Travers Barclay Child of Vrije Universiteit Amsterdam, Carol Graham of the Brookings Institution and the University of Maryland, College Park, and Soumya Chattopadhyay of the Overseas Development Institute in London; Erwin Tiongson and Madita Wiese from Georgetown University; and Hai-Anh Dang and Sebastian James from the World Bank. Mildred Gonsalvez and Cecile Wodon provided invaluable administrative and logistical assistance.

The team benefited from valuable suggestions provided throughout the production process of this report, by colleagues both within and outside the World Bank Group. Special thanks for their participation in an inception workshop goes to Caroline Freund of the Peterson Institute, Ricardo Fuentes-Nieva of Oxfam International, Ravi Kanbur of Cornell University, Homi Kharas of the Brookings Institution, and Erwin Tiongson of Georgetown University, together with Shubham Chaudhuri, Uwe Deichmann, Indermit Gill, Andrew D. Mason, Ana Revenga, Carolina Sanchez-Paramo, Carlos

Silva-Jauregui, and Renos Vakis from the World Bank. Several World Bank colleagues provided guidance and advice at different stages of the process, including Judy Baker, John Giles, Tobias Haque, Steve Jaffee, Somik Lall, Branko Milanovic, Nataliya Mylenko, Ambar Narayan, Philip O'Keefe, Douglas Pearce, Bob Rijkers, Emmanuel Skoufias, Mauro Testaverde, and Rogier van den Brink.

Professor Hal Hill of the Australian National University, Dr. Somchai Jitsuchon of the Thailand Development Research Institute, Professor Shantong Li of the Development Research Center, State Council, China; and Gabriel Demombynes and Aart C. Kraay from the World Bank were peer reviewers. Comments were also received during the review process from Valerie Kozel of the University of Wisconsin–Madison; and from James Anderson, Rocio Castro, Ted Chu, Chorching Goh, Camilla Holmemo, and Tara Vishwanath from the World Bank Group.

The team is also very grateful to Alejandro Cedeno-Ulloa and Livia Pontes-Fialho from the World Bank's East Asia and Pacific External Relations group for their assistance with the outreach and dissemination. Mary Fisk and Patricia Katayama provided excellent advice and guidance on the publication process.

The cover was designed by Debra Naylor, Washington, DC. The graphics were designed by Kristen Dennison. Andrew Johnston and Publications Professionals edited and copyedited the report, respectively.

The team also thanks others who have helped prepare this report and apologizes to those who may have been overlooked in these acknowledgments.

Abbreviations

BPS	Central Bureau of Statistics (Indonesia)
EAP	East Asia and Pacific
ECA	Europe and Central Asia
ECD	early childhood development
ECED	early childhood education and development
FDI	foreign direct investment
FIBOS	Fiji Island Bureau of Statistics
FIES	Family Income and Expenditure Survey (the Philippines)
GDP	gross domestic product
GEP	growth elasticity of poverty
HIES	Household Income and Expenditure Surveys
HIS	Household Income Survey (Malaysia)
HSES	Household Socio-Economic Surveys (Mongolia)
IMF	International Monetary Fund
LAC	Latin America and the Caribbean
LECS	Lao Expenditure and Consumption Surveys
LICs	lower-income countries
LMICs	lower-middle-income countries
LPI	Logistics Performance Index
MNA	Middle East and North Africa
MS	Master Sample
MSF	Master Sampling Frame
NSO	National Statistics Office
OECD	Organisation for Economic Co-operation and Development
PICs	Pacific Island countries
PNGHS	Papua New Guinea Household Survey

PPP	purchasing power parity
PPS	Probability Proportion to Size
SAR	South Asia
s.d.	standard deviation
SEED	Save, Earn, and Enjoy Deposits
SES	Socio-Economic Survey (Thailand)
SMEs	small and medium enterprises
SSA	Sub-Saharan Africa
SUSENAS	National Socio-Economic Survey (Indonesia)
TLSLS	Timor-Leste Survey of Living Standards (second national)
TLSS	Timor-Leste Living Standards Survey (first national)
TOD	transit-oriented development
UCS	Universal Coverage Scheme
UMICs	upper-middle-income countries
VHLSS	Vietnam Household Living Standards Surveys
VIP	ventilated improved pit
VLSS	Vietnam Living Standards Survey
VoIP	voice over IP
WLL	wireless local loop

Overview

Introduction

The East Asian experience has come to symbolize how growth that is both rapid and broadly shared can improve the lives of millions of people.[1] Over the past two decades, a wave of rising prosperity lifted more than 40 percent of the region's population out of poverty. This remarkable experience reflected a growth model that has spread through much of the region over the past half century. Policies that aimed to promote labor-intensive growth and investments in human capital reduced poverty rapidly with little or no increase in inequality—the East Asian "miracle" of growth with equity. This approach was popularized by the 1990 *World Development Report* as the "two-and-a-half-point strategy" for poverty reduction (World Bank 1990). It emphasized two pillars—labor-intensive growth and the accumulation of basic human capital—while putting limited emphasis on a third pillar, social protection, which was seen as needed only by those too disadvantaged to participate in the growth process.

Riding the Wave is about sustaining this progress so that the lives of millions in the East Asia and Pacific region continue to improve despite the challenges that remain. Past success means that expectations are high that growth will continue to deliver unprecedented improvements in welfare. Current trends suggest that more deliberate policy efforts will be needed to meet such expectations.

Analytical approach

To identify a policy agenda to support inclusive growth in the region, this report adopts an analytical framework with three main features. First, it goes beyond a binary classification of the population into poor and nonpoor, offering instead a more nuanced discussion of the entire income distribution. Specifically, it separates households into five economic classes (figure O.1): the extreme poor, the moderate poor, the economically vulnerable (those at high risk of falling into poverty), the economically secure, and the middle class.[2] Second, this analysis of economic class and its evolution is used to highlight similarities and differences between countries. Countries are grouped into categories that reflect how their income distributions have evolved, to identify their policy priorities. Finally, the report adopts a specific definition of *inclusive growth*. Economic growth is characterized as inclusive if it reduces poverty and enhances economic mobility and security across all parts of the income distribution.[3]

FIGURE O.1 **Developing East Asia and Pacific, 2002–15: a wave of prosperity and the evolution of economic class in the region**

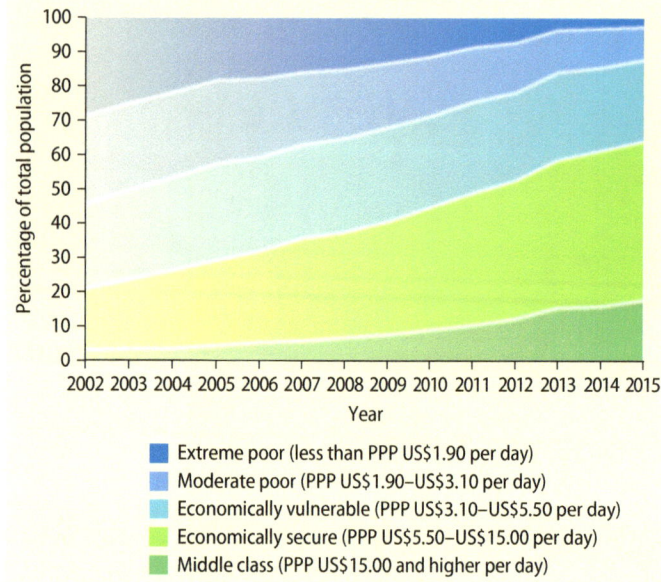

Note: PPP = purchasing power parity.

A look at the evolution of economic classes at the country level between 2002 and 2015 highlights three key facts (figure O.2). First, in 2015, the economically secure and the middle class in developing East Asia and Pacific accounted for nearly two-thirds of the region's population, a significant increase from their share of just over one-fifth of the population in 2002. Because of its size, China accounts for the largest proportion of the two classes. Compared with the regional average, China, along with Malaysia and Thailand, also has a proportionately larger share of its population in these two classes. This contrasts with the larger middle-income countries—Indonesia, the Philippines, and Vietnam—which all have a proportionately lower share of their populations in this group. Second, reflecting the rapid progress in reducing poverty across much of the region, the shares of the extreme and moderate poor have fallen dramatically—from more than half the population in 2002 to less than an eighth in 2015. China, Indonesia, and the Philippines together account for the bulk of this group, with the populations in the latter two disproportionately represented relative

to the regional average. Third, the share of the economically vulnerable has remained almost constant over this period, at roughly a quarter of the total population of the region. The populations in this class in China, Indonesia, the Philippines, and Vietnam are large. Indonesia and the Philippines stand out because their share of economically vulnerable in the population is much higher than average, whereas China's and Vietnam's are very close to the regional average.

The country groupings that emerge from looking at the evolution of economic classes between 2002 and 2015 include the following:

- *Progressive prosperity* countries (Malaysia and Thailand), which have eliminated income poverty while substantially increasing the share of middle-class households
- *Out-of-poverty-into-prosperity* countries (China, Mongolia, and Vietnam), where most people are at least economically secure and the middle class is growing
- *Out-of-extreme-poverty* countries (Cambodia, Indonesia, and the Philippines), where extreme poverty levels are low, but so are the shares of the middle class
- *Lagging-progress countries* (Lao People's Democratic Republic and Papua New Guinea), which still have high levels of extreme poverty
- *Pacific Island countries*, which are a heterogeneous group and are distinct from the rest of the region

The definition of *inclusive growth* used in this report allows it to focus on the constraints that are relevant to each economic class. In turn, this focus helps delineate the elements of a new social contract that could allow countries in the region to sustain inclusive growth. Such a focus on inclusive growth is motivated by the realization that the well-tested approach to "growth with equity" that the region has relied on will be more difficult to implement than in the past and will prove less successful in addressing the needs of many in the population.

For sustaining growth, export-oriented manufacturing appears likely to be a less

FIGURE O.2   Population distribution by economic class and country, 2002 and 2015

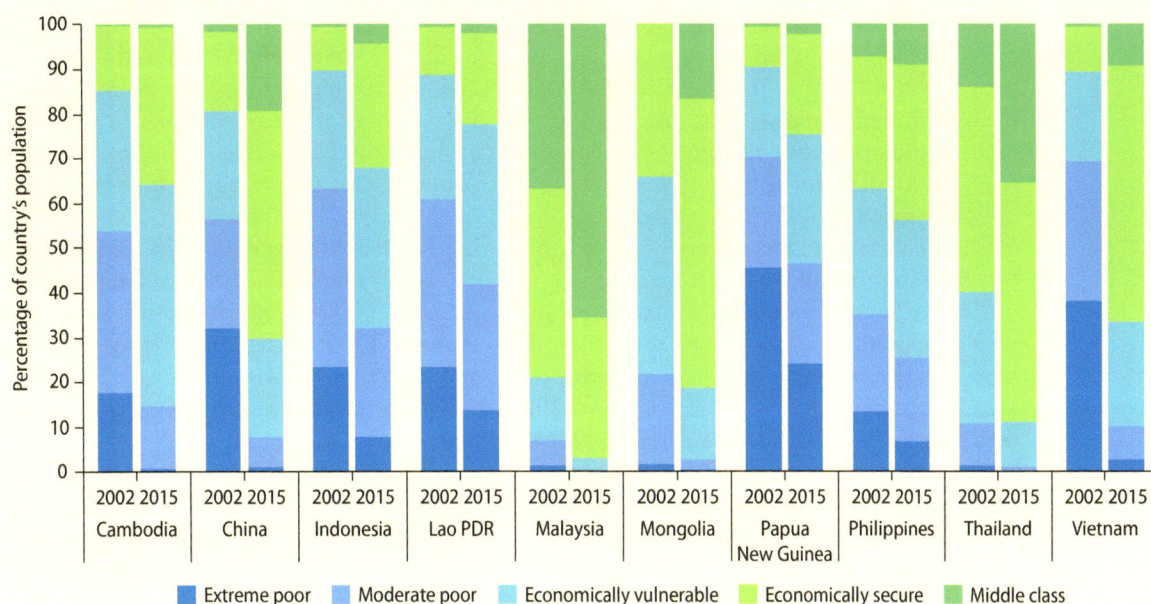

Source: World Bank EAP Team for Statistical Development.

powerful engine than in the past. For the first time since the early 2000s, growth in global trade has slowed below the pace of growth of countries' gross domestic product, and the potential for the region to integrate further through the development of new value chains is not clear. Lower-income countries also face continued competition from China, while they do not have access to some of the export-promoting measures used by countries that industrialized successfully in the past. Higher-income countries, despite their comparatively low wages, see manufacturing shift toward skilled labor and automation—developments that are unlikely to support broad-based growth unless they are well managed.

Adapting to longer-term trends such as the aging of the population and urbanization, which have been sources of opportunity in the past, might require further adjustments to the region's growth model. In the past, a large share of people of working age provided a demographic dividend that helped support the region's growth. In most countries, this demographic dividend will turn into a demographic tax on growth because

by 2025, the region's working-age population is expected to begin to decline. From a policy point of view, the key concern is that much of the region is "getting old before getting rich" (World Bank 2016, 9): social insurance systems have not developed enough and accumulated enough resources to cover the aged population with sufficient incomes to avoid poverty. Even where specific programs for the poorest elderly are provided, such as in China, program coverage will have to expand significantly given demographic trends.

Urbanization, which underpinned broad-based improvements in living standards for the early developers in the region—such as the Republic of Korea and Taiwan, China—and helped support an expansion of basic services, has now turned into a challenge for other economies. Rapid urban growth is being accompanied by growing congestion, environmental strains, and urban squalor because market and policy failures remain unaddressed. Urbanization can also increase exposure to natural disasters, because most large cities in the region are in low-lying coastal areas. Further, urbanization may erode traditional support networks, compounding the challenges posed by the aging populations and reducing living standards on both sides of the urban-rural divide. As people move to cities to take advantage of the opportunities and services that cities provide, and as the poor become increasingly concentrated in those urban areas, a key policy priority will be investing in cities to make them livable and effective sources of opportunities for all.

Recent developments have made groups such as migrants, the elderly, and the unskilled more vulnerable to shocks, while other groups are experiencing unprecedented affluence. In combination with challenges to the region's export-oriented development model, the trend helps to explain why inequality is seen to be rising and is indeed high in many countries. Those perceptions, even if not always borne out by the data, coincide with a sense that income and wealth are now becoming more concentrated in the hands of the wealthiest. As a result, upward income mobility—a hallmark of the East Asian development experience—is now seen to be more elusive, a perception that is reinforced by the gaps in service delivery, including in higher education and in water and sanitation.

A final challenge to the sustainability of the existing model of broad-based growth is that the region has become much more differentiated than it was even three decades ago. Economic success has transformed it from a region largely of poor people in low-income countries to a region of middle-income countries, each characterized to a varying extent by economic classes that range from the extreme poor to the middle class and the very wealthy. That reality makes it very hard to generalize about one model that can bring inclusive growth for all.

Securing upward mobility: removing the constraints to inclusive growth

Riding the Wave makes the case that beyond reducing poverty, upward economic mobility (improving one's lot in life) and economic

security (being able to hold onto the gains made) are defining features of inclusive growth. Indeed, perceptions of growing inequality are closely related to the sense that avenues for moving up are closing for those who are not already well placed. Although systematic evidence on mobility is hard to come by, this report builds on new longitudinal analysis based on data obtained following households over time, either panel data or approximations of panel data (synthetic panels).[4] This evidence covers the period from the early 2000s though the years covered vary, and the lengths of the panels vary by country.

Given developing East Asia and Pacific's high growth and rapid poverty reduction, it can be expected that most households experienced increases in income and that many experienced upward mobility across classes. The analysis confirms this upward mobility but also shows a lot of heterogeneity by country and economic class (figure O.3). Overall, households other than those in the middle class experienced increases in consumption. In addition, for at least one in five people, consumption increased so much that they moved to a higher economic class. That upward mobility appears to be higher in the longer term than in the short term, and it is generally higher than in Latin American countries for which comparable analysis exists. Nevertheless, some countries such as the Philippines saw little mobility.

Despite this good news, most households did not move across economic classes, and in all classes, some people moved downward. The downward mobility reflects both ex ante exposure to risks and limited ex post ability to manage adverse shocks, despite significant resilience. Shocks include economic shocks, which affect prices and returns to household assets such as labor or land or skills, personal shocks such as illness, and natural shocks. The moderate poor and the economically vulnerable are most likely to move down the class ladder when affected by shocks. Even the middle class, despite its relative affluence, faces risks. Conversely, the moderate poor who do not receive a shock are more likely than those who do to move up one or two

FIGURE O.3 Class mobility transition matrix, short run

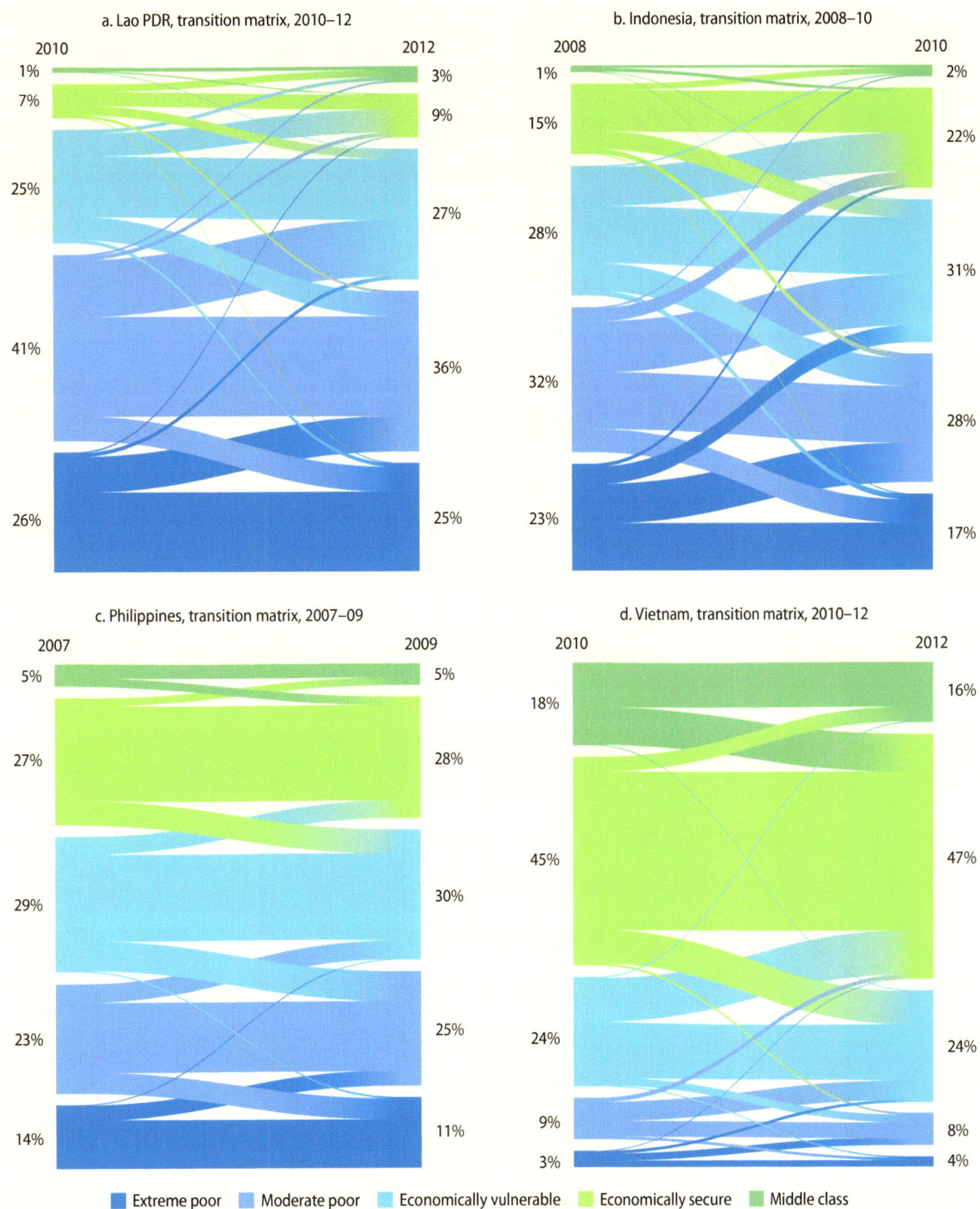

a. Lao PDR, transition matrix, 2010–12

b. Indonesia, transition matrix, 2008–10

c. Philippines, transition matrix, 2007–09

d. Vietnam, transition matrix, 2010–12

■ Extreme poor ■ Moderate poor ■ Economically vulnerable ■ Economically secure ■ Middle class

Source: Cunningham 2016.

classes over a two-year period. More detailed analysis, however, highlights a lot of resilience in the face of shocks, with even households affected by shocks capable of moving to a higher economic class. Ultimately what makes a difference is not whether households experience shocks, but whether they have the asset base they need to avoid sliding into poverty.

The policy tools countries need to secure upward mobility include helping households accumulate assets (for example, by investing in human capital or providing access to credit to invest in physical capital) and preventing the erosion of assets at times of crisis (for example, preventing children from being taken out of school to help sustain the family). Social protection can play a key role in this respect, by reducing poverty and offering all income groups a way of managing risks. Countries in the region differ widely in the range of social protection programs they have in place, and most are starting relatively late to put in place a modern social protection system. Thus they have an opportunity to learn from international experiences and to avoid pitfalls such as disincentives for beneficiaries to graduate from the programs (so-called welfare traps) and excessive taxation of labor incomes.

The key constraints to securing upward mobility for each segment of the income distribution are discussed below, focusing on one class at a time. For some classes, such as those stuck in extreme poverty, the challenge is very much about achieving mobility, whereas for others, such as the economically vulnerable, being able to secure what they have is as important as eliminating constraints to moving up.

The challenge of eliminating extreme poverty

The "last mile" challenge to eradicate extreme poverty can be seen as a special example of low mobility. Although extreme poverty is no longer a challenge for the region as a whole and for most countries, it remains concentrated in the poorer countries and, in some richer ones, among specific population groups, such as ethnic minorities and those in geographically remote areas. In 2015, the extreme poor accounted for less than 3 percent of developing East Asia and Pacific's population. However, the share of the extreme poor varies considerably across countries (figure O.4). In Lao PDR, Papua New Guinea, and the Solomon Islands, the extreme poor still make up a sizable share of the population. In other countries, specific groups or locations account for the bulk of the extreme poor. In Vietnam, for instance, ethnic minorities now account for more than two-thirds of the remaining extreme poor, most of them concentrated in remote and mountainous areas. The same is true in China, and the remaining poor in Indonesia tend to be concentrated in the remote regions of Papua and Kalimantan.

In East Asian countries where economic progress has been lagging, as well as in most Pacific Island countries, broad-based growth that creates demand for low-skilled labor and is complemented by investments to make people more productive will still be effective in eradicating extreme poverty. But where extreme poverty is associated with characteristics such as ethnicity and remote location, growth alone is unlikely to reduce poverty in all its dimensions.

FIGURE O.4 **Extreme poverty in selected countries in East Asia and Pacific, US$1.90-a-day purchasing power parity (PPP), 2015**

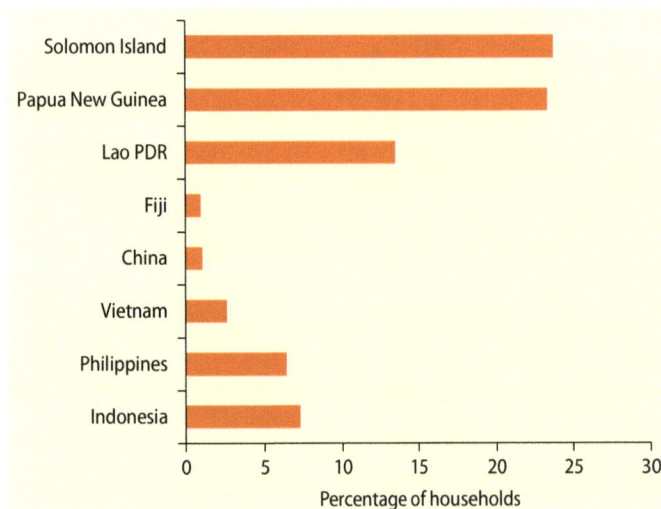

Source: World Bank EAP Team for Statistical Development.
Note: See appendix A for details on the sources.

Addressing the last-mile challenge of eradicating extreme poverty requires identifying and tackling the barriers that prevent specific groups in the population from benefiting from the economic opportunities available to the rest. Such barriers can differ by context and group and can include physical barriers, such as when communities are not served by an all-weather road; administrative barriers, such as when isolated communities face high costs to obtain documents such as birth registrations; legal barriers, such as when unregistered migrants cannot access services; and cultural barriers, such as when there is prejudice or outright discrimination toward ethnic minorities.

The challenge of transitioning to economic security for those living close to the poverty line

Despite the wave of prosperity that has reshaped the region since 2002, about one-quarter of the population continues to be economically vulnerable (figure O.1). Such households face a high likelihood of falling back into poverty, and they have only limited ability to move to economic security, especially over the short run.

This group is not static, however, because a lot of movement occurs across the moderate poverty line in both directions. For example, in Indonesia, 21 percent of those considered economically vulnerable in 2008 were found to be in moderate poverty in 2010, whereas 35 percent of the moderate poor climbed into the economically vulnerable class. In the Philippines, between 2007 and 2009, 22 percent of the economically vulnerable fell into moderate poverty, while 17 percent of the moderate poor climbed above the poverty line to become economically vulnerable. In Vietnam, between 2010 and 2012, only 7 percent of the economically vulnerable slid into moderate poverty, and 46 percent of the moderate poor became economically vulnerable (Cunningham 2017). Longer-term mobility estimates for Indonesia and Vietnam show that slippages from the economically vulnerable group to the moderate poor were more

muted over a 10-year span, compatible with an overall upward trend in incomes over time.

The economically vulnerable also show many signs of dynamism. For example, they have the ability to save to purchase small assets, such as cell phones or motorcycles. And most of this group's employment is through small and medium-size enterprises, where they are often the entrepreneurs. This group is clearly resourceful in the face of missing public goods: in Indonesia's slums, for example, they have organized early warning systems for flooding to make up for the deficiencies in those provided by the government.

The lack of services and of systematic mechanisms to manage risks or cope with the consequences of shocks hinders this group's progress, however. They struggle with a low asset base, including limited education and scarce productive assets, because they lack mechanisms to save for bigger items. Where they are concentrated in rural areas, but often also in urban ones, they suffer from poor health because of the lack of quality health services and limited access to public infrastructure. Weaknesses in the business climate, including insecure property rights and limited access to electricity and other infrastructure, constrain their businesses from expanding. And in many countries, women's participation in the labor force is particularly low among the moderate poor and economically vulnerable, in part because women's domestic labor compensates for the lack of services such as clean water, childcare, and eldercare.

The challenge of matching economic security with high-quality public services

The economically secure and middle classes, which have both grown considerably across the region in numbers as well as in population share, are at low risk of sliding back into poverty. In many countries, however, their economic security has not been accompanied by appropriate provision of public services, let alone high-quality services, in contrast with what has happened in other parts of the world at similar income levels. Despite improved income, health, and education outcomes, one-third of the region's economically secure and 15 percent of its middle class (outside of China) lack access to one or more of the following services: good quality housing, clean water, and to a lesser degree, modern sanitation (figure O.5).

Similarly, in countries where risk management tools are underprovided, even the middle classes are at risk of sliding down the income ladder. Although the middle classes benefit from the social protection measures such as health insurance and pensions that often come with secure jobs, they are not immune to systemic shocks. In Thailand's floods in 2011, for example, 70 percent of the estimated US$47 billion of the damages and losses were in the manufacturing subsector, in which many middle-class workers are employed.

Countries that fail to deliver on some of these classes' needs and priorities risk their turning to an insular world of private service provision. They may be disengaging from the national policy dialogue on service delivery at a time when their higher aspirations could spur improved quality of services. Across countries and at different levels of development, there are already signs that such opting out may be beginning. The middle classes, in particular, are relying significantly on private health care and to a lesser extent on private primary and junior secondary education.

On some issues, however, the middle classes have proved to be powerful catalysts for change. Their push for better consumer safety regulations and better goods and services can benefit all households. For instance, recent food safety scandals in China have led to stronger regulations and better products for all. In addition, given these groups' own vulnerability to shocks, they could have a stake in developing an appropriate system for managing risks.

The elements of a new social contract to underpin inclusive growth

An extraordinary wave of prosperity has improved the lives of millions across East Asia over the past half century. To sustain that success and address the new challenges that have emerged, governments need to address the constraints that different groups in the population now face. *Riding the Wave* identifies a selective policy agenda with three pillars: fostering economic mobility, providing greater economic security, and strengthening the institutions required for inclusive growth.

Fostering economic mobility will require an agenda that focuses primarily on three areas:

- *Addressing existing gaps in access to jobs and services* by reducing barriers to female labor force participation and simplifying or eliminating regulations for obtaining identity documents that are needed to access services or government programs.
- *Improving the quality of jobs available* by defining property rights over agricultural land more clearly and securely, reducing regulatory barriers to rural-urban mobility,

FIGURE O.5 **Nonmonetary poverty by class, 2012**

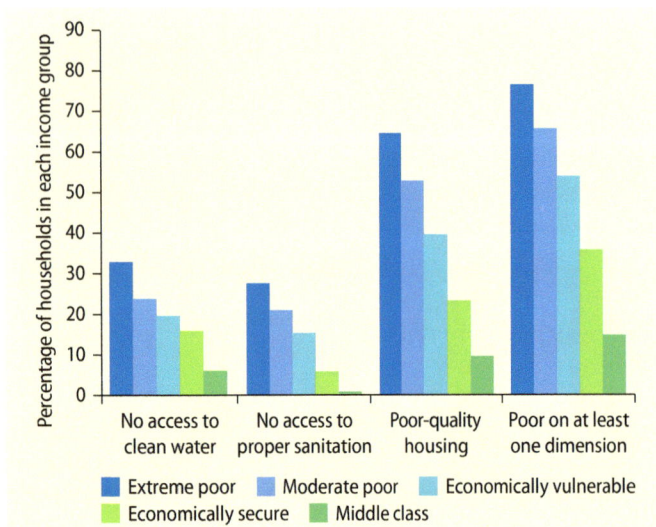

Source: Wai-Poi and others 2016.
Note: Access to clean water denotes piped water, a protected well, or water sold by a vendor. Access to proper sanitation denotes a flush toilet or an improved pit latrine. Good housing quality means the roof is concrete, cement, brick, stone, wood, or tiles; the walls are concrete, cement, brick, or stone; the floor is nonsoil. The sample includes Cambodia, Indonesia, Lao PDR, Mongolia, the Philippines, Thailand, and Vietnam.

improving rural connectivity, and easing the process of formalization for microenterprises and small-scale firms.

- *Furthering financial inclusion* by strengthening legal and regulatory frameworks that balance financial stability, integrity, and inclusion; improving information flows needed to assess creditworthiness and by expanding financial literacy, especially for those at the lower end of the economic spectrum.

Providing greater economic security will call for a focus on strengthening social assistance and social insurance and on increasing resilience to large systemic shocks:

- *Strengthening social assistance* by introducing cash transfer programs (conditional or not) in the lower-income and lower-capacity countries where they do not yet exist and better targeting existing programs to the population groups that remain overrepresented among the extreme and moderate poor.
- *Strengthening social insurance* by expanding more systematically the coverage of measures to help households across the income distribution insure against idiosyncratic risks (such as through pension schemes) while reducing their fragmentation to promote labor mobility; and by expanding the revenue base to sustain the system's expansion.
- *Increasing resilience to large systemic shocks* by complementing household-level risk management measures with country-level mechanisms for managing risks ex ante (such as market-based crop insurance) and coping with them ex post (such as adaptive or scalable safety nets).

Strengthening the institutions required for inclusive growth will involve focusing on several aspects:

- *Mobilizing resources through progressive taxation* by strengthening personal income taxation, including by broadening the tax base, reviewing marginal tax rates, and eliminating the preferential treatment of capital income; by establishing effective property taxes; and by enhancing tax administration.
- *Increasing the effectiveness of pro-inclusion spending programs* by creating better management tools, including social registries (that is, databases of individuals and their socioeconomic situations) and improved targeting mechanisms.
- *Leveling the playing field* by boosting competition, reducing opportunities for capture in the more regulated sectors of the economy, and tackling nepotism and corruption.
- *Adapting to population aging* by supporting lifelong learning to upgrade workers' skills throughout the life cycle, eliminating incentives for older workers to retire too early, opening up aging labor markets to greater inflows of young immigrants, and adapting the health sector to the challenges of aging, including the increased incidence of noncommunicable diseases.
- *Promoting efficient urbanization* by supporting efficient land use in cities of all sizes and by strengthening urban governance to improve service delivery and urban infrastructure, including by improving coordination between different levels of government and different jurisdictions.

The policy agenda will need to be tailored to each country's circumstances because not all the pillars are important for each of the economic classes. For the previously identified country typology, the following priorities may be identified:

- *For lagging-progress countries*, accelerating poverty reduction is the priority. Key policy actions in countries such as Lao PDR and Papua New Guinea should focus, first, on reducing poverty more quickly—by strengthening basic education and financial inclusion, removing barriers to labor reallocation from agriculture to more productive sectors, and tackling obstacles that prevent the marginalized from accessing public services. Second, policies should focus on helping the vulnerable manage the impact of shocks by strengthening social assistance and investing in making economies more resilient to disasters.

- *For out-of-extreme-poverty* countries, the priority is securing progress and fostering upward mobility, while tackling the remaining pockets of extreme poverty. Cambodia, Indonesia, and the Philippines have reduced levels of extreme poverty to single digits. Unlike other countries that now enjoy low levels of extreme poverty, however, the size of the middle class is also in the single digits. The priorities for these countries, therefore, should reflect the needs and aspirations of a diverse population, spanning those in moderate poverty, the vulnerable, and those in economic security. Integrating existing social assistance programs into a stronger social protection pillar is a key priority in these countries, with strengthening mobility a close second. Improving mobility will be particularly important in the Philippines, where the distribution has been static until recently. Given the size of their populations, however, Indonesia and the Philippines cannot neglect the large numbers of extreme poor to which they are still home. These countries need to identify and remove the very specific constraints the extreme poor face in accessing economic opportunities and service delivery.

- *For out-of-poverty-into-prosperity* countries, the priority is removing the remaining vulnerabilities while meeting the needs and aspirations of the middle class. In China and Vietnam, sustained poverty reduction has led to the emergence of a middle class. The first priority is to reduce residual vulnerabilities, including among rural households and groups with special needs (in China, the elderly and children left behind when their parents migrate; in Vietnam, ethnic minorities). The second priority, which is increasingly important, is to meet the needs and aspirations of the middle class. Simultaneously, these economies must prepare for rapid aging.

These priorities require improving the access of migrants to public services, enhancing pension systems in a sustainable manner, and ensuring high-quality, cost-effective health care and education. In China, it is also critical to reform urban planning to promote efficient land use and environmental sustainability.

- *For progressive prosperity* countries, the priority is to satisfy the middle classes' growing aspirations while mobilizing resources to address remaining disparities. The richer countries, which include Malaysia, Mongolia (at a lower income level), and Thailand, have continued to move large numbers of the economically vulnerable into economic security, and they are now characterized by large middle (and rich) classes. The first priority is to satisfy the middle classes' growing aspirations and demands for quality public services, including health and education, which will support continued upward mobility. The second, and related, priority is to implement reforms that narrow rural-urban and cross-regional disparities in economic and social development in these three countries, which in turn will require increased or more efficient resource mobilization.

- *For the Pacific Island* countries, given their specificities, the inclusive growth agenda needs to be especially tailored. Because human resources will remain their principal resource, these countries' priorities for fostering economic mobility include using existing opportunities better, seeking access to international job markets, supporting managed urbanization, and improving agricultural productivity. Priorities to strengthen economic security include investing in disaster loss prevention, mitigation, and managing and improving health and other social programs. Finally, delivering on inclusive growth will require improving the effectiveness of public expenditures and service provision, addressing the challenges of remoteness, and mobilizing development aid.

Implementing this policy agenda will not be easy for any of these groups of countries, particularly in a global context that is likely to remain challenging. Nevertheless, this agenda could form the basis for a new social contract if governments address the priority needs of each economic class while they remain fiscally responsible. To accomplish that, countries must mobilize additional public revenues in an efficient and equitable manner. In so doing, the countries of developing East Asia and the Pacific could ride the wave of prosperity and continue to improve the lives of their citizens well into the 21st century.

Notes

1. Although this statement refers to a broad definition of East Asia and Pacific—comprising the developing countries of East Asia and Pacific, Japan, and the newly industrialized economies—this report's main area of interest is developing East Asia and Pacific that comprises Cambodia, China, Indonesia, Lao People's Democratic Republic, Malaysia, Mongolia, Myanmar, Papua New Guinea, the Philippines, Thailand, Timor-Leste, Vietnam, and the Pacific Island countries. Throughout this report, the Pacific Island countries comprise Fiji, Kiribati, the Marshall Islands, the Federated States of Micronesia, Nauru, Palau, Samoa, the Solomon Islands, Tonga, Tuvalu, and Vanuatu. Data are not available, however, for Kiribati, the Marshall Islands, Nauru, Palau, Samoa, and Tuvalu.

2. The economic classes are defined (in per capita daily consumption expenditures, in 2011 purchasing power parity) as follows: extreme poor—less than US$1.90; moderate poor—between US$1.90 and US$3.10; economically vulnerable—between US$3.10 and US$5.50; economically secure—between US$5.50 and US$15.00; and middle class—more than US$15.00.

3. The report does not refer explicitly to the concept of *shared prosperity* because the term is generally defined on a country-specific basis. The analysis focuses on the entire region rather than on country-by-country developments. Nevertheless, the concept of inclusive growth captures the broad intuition behind shared prosperity.

4. Synthetic panels rely on a methodology of matching households by time-invariant characteristics and their distributions across two comparable cross-sectional data sets. In other words, rather than following the same household over time as in a real panel, they match observed data in one survey with predictions based on the information contained in the second survey.

References

Cunningham, W. 2016. "Class Mobility." Background paper for *Riding the Wave: An East Asian Miracle for the 21st Century.* Washington, DC: World Bank.

Wai-Poi, M., R. Purnamasari, T. Indrakesuma, I. Uochi, and L. Wijaya. 2016. "East Asia's Rising Middle Classes." Background paper for *Riding the Wave: An East Asian Miracle for the 21st Century.* Washington, DC: World Bank.

World Bank. 1990. *World Development Report 1990: Poverty.* Washington, DC: World Bank.

———. 2016. *Live Long and Prosper: Aging in East Asia and Pacific.* Washington, DC: World Bank.

Introduction

Overview

East Asia's progress has come to symbolize how economic growth that is rapid and broadly shared can improve the lives of millions.[1] Since the late 1950s and early 1960s, a succession of economies has experienced the East Asian miracle—rapid economic growth that reduces poverty significantly, with little or no increase in income inequality. The initial success of the newly industrialized economies—Hong Kong SAR, China; Republic of Korea; Singapore; and Taiwan, China[2]—spread in the 1980s to Indonesia, Malaysia, and Thailand, as well as, most dramatically, to China. The poorer Southeast Asian economies of Cambodia, Lao People's Democratic Republic, and Vietnam have followed suit since the early 1990s.

A wave of prosperity has spread across East Asia. Today, three of five people can be considered economically secure in that they face a very low risk of falling into poverty. A solid middle class has emerged in most countries. But those successes do not guarantee inclusive economic growth—growth that reduces poverty and enables upward mobility and economic security for all. Economic progress varies from country to country, and extreme poverty is increasingly concentrated among specific groups. Roughly one-fifth of

the region's population remains at risk of falling into poverty. Upward mobility is increasingly elusive for people in all income groups. Such a decrease in mobility reflects a growing concentration of income and wealth, as well as limited access to basic social services, which are often of poor quality.

Riding the Wave is about sustaining the momentum of the East Asian miracle and continuing to improve the lives of millions—across all income groups—while taking into account their different needs. The report's main area of interest is developing East Asia and Pacific, taken to comprise Cambodia, China, Indonesia, Lao PDR, Malaysia, Mongolia, Myanmar, Papua New Guinea, the Philippines, Thailand, Timor-Leste, Vietnam, and the Pacific Island countries. Past performance has created expectations that growth will continue to deliver unprecedented improvements in welfare and economic security for all. But global and specific challenges—including less certain growth prospects, population aging, and urbanization—will make that task more difficult.

Structure of the report

This introduction presents methods and concepts used throughout the report, including a definition of inclusive growth, a classification of the East Asian population into economic classes, and indicative groupings of countries that are likely to face similar challenges in pursuing inclusive growth.

Chapter 1 examines the region's success in promoting broad-based growth. East Asia and Pacific's development model has resulted in spectacular improvements in living standards and human welfare, as well as prodigiously rapid economic growth compared with other regions. The chapter shows how that success was underpinned by policies that provided the enabling environment for rapid labor-intensive growth, combined with public spending on basic human capital—education, health, and family planning services.

Chapter 2 discusses concerns about the ability of East Asia and Pacific's development model to continue enhancing the welfare of all income groups. Inequality is high or rising in many countries. Large shares of the population increasingly perceive the deck to be stacked against them, with reduced opportunities for upward mobility. And emerging global and regional trends are making it more difficult to achieve and sustain high rates of broad-based growth built on export-oriented manufacturing.

Chapter 3 characterizes the region and its countries in different economic classes, thereby offering a more detailed picture of past progress in improving living standards. This characterization also provides a useful tool to describe the heterogeneity of countries in the region and the changing geography of extreme poverty. Across much of the region, extreme poverty is no longer a significant challenge. However, some countries, including Lao PDR, Myanmar, Papua New Guinea, and the Pacific Island countries, have not yet emulated the success of their peer countries in generating and sustaining rapid and broadly shared growth so as to reduce poverty significantly.

Chapter 4 builds on the characterization of economic classes to analyze the emerging challenges to inclusive growth faced by each income group. The chapter draws attention to several challenges that are common across classes and that will increasingly weigh on

countries' ability to deliver inclusive growth. For instance, every income group faces the risk of sliding back in regard to living standards but with different implications for different classes. That risk may intensify, given the regional and global trends discussed in this report.

Chapter 5 outlines a package of policies designed to tackle the emerging challenges to inclusive growth in developing East Asia and Pacific. The package rests on the two pillars of fostering economic mobility and increasing economic security. In addition, building the capacity to deliver inclusive growth emerges as a cross-cutting priority. Implementing such a policy package will help meet the needs of all economic classes, although each country will need to customize a package to its own circumstances.

New thinking for a new era: economic classes, country groupings, and inclusive growth

Many of the challenges that East Asia and Pacific faces are a by-product of its success. A region of mostly poor countries and poor people in the 1980s has become a region of middle-income countries with a diversity of economic class—from pockets of extreme poverty to a significant number of middle-class households. The specific needs of today's more economically diverse population require a different way of thinking about policy than what served the region so well in the past.

To capture the region's heterogeneity and how it has evolved, this report first introduces the partition of households into economic classes: extreme and moderate poor; economically vulnerable, defined as those at high risk of falling into poverty; economically secure; and the middle class.[3] This approach explicitly aims to avoid a simple dichotomy between poor and nonpoor, which would blur some of the most important developments the region has witnessed over the past two decades. From a methodological viewpoint, the classification aims to strike a balance between relying on well-established indicators, such as the international poverty line of $1.90 per day (based on purchasing power parity) and grounding the economic classes in observed patterns, such as the likelihood of falling into poverty (see chapter 3).

Characterizing the region by economic class has the advantage of throwing into stark relief some of the features that countries share, and that is the second aspect of this report's analysis. The report presents five groupings of East Asia and Pacific countries, based on common features. These groupings are not expected to do justice to all country-level specificities but rather to introduce more nuanced messages than could emerge from a simple regional overview, especially with regard to policies. The five groupings are as follows:

- *The progressive prosperity countries* (Malaysia and Thailand), which have eliminated income poverty while substantially increasing the share of middle-class households
- *The out-of-poverty-into-prosperity countries* (China, Mongolia, and Vietnam), where most people are at least economically secure and the middle class is growing
- *The out-of-extreme-poverty countries* (Cambodia, Indonesia, and the Philippines), where extreme poverty levels are low, but so are the shares of the middle class
- *The lagging-progress countries* (Lao PDR and Papua New Guinea), which still have high levels of extreme poverty
- *The Pacific Island countries*, which make up a heterogeneous group discussed separately here because those countries are distinct from the rest of the region.

The third element that characterizes the analytical approach of the report, together with economic classes and country groupings, is a definition of inclusive growth. Economic growth is regarded as inclusive if it reduces poverty and enhances economic mobility and economic security across all parts of the income distribution.[4] Although this definition of inclusive growth is narrowly described with respect to monetary welfare measures,

it is underpinned by a much broader characterization of human welfare, which is reflected in the report's use of available data. In particular, the definition assumes that poverty is a multidimensional concept, so equal access to social services is needed both directly and instrumentally, to reduce poverty, favor upward mobility, and increase economic security. The report documents systematic differences in access to social services across different areas (for example, rural and urban) and population groups (for example, ethnic minorities) even if it does not suggest any synthetic measure to capture such differences.

By focusing on the challenges and opportunities for inclusive growth as they emerge in relation to every economic class, this report highlights those elements of a new social contract that could reinforce the region's ability to continue delivering inclusive growth. Each country can tailor the elements of such a social contract to its own circumstances, including its development level and its composition by different classes.

Notes

1. This statement refers to a broad definition of East Asia and Pacific, the region that comprises developing East Asia and Pacific, Japan, and the newly industrialized economies. Throughout this report, geographic groupings are defined as follows: the newly industrialized economies comprise Hong Kong SAR, China; the Republic of Korea; Singapore; and Taiwan, China. The Pacific Island countries comprise Fiji, Kiribati, the Marshall Islands, the Federated States of Micronesia, Nauru, Palau, Samoa, Solomon Islands, Tonga, Tuvalu, and Vanuatu. Data are not available for some of those countries—Kiribati, the Marshall Islands, Nauru, Palau, Samoa, and Tuvalu. East Asia is used as shorthand to refer to the countries of developing East Asia and Pacific without the Pacific Island countries.
2. Japan also relied on many of the policies described below. It is not included here because by most measures it was already a relatively advanced economy even before World War II.

3. By focusing explicitly on different classes, this report takes into account the needs and expectations of the whole population. This reflects the realization that, by focusing on the dichotomy of the poor and nonpoor, crucial developments in the region over the past 20 years are missed, such as the rise of the middle class and the fact that the majority of people in developing East Asia and Pacific now face only a slim probability of falling back into poverty; those people are economically secure. This approach also reflects policy makers' concerns about growing inequality (Kanbur, Rhee, and Zhuang 2014), as well as the public's concerns, as evidenced by the perceptions data discussed in chapter 2. It is understood that, on the basis of their specific country situation and preferences, policy makers would want to pay attention to different segments of the income distribution. For example, extreme poverty in Lao PDR is likely to feature in policy debates differently from Malaysia or Thailand.

Alternative approaches are possible, such as adoption of a social welfare function that would attach explicit weights to different parts of the distribution, but the advantages of rigorous ranking of different policy outcomes would come at the cost of a significant loss of simplicity and flexibility.

4. The report does not refer explicitly to the concept of shared prosperity because that concept is generally defined on a country-specific basis. The analysis here focuses on the entire East Asia and Pacific region rather than on country-by-country developments. Nevertheless, the concept of inclusive growth captures the broad intuition behind shared prosperity.

Reference

Kanbur, R., C. Rhee, and J. Zhuang, eds. 2014. *Inequality in Asia and the Pacific: Trends, Drivers, and Policy Implications.* New York: Asian Development Bank and Routledge.

The Building Blocks of East Asia's Economic Miracle | 1

Introduction

East Asia's development model, which has come to be seen as the best way to deliver growth with equity, has resulted in improvements in living standards and human welfare that are nothing less than spectacular. A wave of prosperity has spread throughout the region as a result of prodigiously rapid growth compared with other regions (figure 1.1), driven since the 1980s not only by China but also by other countries (figure 1.2; see also table C.1 in appendix C). Extreme and moderate poverty have declined rapidly and steadily across the region (figures 1.3 and 1.4). Those reductions in income poverty were accompanied by improvements in nonmonetary dimensions of welfare, such as health outcomes (box 1.1). The experience of the Pacific Island countries, however, has differed from that of East Asia (box 1.2).

The development model that underpinned this success combined policies that promoted rapid labor-intensive growth with public spending on basic human capital—education, health, and family planning services. The result was growth that reduced poverty rapidly, without significantly increasing income inequality in most cases.[1] In contrast, there was little emphasis on pursuing redistribution per se[2] or on insuring against risks, other than providing limited public assistance to the severely disadvantaged.

This model was the basis for the "two-and-a-half-point strategy" for poverty reduction put forward by the 1990 *World Development Report* (World Bank 1990). This paradigm has since been broadened into a three-pronged approach to reducing poverty, "Grow, Invest, and Insure," where "grow" refers to the ability to promote labor-intensive growth, "invest" to the provision of quality social services, and "insure" to the ability to manage risks, both ex ante and ex post.[3] In terms of this approach, the unprecedented success of East Asia was built primarily on the growth and investment pillars, with the systematic provision of social assistance and insurance only a supplement to them. The next sections discuss in more detail the key elements of these pillars.

Policies that fostered rapid, labor-intensive growth

East Asia and Pacific economies promoted labor-intensive growth to take advantage of their most abundant resource: unskilled labor. By using their labor more intensely than in

FIGURE 1.1 **Real gross domestic product per capita in developing regions**

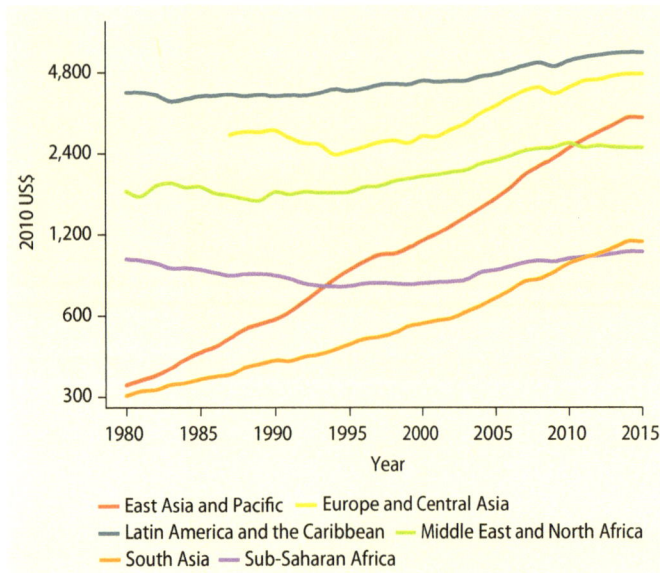

Source: World Bank World Development Indicators (database), https://data.worldbank.org/data-catalog/world-development-indicators.

FIGURE 1.2 **Real gross domestic product per capita in developing East Asia and Pacific**

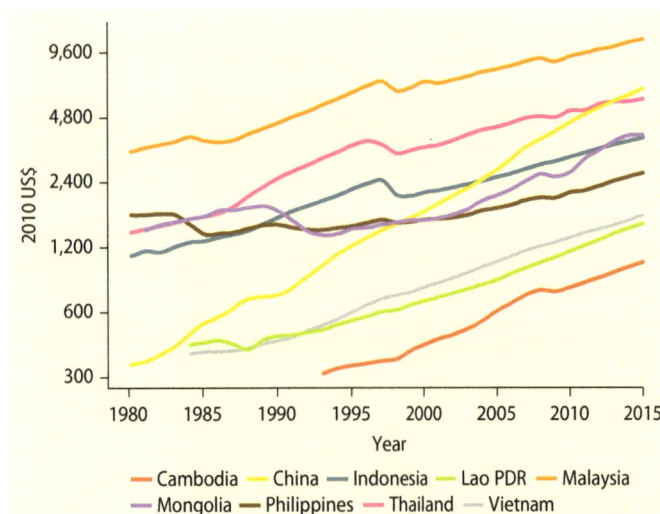

Source: World Bank World Development Indicators (database), https://data.worldbank.org/data-catalog/world-development-indicators.

traditional agriculture, mostly poor populations were able to take advantage of the expansion of opportunities that came with rapid growth, thereby benefiting from higher wages and accumulating assets.

Although policies varied from country to country, reflecting differences in initial political and economic conditions, the successful economies shared several policy and institutional characteristics (see, for example, Birdsall and others 1993; Commission on Growth and Development 2008). Foremost among those characteristics were a commitment to macroeconomic stability; a primary (but not exclusive) reliance on markets to allocate resources; and committed, credible, and capable governance. Market orientation did not prevent governments from intervening to spur development or favor specific industries (Birdsall and others 1993). Rather, such interventions (now commonly termed *industrial policy*) were subject to monitoring and modified if they were deemed ineffective. Governments also ensured that the measures did not become too costly, particularly in fiscal terms (Birdsall and others 1993, 6–7). This emphasis on evaluating and modifying policies was feasible, in turn, because governments were able to build competent civil services that were largely insulated from political interference. Most of the successful East Asian economies also established mechanisms for consultation between the government and the private sector.

Trade openness was a second key element. In general, East Asian economies abandoned import substitution early on in favor of export promotion, in sharp contrast with Latin America up to the 1990s. The result was swift growth in exports—especially of manufactured goods—linked to growing absorption of new technology. East Asia moved rapidly to establish a competitive, pro-export regime, which included duty-free imports for exporters and their suppliers; export credits and export marketing institutions; incentives for foreign direct investment (FDI) and the associated technology transfers; and competitive exchange rates. Selective interventions, as observed in the Republic of Korea, and Taiwan, China, were based on clearly established and well-monitored economic performance criteria (usually exports), were time bound, and were quickly halted when their costs rose. In China, this trade opening was initially confined to selected special economic zones, whose number and size was gradually expanded.[4]

A third common feature was that most of these economies (particularly the early developers and the larger economies of Southeast Asia) were able to achieve high rates of private investment and domestic financial savings. The mobilization of domestic savings was supported by measures such as instituting and supporting banks and development banks; lowering transaction costs and providing incentives for savings; and discouraging consumption (through high interest rates for consumer items and high taxes on luxury goods). Investment was promoted by establishing low tariffs for importing capital goods and increasing public investment in physical infrastructure, such as roads and power, which helped attract private investment by raising returns to it (see Commission on Growth and Development 2008, 34–35).

Finally, these economies all adopted broad-based agricultural policies early in their development process. As low-income economies, they began with a mostly agricultural production base, and a dynamic agricultural sector proved critical to sustaining growth that reduced poverty. Agricultural growth benefited large shares of the population, both directly and by facilitating schooling, migration, urbanization, and expansion of employment in food processing and manufacturing. The outcome was lower rural poverty, less inequality, and containment of urban-rural income gaps.

This progress was made possible by policies such as low levels of agricultural taxation, including implicit taxes through price regulation (Ahuja and others 1997). Agricultural subsidies, such as rice and fertilizer price policies in Indonesia, were used to raise rural incomes. And large-scale public support to agricultural extension helped to absorb the new technologies of the Green Revolution. These measures proved particularly pro-poor when they were accompanied by significant land reform and redistribution, as occurred from the 1960s in Japan, Korea, and Taiwan, China (Acemoglu and Robinson 2002; Boyce, Rosset, and Stanton 2005).

FIGURE 1.3 Poverty rates, across developing regions

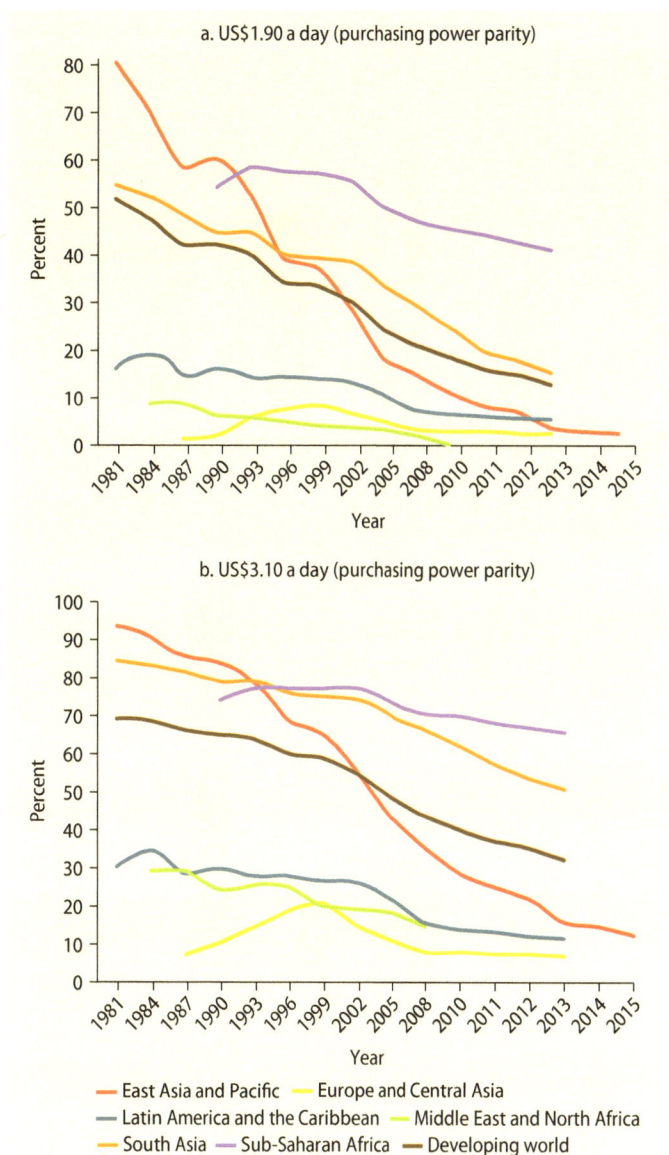

Sources: World Bank PovCalNet (database) http://iresearch.worldbank.org/PovcalNet/povOnDemand.aspx; for 2002–15, World Bank East Asia and Pacific Team for Statistical Development.
Note: See appendix C for details on the methodology.

Between 1978 and 1983, China dismantled its system of collective agricultural production, granting individual farmers land-use rights, although not the right to sell their land. Likewise, Vietnam introduced a new land law in 1993 that dismantled the country's agricultural cooperatives and collectives, allowing transactions in land. In both countries, the

FIGURE 1.4   **Poverty rates, across developing East Asia and Pacific**

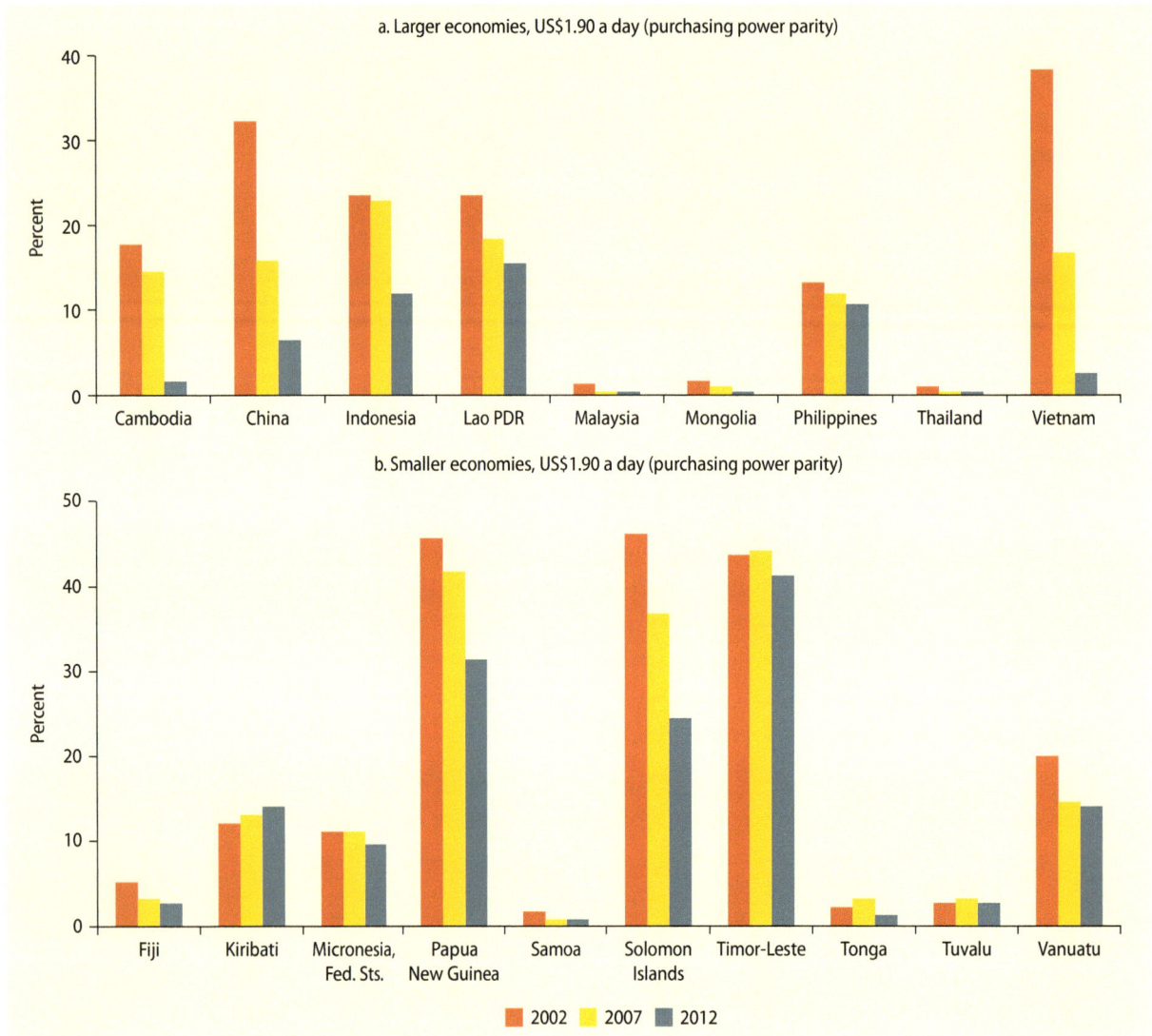

a. Larger economies, US$1.90 a day (purchasing power parity)

b. Smaller economies, US$1.90 a day (purchasing power parity)

■ 2002 ■ 2007 ■ 2012

Source: World Bank East Asia and Pacific Team for Statistical Development.

measures significantly boosted agricultural productivity and reduced poverty (Ravallion and Chen 2007; Ravallion and van de Walle 2008).[5] The poor especially benefited because the initial land allocation in both countries was relatively equitable.[6] In Vietnam, the introduction of a market for land-use rights led to additional productivity gains, as non-farm opportunities expanded rapidly.

Those policies helped the region's economies create formal sector jobs on a large

scale, including jobs for unskilled workers. And they enabled economies based on agriculture to undergo a rapid transformation into economies dominated by manufacturing and services. Millions of rural workers moved into manufacturing jobs. As rapid economic expansion increased the demand for services, rural workers moved into service jobs too. Between the early 1980s and 2012, agriculture's share of the labor force declined in aggregate across developing East Asia, from more than 50 percent to around 35 percent. Meanwhile, industry's share rose from 15 percent to 20 percent, and services' share grew from 25 percent to nearly 45 percent. With these structural changes came rapid productivity growth across sectors. Increasing returns to labor and the expanding number of jobs outside of agriculture helped spread the benefits of growth to large sections of the population.

Policies that built up basic human capital

The successful East Asian economies also invested in the skills, knowledge, and experience of workers—their human capital—by expanding the provision of basic services, particularly primary education, health and nutrition, and family planning. Those investments, which also benefited the poor, complemented the policies that promoted labor-intensive growth by giving the poor the means to take advantage of the expansion in employment opportunities.

From the 1960s onward, many East Asian countries made intensive, sustained investments in human capital. The initial focus on the widespread provision of basic skills, including through universal primary education, was followed by an increase in the availability of secondary education in both urban and rural areas. As growth proceeded, the resulting demographic transition meant that the number of school-age children grew more slowly, reducing the need for additional resources. At the same time, improvements in agricultural productivity and greater urbanization reduced the opportunity cost of children attending school—in other words, such factors alleviated the pressure on families to put children to work—thus increasing the demand for education. Meanwhile, provision of tertiary education was left largely to the private sector, with little public support.

The examples of Korea, an early developer, and Indonesia, a later developer, illustrate this East Asian pattern of human capital investment, which contrasts with patterns seen in comparable countries in Latin America.

At 3 percent of gross domestic product (GDP), public spending on education in 1985 was lower in Korea than in the República de Venezuela (as the country was named before 1999), where it accounted for 4.3 percent of GDP. At the time, the República de Venezuela allocated 43 percent of that spending to higher (tertiary) education, whereas Korea spent only 10 percent on tertiary education. Consequently, Korea was able to spend almost twice as much (2.5 percent of GDP) on basic education as did the República de Venezuela (1.3 percent). Similarly, Bolivia and Indonesia had roughly the same per capita income in the mid-1980s and spent about the same (as a share of GDP) on education. However, Bolivia devoted only about 40 percent of its education budget to basic education, whereas Indonesia's share was almost 90 percent. By 1987, Indonesia had enrolled over 90 percent of rural children in primary school, while the Bolivian school system covered only 60 percent of all children, with fewer than half of all rural schools providing instruction through fifth grade.[7]

East Asian economies similarly expanded efforts to prevent and treat diseases afflicting the poor. As early as the 1960s, Korea established a large number of health centers to provide primary health care and family planning services. It also introduced a national health insurance scheme for urban workers in the 1970s. The scheme was extended to rural areas in the mid-1980s. Across the region, public health expenditure increased markedly from the 1980s onward, with a focus on expanding service provision in rural areas and reducing the cost of treatment for the poor. Improving access to family planning was also emphasized by many successful East Asian economies. Thailand, for instance, implemented one of the world's most effective and innovative family planning programs with the help of public-private partnerships.

Those investments in education, health, and family planning brought a range of benefits (box 1.1). School enrollment rose rapidly in many countries. Overall, the educational attainment of the work force in the region increased fivefold between 1950 and 2010, with rapid increases in labor force skills among broad segments of the population. Efforts were also made to improve the quality of education, which in several countries reached levels comparable with those found in high-income economies (World Bank, forthcoming). Reflecting those trends, students in many economies achieved learning outcomes unmatched anywhere.[8]

Similarly, basic health services and access of the poor to health care were improved. Together with efforts to boost child nutrition and improve access to clean water and sanitation, greater access to health care reduced sharply the incidence of disease and of indebtedness stemming from catastrophic health expenditures. Family planning programs coupled with rapid growth helped reduce fertility rates sharply: the average number of

---

BOX 1.1   **Socioeconomic progress in developing East Asia and Pacific**

The countries in developing East Asia and Pacific[a] have seen significant improvements in various non-monetary dimensions of welfare (figure B1.1.1, panels a and b). School enrollment rose rapidly in many countries, including China, Indonesia, Thailand, and Vietnam, as did educational attainment (that is, average years of schooling). The access of the poor to health services, as demonstrated, for instance, by the share of births attended by skilled health workers, increased sharply. Likewise, access to clean water and sanitation significantly increased. As a result,

child mortality, which overwhelmingly affects the poor, fell particularly sharply. Already in the 1970s and 1980s, much of the region performed better on most indicators than did most of the world's lower-middle-income countries; since then, its performance has improved further to the values observed in upper-middle-income countries.

a. Developing East Asia and Pacific is defined as Cambodia, China, Indonesia, Lao People's Democratic Republic, Malaysia, Mongolia, Myanmar, Papua New Guinea, the Philippines, Thailand, Timor-Leste, Vietnam, and the Pacific Island countries and is the central focus of this report.

FIGURE B1.1.1   **Socioeconomic indicators**

a. 1975, or earliest available

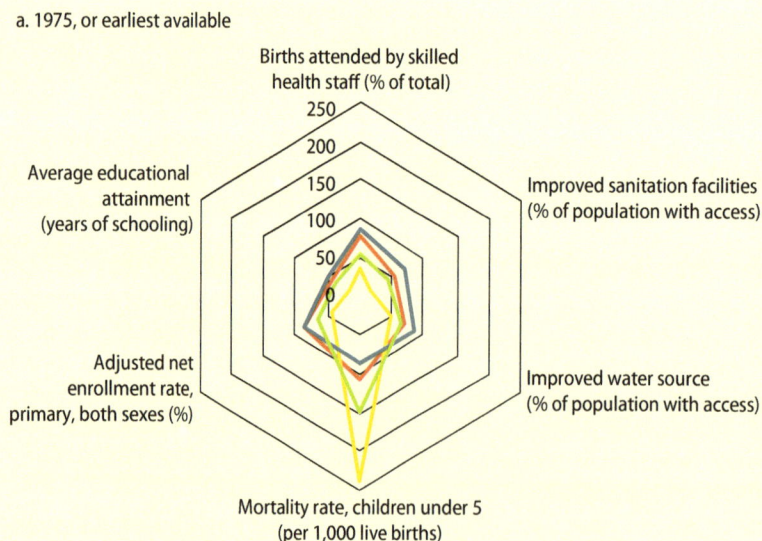

box continues next page

BOX 1.1 **Socioeconomic progress in developing East Asia and Pacific** *(continued)*

FIGURE B1.1.1 **Socioeconomic indicators** *(continued)*

b. 2015, or latest available

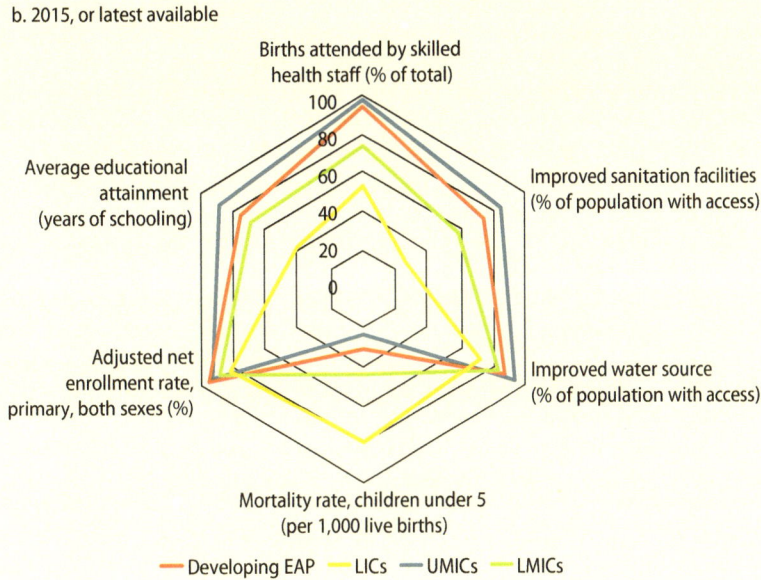

Sources: World Bank World Development Indicators (database), https://data.worldbank.org/data-catalog/world
-development-indicators; Barro-Lee Educational Attainment Dataset, http://datatopics.worldbank.org/education
/wProjection/bpopmodel; World Bank staff calculations.
Note: EAP = East Asia and Pacific; LICs = lower-income countries; LMICs = lower-middle-income countries; UMICs =
upper-middle-income countries. LICs, LMICs, and UMICs include all relevant countries outside developing East Asia
and Pacific with available data. All values refer to unweighted group means; country samples are balanced over time.
Data for panel a refer to 1975 or the earliest available year after then; data for panel b refer to 2015 or the latest available
year before then. For average educational attainment, all values are multiplied by 10 for presentational purposes.

births per woman in Thailand, for instance, fell from six in the mid-1960s to fewer than two by 1996. Similar successes had been seen earlier in Korea and Taiwan, China (Gill, Revenga, and Zeballos 2016).

Limited social protection and redistributive policies

Overall, East Asia's development model placed less emphasis on redistribution than on growth per se.

Social protection systems were underdeveloped, with the state playing a smaller role than in other developing regions at comparable income levels.[9] The limited role of social protection broadly reflected three factors. First, there was a perception that the rising tide from rapid growth would lift all boats. Second, governments sought to minimize the risks facing the population by pursuing macroeconomic stability rather than by systematically providing insurance against adverse idiosyncratic shocks. As a corollary, when sharp economic fluctuations did occur, as during the Asian financial crisis of the late 1990s, the accompanying decrease in real wages and increase in unemployment significantly affected prospects for inclusive growth. Third, the region relied on strong traditional family structures to mitigate the impact of shocks. For instance, early in

BOX 1.2   Growth and poverty reduction in the Pacific Islands and Papua New Guinea

The growth and poverty reduction story of the Pacific Island countries (PICs) differs markedly from the headline-grabbing success of many of their mainland counterparts. With the possible exception of Papua New Guinea, which shares many of the characteristics of the PICs despite not being one, many of these differences have been dictated by the PICs' geography and the limited size of their populations and economies. Their remoteness from large markets and the dispersion of their populations over vast areas of ocean have impeded broad-based growth through labor-intensive and export-oriented manufacturing, because high transport costs make it difficult for the PICs to compete with countries closer to major international markets.

Overall, therefore, the economies of most PICs still have a narrow production base, with semisubsistence agriculture playing a major role, especially in the livelihoods of the poor. Foreign exchange, which is much needed, comes from tourism (in Fiji, Palau, Samoa, Tonga, and Vanuatu); mining and minerals (in Papua New Guinea); logging (in the Solomon Islands); fisheries and commercial agricultural products (coffee in Papua New Guinea and Vanuatu, copra in several of the smaller countries, and sugar in Fiji). The high costs of service delivery to a very dispersed population have made it difficult to invest in human capital; to expand economic opportunities for the population; to support a more diversified economy; and to provide basic needs such as water, sanitation, and electricity. High exposure to natural disasters has increased the risks already inherent in the narrow production base. For example, Cyclone Winston caused total damages in Fiji of around F\$2 billion, equivalent to 25 percent of the country's gross domestic product (GDP).

Although extreme poverty is widespread in Papua New Guinea, the Solomon Islands, Vanuatu, and some atoll countries in the north Pacific, extreme poverty in most of the smaller island countries remains concentrated in smaller communities, which are far from the main cities, are deprived of access to basic services, and are highly vulnerable to natural shocks. The limited employment opportunities outside of subsistence farming and of the smaller government, tourism, and fishing sectors have made international migration an important economic option for many Pacific islanders. In countries such as Samoa and Tonga, where remittances account for more than 20 percent of GDP, migration helps many households to avoid slipping into poverty. Large amounts of foreign aid have similarly contributed to poverty reduction. Strong traditional family and community sharing networks also help to keep extreme poverty at bay, especially in the Polynesian countries. However, the adverse impacts of climate change, the frequent and systemic effects of natural disasters, and the effects of monetization and urbanization are putting stress on those traditional networks.

Sources: World Bank 2016b, 2016c, 2017.

Korea's development process, social assistance programs that offered tax incentives to people who took care of their aged parents were clearly designed to complement and not replace the role of the family. And although a social assistance program was instituted in 1965, it covered only about 5 percent of the population. It was not until after the Asian financial crisis that Korea broadened the scope and coverage of its social protection programs. Taiwan, China, followed a similar course.[10]

This situation has changed recently in some parts of the region. Over the past couple of decades, several countries have introduced elements of a social protection system as their circumstances have changed. Social pensions (noncontributory old-age transfers) have been widely adopted in recent years, though their age thresholds and generosity vary. Such pensions range from those that are universal (Timor-Leste and several Pacific Island countries), to those that are available to everyone without a formal sector pension (Thailand), to those that are more tightly targeted (Malaysia and the Philippines). Similarly, in China, pension schemes for rural and urban residents, which involve large public subsidies, have brought coverage to an additional 350 million working-age people. More generally, countries across the region that had delayed putting in place a modern social protection system (box 1.3) have the opportunity to learn from the experiences of other countries in the region and beyond, thereby avoiding pitfalls such as the creation of welfare traps and excessive labor taxation (see chapter 5).

Better-targeted social assistance programs offering cash transfers have also been gradually established in the region. Examples include the conditional cash transfer schemes in Cambodia, Indonesia, and the Philippines;[11] the programs that were consolidated in Fiji; and China's *dibao* program, which now reaches around 70 million people. In addition, several countries, including Indonesia and the Philippines, have made substantial investments in improving and modernizing social protection delivery systems. Greater use of technology, the introduction

of national identification schemes, and significant initiatives in areas such as payment systems have produced positive results (see chapter 5). In several countries, including Indonesia and Malaysia, recent measures to reduce spending on subsidies for food and fuel are creating the fiscal space for a more appropriate social protection system.

Just as they had relied little on social protection to redistribute wealth, most economies in the region have tended to use redistributive taxes less frequently than developed economies do. For instance, direct taxes account for only 41 percent of total taxes in developing East Asia, compared with 65 percent in member countries of the Organisation for Economic Co-operation and Development (OECD), and capital income accounts for only around 5 percent of personal income tax revenues (World Bank 2016a; see also table C.2 in appendix C).

In addition, tax policy and tax administration both suffer from significant shortcomings.

BOX 1.3   **East Asia lags behind other middle-income regions in providing social protection**

East Asia still has fewer and less effective social programs than do other mostly middle-income regions (table B1.3.1). Except in Malaysia and Thailand, program coverage is generally narrower than found in, for example, countries in Eastern Europe and Central Asia or in Latin America and the Caribbean.

TABLE B1.3.1   **Performance of social protection programs in different developing regions**

	Coverage[a] (%)	Extent of benefits[b] (%)	Extent of benefits, poorest quintile[b] (%)	Beneficiary incidence, poorest quintile[c] (%)	Benefit incidence, poorest quintile[d] (%)
East Asia and Pacific	49.8	17.5	11.9	28.1	3.1
Eastern Europe and Central Asia	62.1	27.1	32.1	24.2	7.8
Latin America and the Caribbean	60.9	29.8	31.8	20.1	5.4
Middle East and North Africa	51.4	12.8	11.2	21.9	7.6
South Asia	27.5	3.2	2.5	21.2	1.8
Sub-Saharan Africa	19.4	14.6	28.7	18.3	4.0

Sources: Atlas of Social Protection Indicators of Resilience and Equity (database), http://datatopics.worldbank.org/aspire; World Bank World Development Indicators (database), https://data.worldbank.org/data-catalog/world-development-indicators.
Note: Regional aggregates denote population-weighted means. Data for China and Lao PDR are not available.
a. *Coverage* denotes the percentage of population participating in social assistance programs (including direct and indirect beneficiaries).
b. *Extent of benefits* denotes the total transfer amount received as a share of the total welfare of beneficiaries.
c. *Beneficiary incidence, poorest quintile* denotes the percentage of program beneficiaries belonging to the poorest quintile (of the posttransfer welfare distribution).
d. *Benefit incidence, poorest quintile* denotes the percentage of total program benefits received by the poorest quintile.

The tax base for both direct and indirect taxes is small, reflecting the large size of the informal sector and the numerous exemptions, deductions, and incentives allowed by tax legislation in the region. Personal income taxes are particularly low and display little de facto progressivity, owing to the widespread exemptions allowed, to the small share of the population to which the maximum marginal rate applies,[12] and to minimum threshold levels that exclude significant proportions of even well-off households. In most countries, a limited number of workers are registered as taxpayers, further restricting the pool to which taxes are applied.[13] Compliance is further reduced by the restricted use of withholding taxes on capital income.[14]

Personal capital income and wealth largely escape taxation, thereby reducing the overall progressivity of the tax system. Interest, dividends, and capital gains are typically taxed at much lower rates than is labor income,[15] which creates the potential for wealthier households to reduce their tax burden by disguising labor income as capital income. Recurrent property taxes are very limited, despite being efficient[16] and equitable;[17] even with the low existing taxes, compliance is poor.[18] The lack of compliance reflects the considerable political and social resistance to such taxes, as well as their significant administrative requirements. Countries are more reliant on corporate income taxes, including those paid by multinational companies.[19] However, the growing international mobility of capital threatens this revenue source, owing to rising tax competition among developing countries, and implies that much of the incidence of corporate income taxes falls on wages, reducing its progressivity.

In general, revenue relies heavily on indirect taxation, which is easy to administer but less progressive (as measured by incidence of taxes as a proportion of the income or consumption of a given group) than is direct taxation. Equity concerns have led to some of the lowest indirect tax rates in the world, limiting tax yields, and to reduced rates on sensitive commodities. However, better-off households appropriate most of the benefits of these reduced rates in absolute terms. Within indirect taxes, there is high reliance on trade taxes, particularly in the Pacific, even though these taxes are inefficient and regressive.

Notes

1. As noted in chapter 2, China constituted an exception to this trend, although the initial level of inequality was much lower than in many other developing East Asian countries.

2. There were, however, notable exceptions. A few economies implemented radical land reform (Taiwan, China; the Republic of Korea; and Vietnam), and a few pursued extensive nationalization (China, Indonesia, and Vietnam). Whatever their immediate effects (nationalization, for example, boosted equality but reduced incomes), these policies can be seen more as one-off interventions than as careful efforts to redistribute the benefits of growth. The most notable exception is Malaysia, which for decades has had in place ethnically targeted programs.

3. See Gill, Revenga, and Zeballos (2016) for a detailed exposition of this point.

4. After the Shenzhen Special Economy Zone was established in 1980, a further 14 coastal cities (including Fuzhou, Guangzhou, and Shanghai) were opened to overseas investment in 1984, and the Hainan Island Special Economic Zone was created in 1988.

5. Agricultural total factor productivity growth was particularly high in China, reflecting also significant public investment in agricultural research and development.

6. Even now, inequality in land distribution is much lower in China's eight most important agricultural provinces than in India or Brazil (the respective Gini coefficients equal 17, 75, and 89 percent).

7. See Birdsall and others (1993, 199–201), for more details about these cases.

8. For example, Vietnamese students, including those from poor backgrounds, regularly outperform peers from member countries of the Organisation for Economic Co-operation and Development. See also Hanushek and Woessmann (2011, 2015).

9. *Social protection* refers to measures that help reduce poverty and vulnerability by (a) diminishing people's exposure to economic risks, (b) enhancing their capacity to manage such risks, and (c) promoting

efficient labor markets. There are three common types of social protection. The first type, *social assistance*, consists of noncontributory transfers in cash or kind, conditional or nonconditional, aimed at the poor and the economically vulnerable. The second type, *social insurance*, comprises programs that minimize the impact of economic shocks on individuals and families by providing benefits and services in recognition of contributions to an insurance scheme. Social insurance schemes include publicly provided or mandated insurance schemes that provide coverage for old age, disability, and death of the main household provider; maternity leave and sickness cash benefits; and health insurance coverage. The third type, *labor market intervention*, is designed to promote employment, efficient operation of labor markets, and protection of workers.

10. See Gill, Revenga, and Zeballos (2016) for more details.

11. In the Philippines, population coverage is now around 20 percent. In Indonesia, the target is to triple coverage.

12. The top marginal personal income tax rate is applied at a threshold level exceeding 20 times GDP per capita in China, Myanmar, and Thailand and 10 times GDP per capita in Indonesia. In contrast, the average threshold level in the OECD is four times GDP per capita (Claus, Martinez-Vazquez, and Vulovic 2012; Kanbur, Rhee, and Zhuang 2014; Lam and Wignender 2015).

13. For instance, in China, the effective share of individuals who pay personal income tax is less than 3 percent of the working population.

14. In Indonesia, there are no withholding taxes on capital gains, even though such gains are subject to personal income tax. As a result, only 5 percent of personal income tax revenues in Indonesia stem from capital income, with the rest coming from withholding on salaries. A similar situation exists in Thailand.

15. Tax rates on dividends range from 5 percent in Vietnam to 20 percent in China and Korea. In Indonesia, tax rates on dividends and interest equal 10 percent and 20 percent, respectively—substantially less than the 30 percent top marginal tax rate on salary income.

16. An efficient tax is one that generates limited distortions.

17. Revenues are particularly low in Indonesia (0.35 percent of GDP), Mongolia (0.15 percent of GDP), and Thailand (0.45 percent of GDP). In contrast, in China, property taxes account for 1.5 percent to 2.0 percent of GDP, a level that is comparable to those observed in OECD countries (Norregaard 2015).

18. In the Philippines, the collection rate for property taxes stands at 50 percent.

19. Commodity producers, including Indonesia and Malaysia, derive a substantial share of revenue from the hydrocarbon sector.

References

Acemoglu, D. and J. A. Robinson. 2002. "The Political Economy of the Kuznets Curve." *Review of Development Economics* 6 (2): 183–203.

Ahuja, V., B. Bidani, F. Ferreira, and M. Walton. 1997. *Everyone's Miracle? Revisiting Poverty and Inequality in East Asia.* Washington, DC: World Bank.

Birdsall, N., J. E. Campos, C.-S. Kim, W. M. Corden, H. Pack, J. Page, and J. E. Stiglitz. 1993. *The East Asian Miracle: Economic Growth and Public Policy.* New York: Oxford University Press.

Boyce, J. K., P. Rosset, and E. A. Stanton. 2005. "Land Reform and Sustainable Development." PERI Working Paper 98, Political Economy Research Institute, University of Massachusetts at Amherst. http://works.bepress.com /james_boyce/15.

Claus, I., J. Martinez-Vazquez, and V. Vulovic. 2012. *Government Fiscal Policies and Redistribution in Asian Countries.* Manila: Asian Development Bank.

Commission on Growth and Development. 2008. *The Growth Report: Strategies for Sustained Growth and Inclusive Development.* Washington, DC: World Bank. http://hdl .handle.net/10986/6507.

Gill, I. S., A. Revenga., and C. Zeballos. 2016. *Grow, Invest, Insure: A Game Plan to End Poverty by 2030.* Washington, DC: World Bank.

Hanushek, E., and L. Woessmann. 2011. "The Economics of International Differences in Educational Achievement." In *Handbook of the Economics of Education*, vol. 3, edited by E. Hanushek, S. Machin, and L. Woessmann. Amsterdam: North-Holland.

———. 2015. "The Economic Impact of Educational Quality." In *Handbook of International Development and Education,* edited by P. Dixon, S. Humble, and C. Counihan. Cheltenham, UK: Edward Elgar.

Kanbur, R., C. Rhee, and J. Zhuang, eds. 2014. *Inequality in Asia and the Pacific: Trends, Drivers, and Policy Implications.* New York: Routledge and Asian Development Bank.

Lam, W. R., and P. Wignender. 2015. *China: How Can Revenue Reforms Contribute to Inclusive and Sustainable Growth?* Washington, DC: International Monetary Fund.

Norregaard, J. 2015. "Taxing Immovable Property: Revenue Potential and Implementation Challenges." In *Inequality and Fiscal Policy.* Washington, DC: International Monetary Fund.

Ravallion, M., and S. Chen. 2007. "China's (Uneven) Progress against Poverty." *Journal of Development Economics* 82 (1): 1–42.

Ravallion, M., and D. van de Walle. 2008. *Land in Transition: Reform and Poverty in Rural Vietnam.* Washington, DC: Palgrave Macmillan and World Bank.

World Bank. 1990. *World Development Report 1990: Poverty.* Washington, DC: World Bank.

———. 2016a. *Reducing Vulnerabilities: East Asia and Pacific Economic Update, October 2016.* Washington, DC: World Bank.

———. 2016b. *Pacific Islands—Systematic Country Diagnostic for the Eight Small Pacific Island Countries: Priorities for Ending Poverty and Boosting Shared Prosperity.* Washington, DC: World Bank. http://documents.worldbank.org/curated/en/313021467995103008/Pacific-Islands-Systematic-country-diagnostic-for-the-eight-small-Pacific-Island-Countries-priorities-for-ending-poverty-and-boosting-shared-prosperity

———. 2016c. "Papua New Guinea Systematic Country Diagnostic Concept Note." Unpublished paper, World Bank, Washington, DC.

———. 2017. "Kiribati, Nauru, Marshall Islands, Micronesia, Palau, Samoa, Tonga, Tuvalu and Vanuatu Regional Partnership Framework," Report 100997-EAP, World Bank, Washington, DC. http://pubdocs.worldbank.org/en/118921488323842915/R2017-0028.pdf.

———. Forthcoming. *Growing Smarter: Learning and Growth in East Asia and the Pacific.* Washington, DC: World Bank.

Ready for the Challenges of the 21st Century? | 2

Introduction

Developing East Asia and Pacific has long been synonymous with a development model of economic growth with equity, a model that has delivered better lives for millions. To continue to benefit from the wave of prosperity that has changed the region, however, governments need to invest now more evenly than they did previously across all three pillars of the grow-invest-insure paradigm. Such a shift is needed because the evolving regional and global contexts pose several challenges to the region's development model. In many countries in the region, inequalities are rising, jeopardizing growth and raising the risk of wasted production potential and of inefficient allocation of resources. Perceptions of inequality, whether justified or not, influence people's behaviors, choices, and investments, with wider effects on societies and economies. Achieving or sustaining high levels of growth may become more difficult because trade is expanding more slowly, the expansion of global value chains is uncertain, and countries need to navigate structural, technological, and institutional transitions. Furthermore, population aging and urbanization, which were sources of opportunity for growth, are now turning into potential threats. Aging is

slowing growth, with much of the region "getting old before getting rich." Rapid urban growth risks entrenching inequalities and can lead to congestion, environmental strains, and poor living conditions.

Concerns over the inclusiveness of the region's development model are growing

Income inequality is high[1] or rising in most countries in the East Asia and Pacific region, particularly in the large ones. As a result, the average person in the region lives in a country where inequality has been increasing over the past couple of decades, which is quite a different experience from what has happened in most other parts of the world, particularly in Latin America (figure 2.1). In addition to any other concerns that high inequality may generate (box 2.1), the rising inequality means that economic growth is becoming less effective in reducing poverty.

Perceptions that inequalities are too high and still growing have been on the rise across the East Asia and Pacific region and are now very visible in policy debates. An informal survey of policy makers identified inequality as a key concern for the region (Kanbur, Rhee, and Zhuang 2014). Much data also

FIGURE 2.1   **Inequality across developing regions of the world**

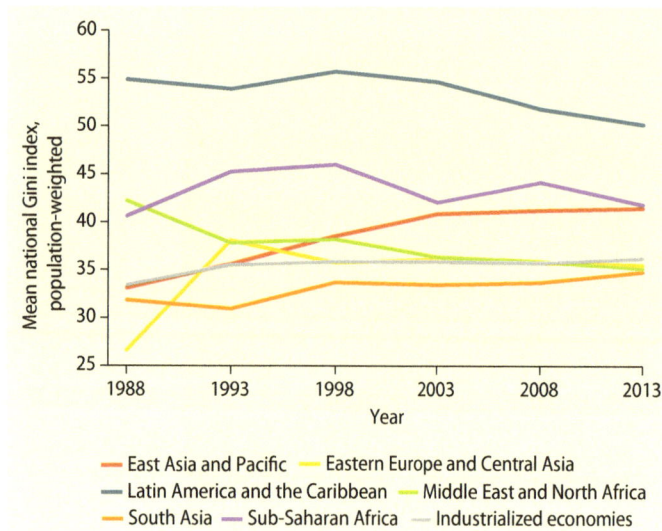

East Asia and Pacific   Eastern Europe and Central Asia
Latin America and the Caribbean   Middle East and North Africa
South Asia   Sub-Saharan Africa   Industrialized economies

Source: World Bank 2016c.
Note: Mean national Gini index, population-weighted. The national Gini indexes are estimated from household surveys of consumption expenditure or income.

suggests that several countries in the region are experiencing an increasing concentration of wealth in the hands of the richest, albeit from a generally low base and to an extent that is still lower than in other parts of the world. This development contributes to perceptions that for many people the opportunities for upward mobility may have declined.

Changing perceptions about inequality and mobility

Today, large majorities of the region's population (more than 90 percent in China, Republic of Korea, and Taiwan, China; around 80 percent in Japan; and more than 50 percent in the Philippines) think that income differences in their own country are too large.[2] In Indonesia, 89 percent of the population thinks that it is quite or very urgent

BOX 2.1   Inequality can be damaging—and so can perceptions of inequality

In the past decade, inequality has returned to the center of policy debates in both advanced and developing economies. Apart from the philosophical focus on redistributive justice and the moral case against inequality, an important strand in this discussion is the instrumental impact of inequality in outcomes. Specifically, inequality can harm development in two major ways. First, "with imperfect markets, inequalities in power and wealth translate into unequal opportunities, leading to wasted productive potential and to an inefficient allocation of resources" (World Bank 2006, 7). Such inequality can reduce growth if the poor do not earn enough, lack sufficient savings, or are unable to borrow to invest in the acquisition of human capital or productive physical capital (Banerjee and Newman 1993; Galor and Zeira 1993), a point indirectly supported by the evidence that countries with a larger middle class tend to grow faster (Easterly 2001).[a]

Second, "economic and political inequalities are associated with impaired institutional development. [...] unequal power leads to the formation of institutions that perpetuate inequalities in power, status,

and wealth—and that typically are also bad for the investment, innovation, and risk-taking that underpin long-term growth," (World Bank 2006, 8–9). Elite capture—the processes by which small minorities appropriate large shares of resources—and crony capitalism—an economic system where public officials and business leaders collude for their mutual benefit—for example, may shape institutions that serve only the needs of the few, hindering a society's ability to solve widespread problems cooperatively and to manage common resources and public services. Those citizens who are left behind may resort to violence to affirm their claims or, on a smaller scale, may resort to crime to improve their lot in life.

A key element of such impacts is that for many adverse behavioral responses to materialize, the perceptions of inequality have economic implications, whatever the objective reality. For example, if social stereotyping exists, inequality can affect motivation and choices with negative effects on lifelong opportunities.[b]

Analysis of data on perceptions of inequality highlights what objective inequality means to people in

box continues next page

BOX 2.1   Inequality can be damaging—and so can perceptions of inequality *(continued)*

at least two respects. First, it helps identify whether people see inequality as a source of opportunity (that is, there is a big payoff to doing well in life) or as a sign that opportunities for upward mobility are limited (that is, economic advantages are limited to those already at the top). Different interpretations can affect people's choices about investments, for example, and therefore their life chances and outcomes. Second, perceptions of inequality are important drivers of public policy preferences, particularly regarding redistribution. Recent work in the East Asia and Pacific region found that the *actual* level of inequality is generally not significantly related to the preference for redistribution, whereas the *perceived* level of inequality is positively and

significantly correlated with the demand for redistribution (Gimpelson and Treisman 2015; Tiongson and Weise 2016). A wrong (lower) perception of the levels of inequality and a negative correlation between perceiving (high) inequality and turning out to vote may have contributed to countries in the region not having adopted a more redistributive policy stance (Tiongson and Weise 2016).

a. A large body of literature has examined the relationship between inequality and subsequent economic growth both theoretically and empirically by using cross-country data. The results have generally been inconclusive and have tended to vary depending on country samples, measures of inequality, econometric methods, and time period (World Bank 2016b).
b. For example, junior-high school students in villages in India, when their status as belonging to a disadvantaged group was made noticeable, would put in less effort in performing a task (Hoff and Pandey 2004).

to address inequality (World Bank 2016a). In Vietnam, "a majority of those surveyed and eight in ten urban residents worry about disparities in living standards" (World Bank 2014b, 47), with young people more likely to worry about inequalities in all spheres of life—health, education, incomes—and by geographical levels (local, national).

These perceptions are more marked in East Asia and Pacific than in other regions of the world[3] and are common across subgroups identified by age, gender, rural or urban residence, and education level. The same perceptions are even more marked for lower-income groups and for those who identify themselves as being in the lower class.

In addition, there has been a significant decline since the 1990s in the number of people who see income inequality as providing desirable incentives for individual effort.[4] The reversal in attitudes has been particularly sharp in China,[5] although a belief in hard work remains stronger there than in richer countries outside developing East Asia and Pacific, such as Japan and the Republic of Korea.

Perceptions of rising inequality are likely driven by several factors, including rising aspirations, which may be only weakly correlated with objective measures of inequality. When

people are increasingly able to meet their basic everyday needs, longer-term ambitions that are harder to achieve—such as improving one's health or job prospects—play a greater role and lead to frustration—the paradox of the happy peasant and frustrated achiever (Graham and Pettinato 2002). In this sense, the East Asia and Pacific region may be a victim of its own success: citizens who become better off also become increasingly aware that they may be falling short of the new standards they set for themselves (Graham 2017; Graham, Chattopadhyay, and Zhang 2016). Again, to the extent that economic growth has resulted in a very visible emerging middle class, poorer households may question whether they have a fair chance of reaching similar levels of economic security or whether the odds of catching up are becoming slimmer. Similarly, perceptions of inequality, and of the link between effort and upward mobility, partly reflect the increased visibility of various aspects of inequality, including conspicuous consumption by the rich. Those perceptions are accompanied by evidence that large accumulations of wealth reflect not only the payoff for innovation and creativity but also significant persistence and concentration in sectors where economic rents are high.

Rising inequality, high inequality, and both

Increased concerns about economic inequality are justified in general by trends in objective inequality in the East Asia and Pacific region, as captured by data from household surveys. Overall inequality has been rising, driven by increases in large populous countries, although over time China's growth moderated its contribution to regional inequality, while the opposite happened in the Philippines. Few countries experienced large drops in inequality of the kinds witnessed over the past decade in other parts of the world (especially Latin America). In addition, inequality at the top is rising, although starting from a low basis. Detailed country-level evidence shows that monetary disparities are underpinned by disparities in nonmonetary welfare indicators (box 2.2).

Inequality among residents in developing East Asia and Pacific (that is, inequality among all its residents, ignoring national boundaries) as captured by the Gini coefficient has been increasing since 1988.[6] Relatedly, growth over the past three decades has favored those at the top of the income distribution more than those at the bottom (figure 2.2, panel a),[7] particularly in China.[8] Small differences in growth rates have resulted in substantial differences in absolute gains (figure 2.2, panel b). Between 1988 and 2012, the consumption expenditure of the top 5 percent of East Asia and Pacific citizens increased by almost US$400 per annum, compared with less than US$30 for the bottom 20 percent and around US$60 for the median group (all figures in 2011 terms of purchasing power parity [PPP]).

Changes in the aggregate regional distribution reflect different underlying growth experiences across countries. The cross-country composition of the different income groups has changed significantly. China, for example, doubled its share in the top 5 percent

---

BOX 2.2   Beyond monetary inequalities: disparities in access to services and curtailed opportunities for future generations across developing East Asia and Pacific

Monetary inequalities are underpinned and often reinforced by persistent disparities in access to education and other services, as well as in the quality of such services (see appendix C, table C.4 for the case of disparities between rural and urban areas in access to services). In Indonesia, for example, more than one-quarter of inequality can be explained by differences in educational attainment across groups. Similarly, the existence of a social gradient in health, with mortality rates declining significantly across economic classes, has long been established in the international literature (Marmot 2015). These considerations become all the more important when disparities in access to services (such as education or perinatal care) curtail the opportunities of the disadvantaged, limiting their future economic mobility. In Indonesia, the incidence of children who are stunted, or short for their age, is higher than in comparable countries in the region and is particularly high for children of less educated parents. Stunted growth results from protracted, rather than acute, malnutrition and is correlated with poorer achievement later in life in many areas, from cognitive skills to health to income.

Evidence from Indonesia also highlights the difficulties of reversing overlapping disparities. The influence of birth circumstances (that is, a set of factors over which an individual had no control, among which education plays the largest role, followed by being born in an urban area and the province of birth—all of which are likely to determine the opportunities for an individual to have access to services) declined from 39 percent for people born in the 1950s to 34 percent for people born in the 1970s, as access to services increased over the years. Yet despite continued expansion of services since the 1980s, the decline in the influence of birth circumstances has stalled or even reversed.

Source: World Bank 2016a.

FIGURE 2.2 **Growth incidence curve and absolute consumption gains for aggregate developing East Asia and Pacific, 1988–2012**

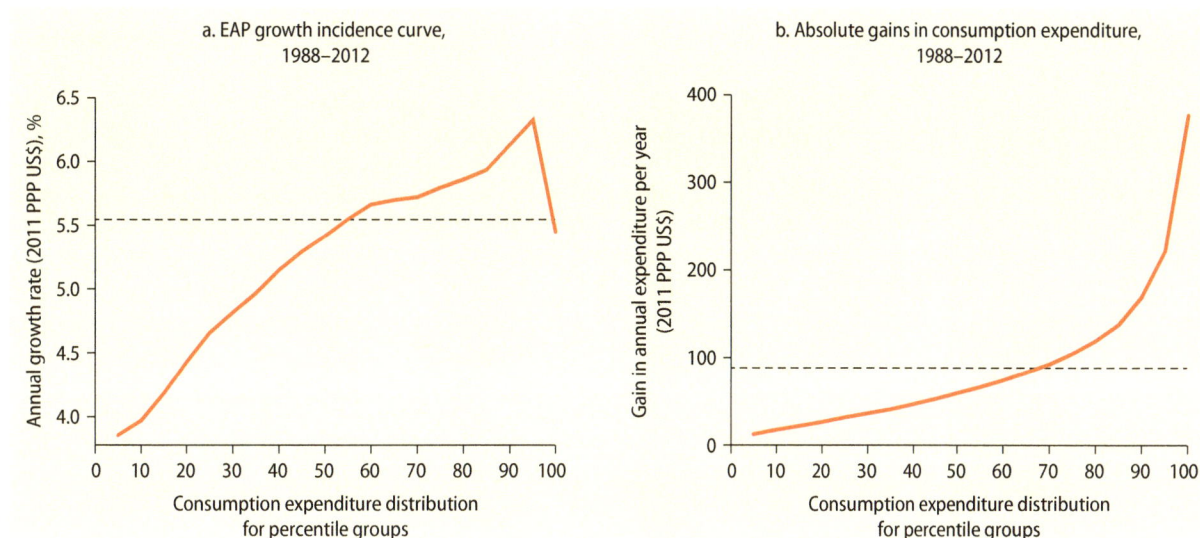

a. EAP growth incidence curve, 1988–2012

b. Absolute gains in consumption expenditure, 1988–2012

Source: Jirasavetakul and Lakner 2017.

Note: The horizontal axis in panel a shows a growth rate in mean consumption of 5.54 percent. The horizontal axis in panel b shows an absolute gain in developing East Asia and Pacific mean consumption of approximately US$88 (2011 PPP adjusted). EAP = East Asia and Pacific; PPP = purchasing power parity. For each fractile group, panel a shows the annualized growth rate in average consumption expenditure and panel b shows the absolute gain. The horizontal lines show the respective values for the regional mean: a growth rate in mean consumption of 5.6 percent in panel a, and an absolute gain in mean consumption of approximately US$88 (2011 PPP adjusted). The distribution is evaluated at 20 ventile groups (for instance, the bottom 5 percent). Because of churning, these growth incidence curves must be interpreted with caution as, say, the bottom 5 percent of the population at the beginning of the period might be composed of a different set of individuals at the two points in time for which the growth incidence curve is constructed. Population weights are used throughout. The database includes microdata and grouped data in combination with a parametric Lorenz curve.

of the distribution between 1988 and 2012 (figure 2.3).

The increase in aggregate regional inequality between 1988 and 2012 was driven by increased within-country inequality in large countries, particularly in China and Indonesia.[9] Conversely, the impact of between-country inequality has declined, largely reflecting China's rapid convergence toward regional average consumption levels (box 2.3). That pattern contrasts with patterns in other regional analyses.[10]

Analysis at the country level enables a more detailed understanding of the rise of inequality at the regional level. The unweighted mean of country-level Gini coefficients, which treats each country as one observation, remained approximately unchanged from 2002 to 2014. Yet in many countries in the region, particularly some of the most populous ones, inequality increased or remained high (figure 2.4,

panels a and b). In Indonesia, inequality increased significantly after 2000, after remaining steady for the previous 15 years. Inequality in China remained stable since the early 2000s but at a much higher level than at the beginning of its expansion in the early 1980s. Likewise, over the same period, inequality rose significantly in Lao People's Democratic Republic and remained high in Malaysia and the Philippines. Thailand and—based on limited data—Papua New Guinea were the only countries where inequality displayed a significant downward trend.

Spatial disparities—between regions and between rural and urban areas—have been a key factor behind inequality at the country level, especially in China (World Bank 2015a; World Bank and Development Research Center of the State Council, People's Republic of China 2014). The rural-urban divide now accounts for 45 percent of

FIGURE 2.3 Regional composition of developing East Asia and Pacific distribution of consumption expenditure, 1988 and 2012

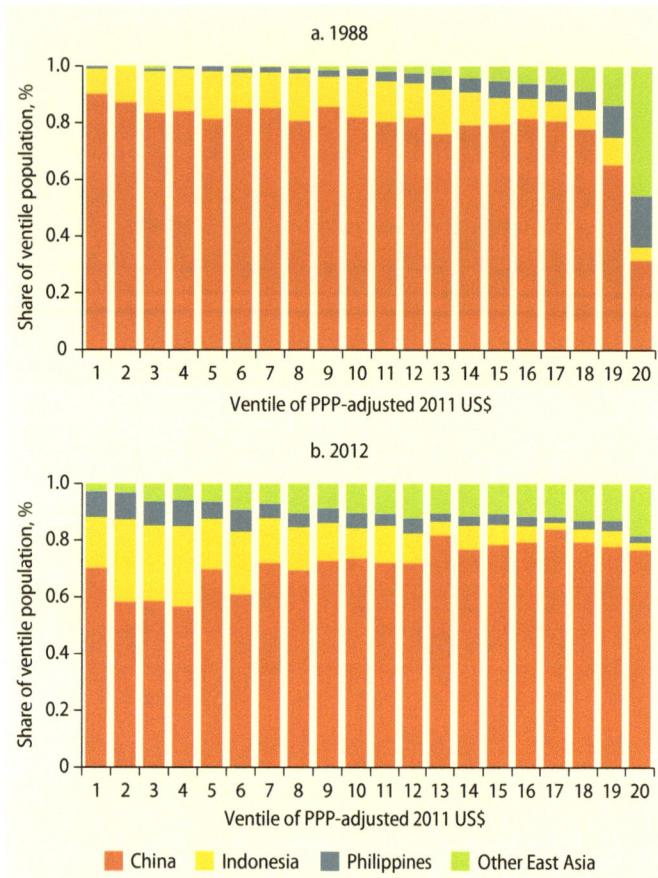

a. 1988

b. 2012

China Indonesia Philippines Other East Asia

Source: Jirasavetakul and Lakner 2017.
Note: PPP = purchasing power parity. For ease of interpretation, the figure does not show Pacific countries separately, although they are included in the calculations. Population weights are used throughout.

overall inequality in China (Kanbur, Rhee, and Zhuang 2014). In other countries, rural-urban disparities are much more contained, accounting for 10–20 percent of economy-wide inequality.[11] Similar results also broadly apply to inequalities between regions. Those spatial inequalities and the unequal distribution of economic activity may reflect positive or neutral factors, such as higher productivity in parts of a country owing to economies of agglomeration[12] or the size distribution of cities.[13] Or they may reflect institutional constraints such as significant de jure and de facto restrictions on internal migration, or distortions in land markets[14] and barriers to connectivity.

Overall, spatial disparities within countries are compatible with, and indeed may be instrumental to, the achievement of continued development and long-run convergence in living standards (World Bank 2009). Such convergence is not automatic, however. It requires policies that focus on tackling the obstacles hampering lagging regions. A key question is whether poor regions are poor because of their intrinsic characteristics or because of the characteristics of those who (choose to) live there (Ravallion and Wodon 1999). A useful way to analyze the issue is to frame it in terms of whether spatial disparities reflect differences in household characteristics, or rather the returns to such characteristics. The former would suggest

---

BOX 2.3   China as a driver of inequality trends across developing East Asia and Pacific

China accounts for 70 percent of the population of East Asia and Pacific, so its income dynamics strongly shape regional inequality. Between 1988 and 2012, China's average consumption moved from below mean consumption to above mean consumption for the region (figure B2.3.1). That change helped equalize the regional distribution of consumption.

Another way to visualize the impact is to separate regional inequality into its within-country and between-country components (figure B2.3.2). By 2012, China was reducing between-country inequality, and thus overall regional inequality, but rising inequality in China had made a major contribution to inequality across the East Asia and Pacific region.

box continues next page

BOX 2.3 **China as a driver of inequality trends across developing East Asia and Pacific** *(continued)*

FIGURE B2.3.1 **Developing East Asia and Pacific region distribution of consumption expenditure, by subregion, 1988–2012**

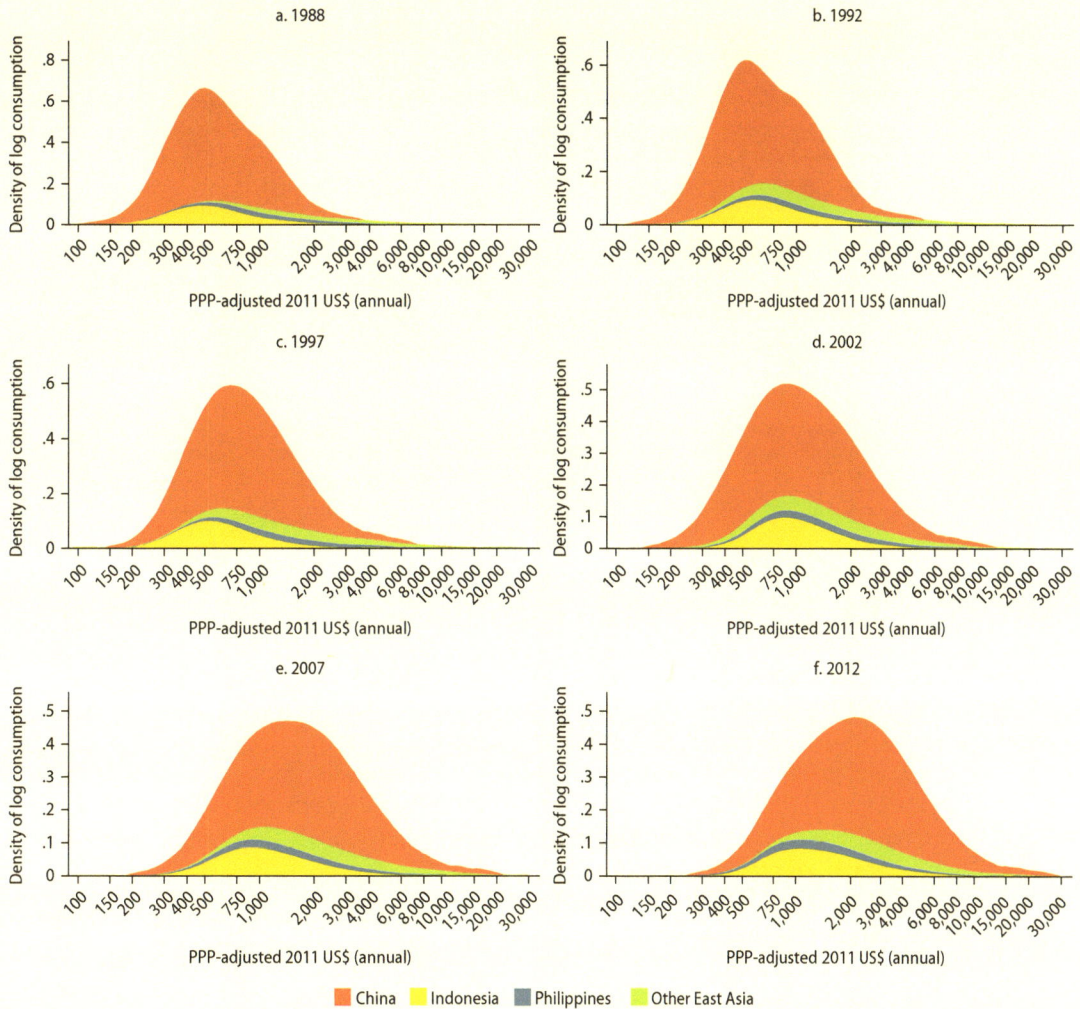

Source: Jirasavetakul and Lakner 2017.
Note: PPP = purchasing power parity. Population weights are used throughout.

box continues next page

BOX 2.3   **China as a driver of inequality trends across developing East Asia and Pacific** (continued)

FIGURE B2.3.2   **Contribution of within- and between-country differences to inequality across developing East Asia and Pacific, 1988–2012**

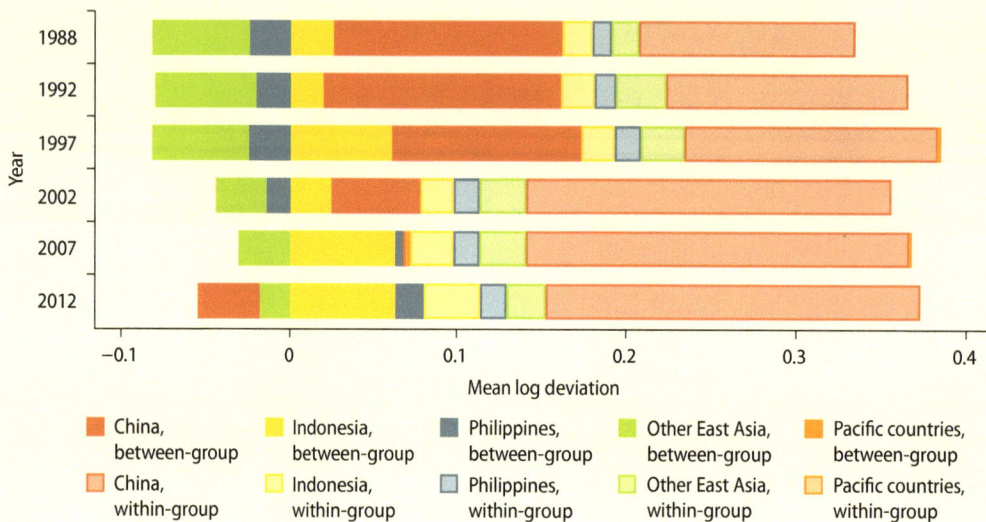

Source: Jirasavetakul and Lakner 2017.
Note: Figure shows the components of a country-level decomposition of East Asia and Pacific–wide inequality (as measured by the mean log deviation).

that public policy should focus on investing in people, the latter that tackling disparities may require area-specific interventions that would equalize returns across geographical areas, such as improving infrastructure and connectivity and reducing the cost of migration.

In general, characteristics and returns both play a role in the East Asia and Pacific region, although their relative importance varies by country (figure 2.5). Much of the rural-urban welfare gap, at the level of both countries and their individual subregions, is due to differences in characteristics, particularly occupation and education. In Thailand and Vietnam, the impact of differences in returns has diminished over time even if it remains significant, suggesting that there has been progress in integrating markets. But in

Cambodia, Indonesia, Lao PDR, and many Pacific Island countries, differences in returns have increased over time.

Income and wealth are increasingly concentrated at the top

As significant as measured increases in inequality in several countries may be, those increases are based on data from household surveys, which tend to underestimate inequality; also, new research suggests that wealth is even more concentrated in the hands of the richest than previously thought.[15] For example, combining data on the top tail from tax records with data on the rest of the distribution from a 2013 household survey for Indonesia raises the estimated Gini coefficient from 41 percent to 46 percent (Wai-Poi and

FIGURE 2.4   Inequality across developing East Asia and Pacific, 2002–14

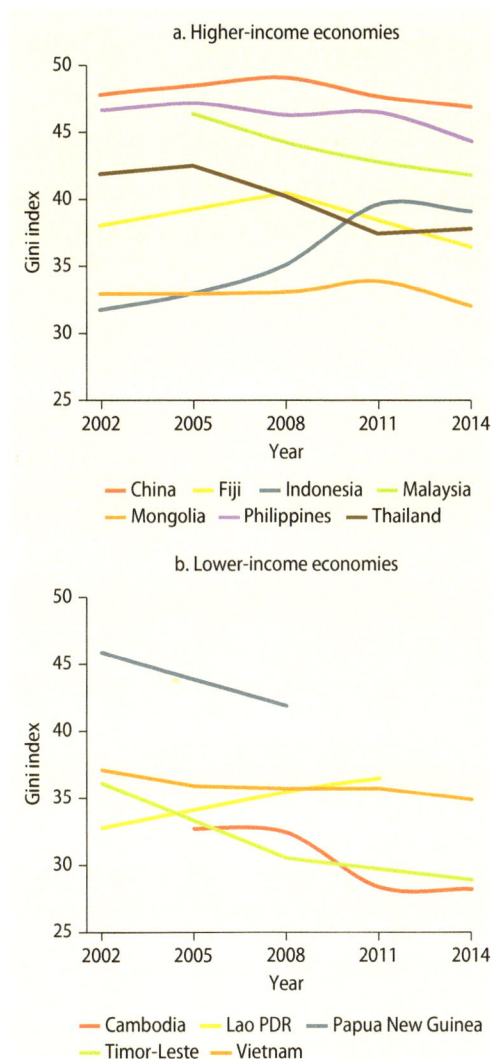

a. Higher-income economies

— China   — Fiji   — Indonesia   — Malaysia
— Mongolia   — Philippines   — Thailand

b. Lower-income economies

— Cambodia   — Lao PDR   — Papua New Guinea
— Timor-Leste   — Vietnam

Sources: World Bank EAP Team for Statistical Development, for EAP 2002–14; World Bank PovCalNet (database), http://iresearch.worldbank .org/PovcalNet/povOnDemand.aspx; World Bank World Development Indicators (database), https://data.worldbank.org/data-catalog/world-development-indicators.

FIGURE 2.5   Welfare disparities between rural and urban areas for select East Asia and Pacific countries: characteristics versus returns, 2000 and 2010

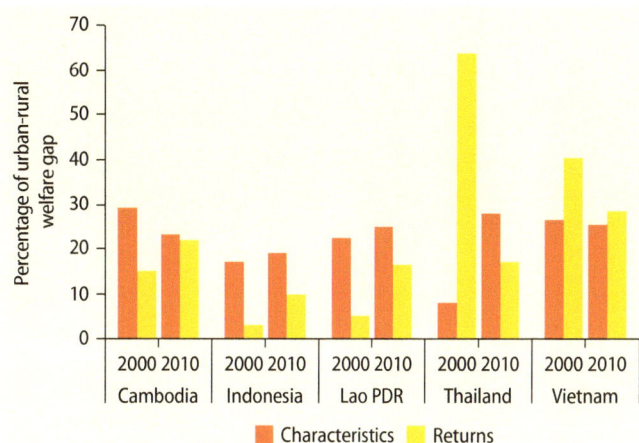

■ Characteristics   ■ Returns

Sources: Lozano-Gracia, Walker, and Antos 2016.
Note: Welfare is measured as the log of (consumption versus regional poverty line). The rural-urban welfare gap is measured as (urban welfare minus rural welfare). This gap is decomposed, using the Blinder–Oaxaca procedure, into the contribution of differences between rural and urban areas in (a) the characteristics of households, such as education, versus (b) the returns to such characteristics, such as the returns to education.

others, forthcoming). Although such detailed evidence is hard to come by, a variety of data sources beyond standard household surveys provide useful pointers on the extent of wealth concentration at the top for the East Asia and Pacific region.

According to the World Wealth and Income Database, inequality at the top of the distribution tends to be lower in East Asia

than in the United States, even though most countries for which data are available have seen an increase in top-income shares since the Asian financial crisis in 1997. The evolution of the income of the top 1.0 percent (figure 2.6, panel a) is broadly similar to that of the income of the top 0.1 percent (figure 2.6, panel b).

Wealth inequality at the top is high in several East Asia and Pacific economies. China and Hong Kong SAR, China, recorded the largest increases since 2000 among all economies in the region (Credit Suisse Research Institute 2015). In contrast, the wealth share of the top percentile fell in Japan and Singapore (low- to middle-inequality countries), as well as in Malaysia and the Philippines (high-inequality countries).

East Asia and Pacific is the region of the world where billionaire wealth has been increasing most rapidly—30 percent annually between 2002 and 2014.[16] Despite the strong increase, the region still accounts for only around 10 percent of global billionaire wealth. As in almost all regions, billionaire wealth in East Asia and Pacific has been

FIGURE 2.6   **Income share of the top 1 percent and of the top 0.1 percent: selected economies of East Asia compared with the United States, 1980–2015**

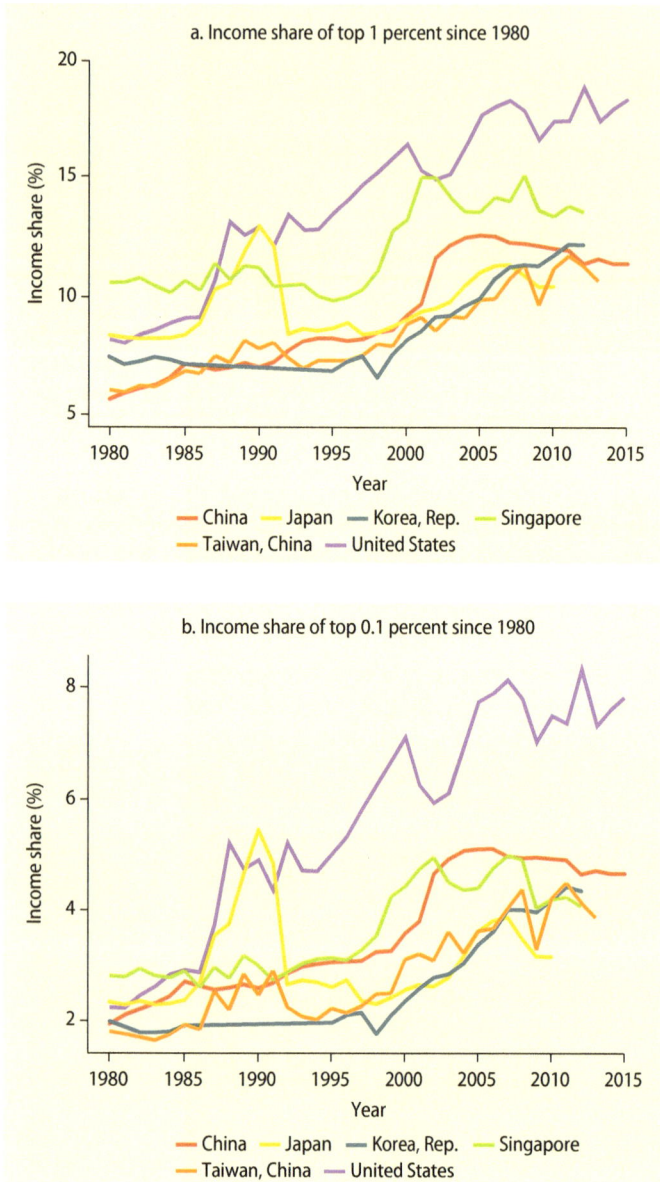

a. Income share of top 1 percent since 1980

b. Income share of top 0.1 percent since 1980

Source: World Wealth and Income Database, http://www.wid.world. (accessed March 17, 2017)
Note: Estimates are typically derived from tax records data. The United States is included for comparison. Indonesia was excluded because of wide fluctuations in top income.

growing faster than gross domestic product (GDP). Today, billionaire wealth is equivalent to almost 9 percent of the GDP of the East Asia and Pacific economies that have billionaires. Six East Asian economies—Hong Kong SAR, China; the Malaysia; the Philippines; Singapore; Taiwan, China; and Thailand—are among the top 20 global economies in billionaire wealth compared with GDP. In Thailand, the combined wealth of the country's billionaires equals around 10 percent of GDP.

Although these different sources point to rising concentrations of wealth, albeit from a low base, there is significant debate on what to make of this finding. A growing class of billionaires, for example, may be seen as the result of innovation and dynamism being rewarded. If that dynamism solidifies over time into elite capture and wealth concentrated in sectors from which high rents could be extracted, however, the growth-with-equity model may face a worrisome challenge (box 2.4). This latter concern is particularly strong with regard to large family firms or family conglomerates with strong political connections—one of the key channels for concentration of wealth. Such firms may have been able to solve serious coordination failures in underdeveloped markets when many East Asia and Pacific economies took off, but they may no longer be appropriate for the new challenges ahead.

Without adjudicating whether the concentration of high incomes at the top is good or bad, especially given that the situation most likely varies by country and sector of activity, two main elements of this concentration of wealth are worth highlighting. First, it is difficult to draw a clear picture of overall inequality without considering both information on top incomes and standard inequality measures. Yet in none of the 10 economies for which both household survey estimates and top-income data are available do all measures point toward decreasing inequality.[17] Second, the growing concentration of wealth is likely to shape perceptions of overall inequality when it fuels very conspicuous consumption. For example, data on sales of high-performance Italian cars in China, Malaysia, and Thailand show that spending grew faster than GDP between 2000 and 2014.[18] Similarly, consumer spending on Swiss watches in East Asia and Pacific grew faster than GDP over the same period, and the average value of Swiss watches sold in the region almost doubled.

BOX 2.4 Growth of the super rich across developing East Asia and Pacific: economic dynamism or elite capture?

The growth of a very rich segment of the population may be seen as a sign of economic dynamism. In China, a new class of high-net-worth individuals with investable assets in excess of RMB10 million (or approximately US$1.6 million) has emerged, and this segment is distributed along a wide spectrum of areas of the country. These individuals made their fortunes in modern sectors such as information technology and biotechnology (Zeng, Shang, and Chishty 2015). They appear to have a different outlook than that of their more established older counterparts, thereby being more keen to invest in new industries rather than traditional ones and paying close attention to "government policies regarding domestic reforms, market openings and innovation" (Zeng, Shang, and Chishty 2015, 11). A similar assessment is made of the new billionaires on the Forbes list; increasingly, they are wealth creators—company founders outside of finance and company executives or owners—as opposed to individuals who are politically connected or who inherited their wealth (Freund 2016). In that light, as of 2014, emerging East Asia and Pacific was doing particularly well, with 48 percent of billionaires identified as company founders (nonfinancial sectors) or as owners and executives.

Yet there are concerns that concentrated ownership structures, even if initially spurred by innovation,

may generate inefficiencies and create a potential for elite capture. Evidence from a broader group of rich people than only the billionaires analyzed by Freund (2016)[a] suggests that even companies founded by entrepreneurs show a tendency to become family dynasties and that large family firms are more likely to enjoy more plentiful political connections than equally large publicly held firms. Similarly, regarding the potential for elite capture, some indication can be obtained by classifying billionaires' sources of wealth on the basis of whether they are primarily in sectors linked to rent extraction[b] or whether they became rich through sectors that benefit from globalization. In the average developing country in East Asia and Pacific, 42 percent of billionaire wealth is generated in rent-seeking sectors. Further, on the basis of the size of rent-seeking sectors as a share of GDP, 6 of the top 10 economies in the world are in East Asia. Firms that operate in rent-seeking industries are more likely to have family members who hold political office, as shown by evidence for Thailand (Bunkanwanicha and Wiwattanakantang 2008).

a. This analysis was based on a sample selected from the 200 largest firms listed on the main stock exchanges of nine East Asian economies in 1996 and 2008 (see Carney and Child 2013; Claessens, Djankov, and Lang 2000).
b. Based on the definition of rent-seeking sectors used by the *Economist's* 2014 index of crony capitalism.

Factors that were once opportunities are turning into challenges

Several global and regional developments suggest that it will be difficult for countries in developing East Asia and Pacific to sustain (or achieve) high levels of growth following their recent period of broad-based, labor-intensive, export-oriented development. Manufacturing-based growth is threatened by a slowed expansion in trade and uncertain prospects for global value chains. The demographic transition and urbanization, which have been sources of opportunity in the past, are now turning into potential threats. These challenges are likely to be compounded

by features of the East Asia and Pacific region's past development model, including the lack of a systematic approach to social protection in many countries, low levels of resource mobilization, and regressive taxation (see chapter 1). Unless countries address those challenges, their abilities to support long-term inclusive growth will progressively narrow.

Can export-oriented manufacturing still support growth with equity?

Although openness and absorption of new technologies continue to be important for the region, particularly for lower-income countries such as Cambodia, Lao PDR, and Myanmar, the global environment appears less conducive to manufacturing-based export-led development.

Current forecasts suggest a reversal in the patterns observed in the past 15 years, with growth in trade slowing below expected GDP growth (World Bank 2017b). Slower growth appears to be driven by the continuation of factors that have manifested themselves over the past few years, both cyclical (such as the lack of buoyancy in the world economy) and structural (such as China's shift from an export- and investment-led growth model to a consumption-led one). Growing protectionism also is part of the picture, although it has not yet played a major role in driving global trends.

Other factors are less clear, such as the potential for further expansion of global supply chains to countries that so far have not been able to participate. Although the decline in the costs of doing business across borders has likely stalled at the global level, lower-income countries in East Asia and Pacific may be able to reap the benefits of China shifting some of these activities such as electronics, as its labor costs continue to increase, to neighboring countries with lower wages. Given current infrastructure and skill constraints, however, a concerted policy effort may be needed to realize these opportunities (World Bank 2015b). In particular, global value chains increase the importance of both efficient logistics and a favorable business environment. While Malaysia has been able to improve its logistics performance and currently ranks 32nd in the World Bank's global benchmarking tool, the Logistics Performance Index (LPI), other countries have found it difficult to keep up. Indonesia's ranking fell from 43rd in 2007 to 63rd in the 2016 LPI.

These developments are a concern for lower-income countries in the East Asia and Pacific region, not least as China continues to be a significant source of competition for would-be industrializers. In addition, some of the export-promoting measures adopted by previous industrializers, including export subsidies and currency undervaluation, may

no longer be feasible under international trade rules. If lower-income countries are not able to rely on export-oriented manufacturing as an engine for growth with equity, they might find themselves relying on exports from other sectors, such as natural resources and services, which tend not to create significant opportunities for broad segments of the population.

While dark clouds gather on the horizon for lower-income countries, richer countries face threats of their own that will require government policies designed to support growth. Technological innovation is disrupting production patterns and business models worldwide, which could lead to what Rodrik (2015) termed "Premature Deindustrialization." Thus, while low wages remain a source of comparative advantage, manufacturing is becoming more skill intensive and increasingly automated. Those changes may offer opportunities for some workers, particularly those with better skills, but may render many jobs out of reach of others, unless properly managed. The sustainment of high economic growth in upper-middle-income countries will involve navigating three key transitions to avoid a middle-income trap (Gill and Kharas 2015):

- The *structural transformation transition* tightens the market for unskilled labor when the supply of surplus labor from agriculture starts to disappear.
- The *technological upgrading transition* centers on the need to move up the value chain. This transition involves the intraindustry reallocation of resources, and it differs from earlier phases of the growth process, when moving into new industries was key to growing productivity. A few countries in the region, such as Singapore, have managed this transition well by upgrading their skill base.
- The *institutional transition* involves the development of effective and responsive government bureaucracies, particularly as the weight of government structures becomes sizable.

Together, these challenges suggest that lower- and higher-middle-income countries in the East Asia and Pacific region may face lower overall economic growth as they seek to adjust to the new global environment and seize its opportunities. In addition, two long-term global trends that are particularly salient for the region and that have been a source of opportunity in the past will complicate the picture and necessitate further adjustments to the economic growth model: population aging and urbanization.

Population aging could slow economic growth and increase household vulnerability

The populations of developing East Asia and Pacific are aging rapidly—a reflection of sharp declines in fertility and increased longevity—and the topic is a major challenge worthy of its own report (World Bank 2016b). China alone is already home to more people age 65 and older than any developing region in the world. In many countries, population aging is occurring at low-income levels. Although in the past a large share of working-age people provided a demographic dividend that helped support the region's growth, the demographic dividend in most countries is about to reverse. By 2025, it is expected that the size of the region's working-age population will have begun to decrease. The impact of that decrease may be intensified by the fact that most countries in East Asia and Pacific lack the requisite mechanisms to adjust their policies to accommodate longer work lives (World Bank 2014a).

Both the pattern and the pace of demographic change differ widely by country (figure 2.7). A group of countries is composed of the rich, already aged economies of Hong Kong SAR, China; Japan; Korea; and Singapore (panel a); in these economies, the old-age dependency ratio will continue to rise to unprecedented levels (Chomik and Piggott 2015). A second group comprises rapidly aging middle-income economies—China, Indonesia, Malaysia, Mongolia, Thailand, and Vietnam (panel b).[19] A third group of generally poorer countries—Cambodia, Lao PDR, Myanmar, Papua New Guinea, the Philippines, and Pacific Island countries (panel c)—is still

young, and it will take much longer for those countries to experience significant increases in the old-age dependency ratio.[20]

In addition to slowing economic growth, population aging is likely to increase households' vulnerability to shocks, particularly health shocks.[21] This effect is especially found in rural areas, where population aging tends to accompany shrinking family size and migration, as well as a weakening of traditional support networks.[22] The lack of pension coverage and insufficient accumulated savings mean that the elderly, especially those who live in rural areas, tend to continue working until they are very old. In addition, the lack of well-developed social insurance systems diminishes households' ex post ability to manage health and income shocks in both urban and rural areas, particularly where informal employment represents a large share of total employment.

From a policy viewpoint, the key concern is that much of the East Asia and Pacific region is getting old before getting rich. Social insurance systems are not sufficiently developed, nor have enough resources accumulated, to provide the elderly population with sufficient income to avoid poverty.[23] Even where specific programs for the poorest elderly are in place, such as in China, in the near term, program coverage will need to be expanded significantly to address demographic trends.

Urbanization may entrench inequalities

Developing East Asia and Pacific is urbanizing rapidly, though there is significant variation across countries.[24] Indeed, the increase in the region's urban population from 2000 to 2010 was enough to constitute the equivalent of the sixth-largest country in the world (World Bank 2015a). Urbanization is expected to continue.[25] In many countries, such as Japan, in the newly industrialized economies, and in many advanced economies, urbanization has been an opportunity for inclusive economic growth, rather than a threat to it. The rapid growth of cities has generated significant agglomeration economies, enabling finer specialization and greater competition in labor

FIGURE 2.7   Population aging across developing East Asia and Pacific
(Old-age dependency ratio [population age 65 and older to population age 25 to 64])

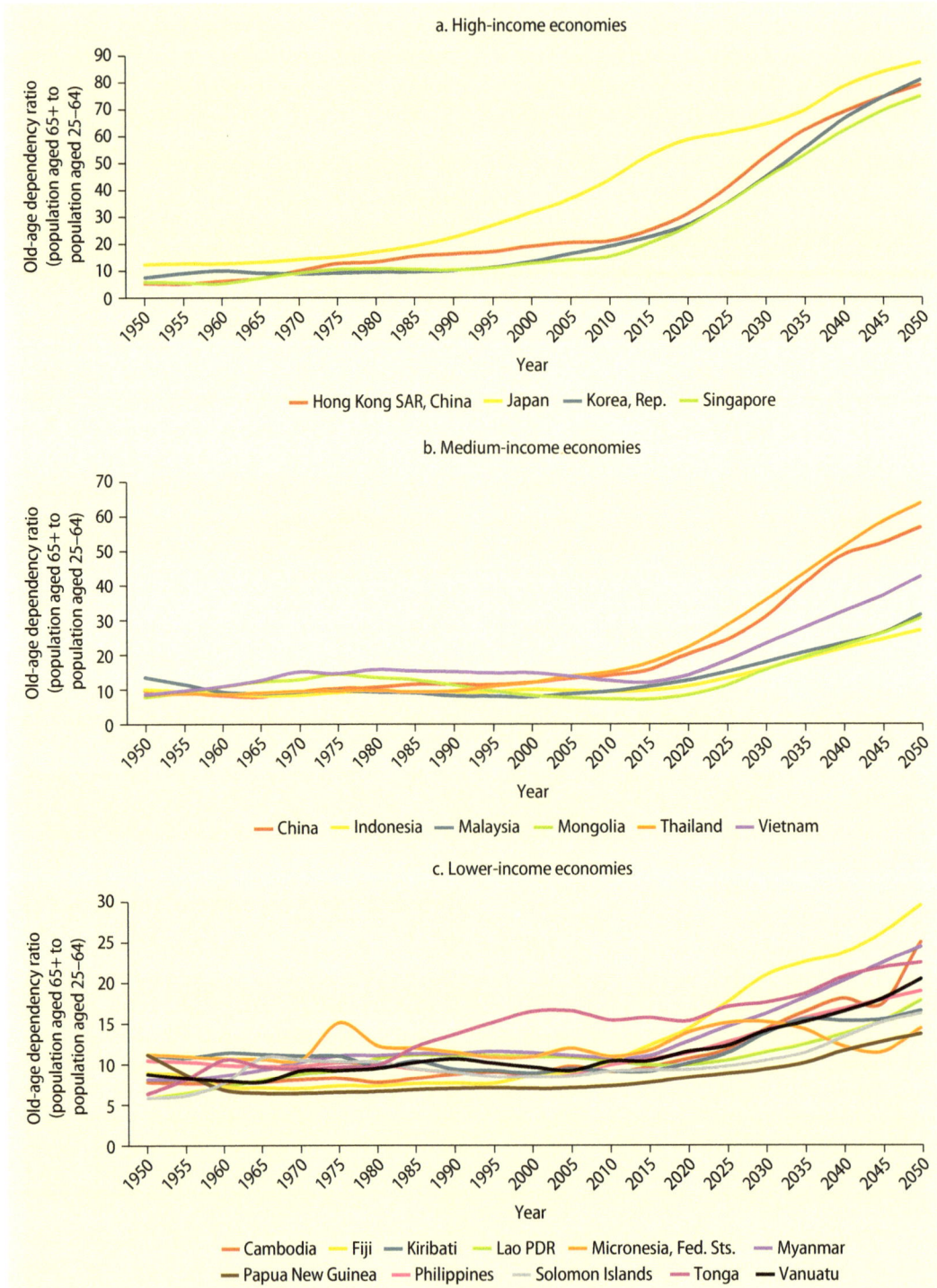

Source: United Nations, United Nations Department of Economic and Social Affairs, Population Division, 2014.
Note: Medium variant population projection.

and product markets, as well as increased knowledge spillovers. In turn, that growth has enhanced productivity and has spurred innovation and economic diversification. As a result, urbanization has been accompanied by broad-based improvements in living standards and has helped support the expanded provision of basic services across all areas.

Yet in the East Asia Pacific region, there are growing concerns over the pattern of growth in urban areas and the role growth can play in entrenching inequalities (Baker and Gadgil 2017). These concerns are not just because the concentration of the poor in urban areas is increasing with urbanization, as people are attracted to urban areas by the opportunities and services that cities provide. Rapid urban growth can be accompanied by congestion, environmental strains, and urban squalor. Given typical urbanization patterns in the region—as elsewhere—the less urbanized, lower-middle-income countries of today are likely to see large increases in the population of their large urban agglomerations. As a result, more people will be living in congested spaces, with poor access to services. In contrast, upper-middle-income countries will see large expansions in built-up areas as cities spread to accommodate the needs of their large populations.

It is of particular concern that an estimated 250 million people in East Asia and Pacific today still live in slums.[26] In addition, the region's urban poor are vulnerable to economic shocks and especially vulnerable to natural disasters, which are frequent in East Asia and Pacific and cause significant economic disruption.[27] The vulnerability of the urban poor is compounded by their dependence on cash income, the higher-risk locations where they often live (including hillsides and flood-prone areas), and their limited access to social services and infrastructure.

Certain groups, such as women, the elderly, and migrants, face specific sources of exclusion and vulnerability (World Bank 2017). Migrants might remain trapped in urban poverty if they are not fully integrated into modern urban labor markets. In some cases, particularly in China, regulations on migration and residence permits prevent migrants from gaining access to the same types of jobs and social services as other urban residents (box 2.5). Migrants earn systematically less than nonmigrants in urban centers because of such restrictions.[28] Urbanization may also weaken extended family structures and traditional support networks, compounding the challenges posed by population aging[29] and thus reducing living standards on both sides of the urban-rural divide. Furthermore, where urbanization is associated with highly visible intraurban and urban-rural disparities, it is likely to reinforce perceptions of growing inequality.

BOX 2.5   Regulatory barriers to migration

Internal migration has played a key role in reducing poverty in many East Asia and Pacific countries by reallocating resources from agriculture to higher-productivity sectors, such as export-driven, low-cost manufacturing in China. Yet the movement of people to different parts of a country and the creation of new jobs can be hindered by the monetary, social, and emotional costs of moving, as well as by regulatory barriers. Registration requirements that assign people to specific rural or urban locations and limit their access to social services to those locations are the most obvious barriers.

Since 1958, China has enforced a household registration (*hukou*) system that assigns individuals

box continues next page

BOX 2.5   Regulatory barriers to migration *(continued)*

an agricultural (rural) or nonagricultural (urban) location, along with either farmland or jobs, housing, food, and state-sponsored benefits (Fan 2008). Similar registration requirements are in force in Vietnam. Although strict application of the original legislation made it essentially impossible for rural migrants in China to survive in urban areas, reforms of the *hukou* since the mid-1980s[a] have resulted in an estimated 260 million people moving to the cities (National Bureau of Statistics of China 2010). In fact, "in 2011, the State Council encouraged the registration of temporary populations in cities [and] the adoption of a residence permit system, and [it] formulated *hukou* reform policy that was linked to the city's administrative level" (World Bank 2017b, 92). This led to large regulatory disparities between cities.

The current system in China appears to have created a group of second-class citizens who benefit from accessing better earning opportunities in the cities than they would have at home, but who have problems accessing (or must pay more to access) urban services. On average, migrant workers work nine hours longer per week than their urban peers, but their mean monthly wage is only 76 percent of that of other urban workers (Li, Li, and Chen 2010). Migrants and urban citizens are treated differently in terms of political, economic, and social rights, particularly in accessing education and health services. Thus, the net subsidy for migrants can be negative, as any public transfers they receive are offset by the taxes and fees they are required to pay (Khan and Riskin 2005). An analysis using data for 2002 from the China Household Income Project (Gao and Riskin 2009) revealed that only 5 percent of migrant workers were covered by the country's pension system, less than 5 percent were covered by unemployment insurance, only 3 percent were covered by medical insurance, and less than 10 percent benefited from public housing. Moreover, migrants in Beijing, Guangzhou, Shanghai, and Tianjin were discriminated against in obtaining unemployment insurance, pensions, medical insurance, and workplace injury insurance. Most did not receive any

FIGURE B2.5.1   Number of migrants in Vietnam

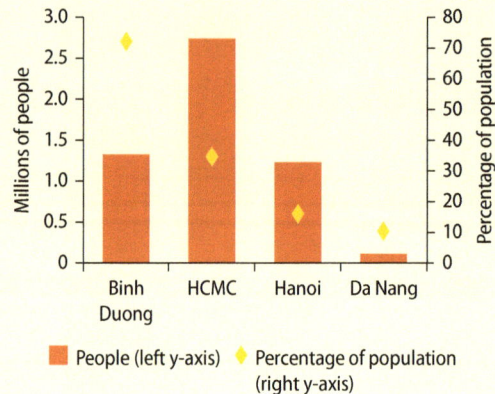

Source: World Bank and Ministry of Planning and Investment of Vietnam 2016.
Note: HCMC = Ho Chi Minh City.

paid holidays, and some did not even have weekends off (Wang and Chen 2010).

A similar situation exists in Vietnam under the *ho khau* system. More than 5 million Vietnamese do not have what is called permanent registration where they live (figure B2.5.1). As in China, citizens in major Vietnamese urban centers who do not enjoy permanent registration face higher living costs and difficulties accessing health care, education, social protection, and utilities, and they experience discrimination in employment and social connections. To obtain permanent registration, it is often necessary for people to make large unofficial payments to local officials.

a. Changes introduced at the city level included high fees for migrants from rural areas to obtain a city *hukou* and to access urban services (Fan 2008). Later, a different type of *hukou*, known as blue-stamp *hukou*, was introduced in Shanghai and Shenzhen for migrants who met high skill requirements and who had sizeable resources that could be invested (Wong and Wai-po 1998). The blue-stamp *hukou* could then be converted into a permanent urban *hukou* after a specified period of time. In 2001, the state council approved a scheme to grant urban *hukou* to migrants from rural areas who held stable jobs and who had resided in small cities or towns for more than two years (Fan 2008). Later, in 2003, the state council issued a directive that affirmed the rights of rural migrants to work in cities (Cai 2003).

Notes

1. As in much of the literature, here inequality is defined as being high if the Gini index exceeds 40.
2. Among developing regions, East Asia and Pacific has the second-highest share (after Latin America and the Caribbean) of respondents who strongly perceive income inequality as being too high in their country (in the International Social Survey Program, ISSP, respondents were asked whether they agree or disagree on a 5-point scale that "differences in income are too large," Weise 2016, 2) and whether incomes in their country should be made more equal. In the World Value Survey, respondents were asked to identify on a 10-point scale whether "incomes should be made more equal" or whether "we need larger income differences as incentives for individual effort" (Weise 2016, 2).
3. When shown different types of distribution, East Asians preferred distributions that would result in Gini indexes of 20 percent to 25 percent (Tiongson and Weise 2016, using ISSP data). The preference for greater equality is not rooted in a correct assessment of current inequality levels, as respondents consistently underestimated true inequality (although less so in richer countries such as Japan).
4. Results from the World Values Survey (2005–14) show that respondents gravitate toward "incomes should be made more equal" rather than "we need large income differences as incentives for individual efforts." However, in some cases, such as China, respondents display a full reversal of preferences toward greater equality, between 2005 and 2014 (Weise 2016).
5. Relatedly, the increases in inequality that were part and parcel of China's growth boom in the 1990s and early 2000s are, in part, thought to be the cause of the sharp declines in life satisfaction at the time that growth took off (Graham, Chattopadhyay, and Zhang 2016, 10).
6. As the Lorenz curve for 2012 crosses to the left of the one for 1988 at around the 95th percentile, this increase in inequality appears to be driven by an increase in inequality at the bottom of the distribution. Although there was no strict Lorenz dominance between 1988 and 2012, inequality measures with

reasonable parameter values have all found increasing inequality. For a fuller discussion, see Jirasavetakul and Lakner (2017).
7. These patterns have changed over time. Between 2007 and 2012, the growth incidence curve for the region was almost flat (Jirasavetakul and Lakner 2017).
8. These findings also broadly hold over different subperiods, with the exception that those at the very top of the income distribution saw large income losses immediately following the 1997–98 Asian financial crisis.
9. Together, these two countries account for most of the region's population and therefore receive a relatively high weight in calculations of regional inequality.
10. A similar analysis for Africa (Jirasavetakul and Lakner 2017) shows that, in contrast to East Asia and Pacific, the within-country component gradually and continuously declined, although, similarly to East Asia and Pacific, it still explains most of overall Africa-wide inequality—around 60 percent. Findings for East Asia and Pacific are also in contrast with global findings that *between-country* differences remain the dominant source of inequality even if the overall weight of within-country inequality increased (Lakner and Milanovic 2016). It is perhaps not surprising that between-country differences matter more at the global level compared with an analysis at the regional level such as the present one (countries' average income or consumption levels may be expected to be more similar within a region). For details, see Jirasavetakul and Lakner (2017).
11. This is the case in, for example, Cambodia, Lao PDR, the Philippines, Thailand, and Vietnam. These results are based on decompositions of the Theil T index (that is, GE(1)).
12. This is the case when, for example, certain industries locate close to one another to exploit the economies of scale and scope that can result from proximity to one another and to large markets.
13. For instance, an urban distribution characterized by many small towns, closely integrated with the rural economy, would result in much smaller urban-rural disparities than the same rate of urbanization concentrated in a few large urban agglomerations.

14. For example, in China, inadequate property rights for farmers, low levels of compensation for land requisition, and nonmarket-based land pricing have exacerbated urban-rural inequalities of income and wealth and have reduced the efficiency of both urban and rural land use. For details, see World Bank and Development Research Center of the State Council, People's Republic of China (2014).

15. Household surveys tend to underestimate overall inequality for several reasons. Rich people are less likely to open the door to an interviewer or to respond directly, or truthfully, to a questionnaire. In addition, such surveys are likely to fail to capture rare income events or income (and wealth from it) that is obtained illegally or hidden offshore. Furthermore, the sampling frame of a typical household survey is not designed to be representative for the extreme upper tail, so any estimates obtained from a typical household survey would be imprecise. It is worth underscoring that, because rich people actually spend only a small fraction of their income, household surveys that use consumption expenditure data report lower estimates of inequality than if income were measured. Entrepreneurial and capital incomes, which are important for those at the top, also are difficult to capture, even in a well-designed household survey. See Lakner and Ruggeri Laderchi 2016.

16. See the 2016 Forbes billionaires list, https://www.forbes.com/billionaires/list/.

17. The East Asia and Pacific economies that show an increase in both the Gini index and all available top income or wealth measures are China; Indonesia; Korea; and Taiwan, China. For all other economies for which both household surveys and top-income data are available, the conclusions are mixed, with household surveys and (at least some) top-income data going in opposite directions. For instance, for Thailand, the Gini measure declined by 0.7 percent annually between 2002 and 2012, whereas billionaire wealth in GDP grew 16.9 percent annually between 2002 and 2014. For more details, see Lakner and Ruggeri Laderchi 2016.

18. This spending on high-performance Italian cars has resulted in a rising share of luxury cars' total import value to GDP, even though rising incomes have made the cars much more affordable. In China, the average cost in 2000

of such an Italian car was around 80 times GDP per capita, but the cost fell to around 30 times GDP per capita by 2014.

19. For example, in China, low fertility and declining mortality are translating into a rapidly aging society. In 2013, there were 202 million people over the age of 60, accounting for 15 percent of the country's total population. By 2030, the number is expected to double in absolute terms, accounting for 24 percent of the total population (World Bank 2016b).

20. In the first group, the old-age dependency ratio (that is, the ratio of people ages 65 and older to those ages 15 to 64) will reach 58 percent to 70 percent by 2050. This is well above the value for European countries (47 percent) or the United States (37 percent). In the second group, the ratio will reach 30 percent to 43 percent, with China at the upper end. In the third group, the ratio will broadly remain below 25 percent.

21. Older workers, even with high human capital, are relatively less likely to find work following negative shocks, especially to their health.

22. For instance, coresidence with children has been declining rapidly in China, Korea, and Thailand (Giles and Huang 2015).

23. For an analysis of policy issues related to pension systems and old-age protections in the region, see World Bank (2016b).

24. The most urbanized countries in the region are Malaysia (73 percent) and Mongolia (71 percent). Urbanization rates are below 30 percent in 8 of 19 countries for which data are available.

25. For example, in Latin America, a region of mostly middle-income countries, the urbanization rate equals approximately 80 percent, suggesting the urbanization rate of the East Asia and Pacific region is lower than would be expected given its level of development. China, Indonesia, and the Philippines are projected to reach urbanization rates between 60 percent and 70 percent by 2050, which implies that those countries will experience further rural-urban migration of around 350 million people. Among the other regional economies, only Thailand is projected to reach an urbanization rate above 50 percent by 2050 (United Nations, United Nations Department of Economic and Social Affairs, Population Division 2014).

26. The share of the urban population living in slums has declined, but it remains higher than in large Latin American countries. Between 1950 and 2009, the share declined in China from 41 percent to 29 percent, in Indonesia from 43 percent to 23 percent, in the Philippines from 50 percent to 40 percent, and in Vietnam from 54 percent to 35 percent. For comparison, the share of the urban population that lives in slums is estimated to be only 14 percent in Mexico, 21 percent in Argentina, and 27 percent in Brazil (Baker and Gadgil 2017). Slums are defined by residents' access to improved water, improved sanitation, durable housing, and sufficient living area (UN-Habitat 2013, table 2).

27. In 2011, one of the most expensive years on record for natural disasters, losses in East Asia and Pacific from natural disasters totaled US$259 billion. Most costs accrued in the first nine months of the year and accounted for 80 percent of global losses that were due to natural disasters that year (Jha and Stanton-Geddes 2013).

28. In China, migrants in urban centers earn up to 40 percent less hourly (Frijters, Kong, and Meng 2011).

29. Urbanization makes it more difficult for people to rely on family members or neighbors for help. And weaker ties to rural areas make it more difficult for people to migrate back to family farms in the wake of urban job losses.

References

Baker, J., and G. Gadgil. eds. 2017. *East Asia and Pacific Cities, Expanding Opportunities for the Urban Poor.* Washington, DC: World Bank.

Banerjee, A. V., and A. F. Newman. 1993. "Occupational Choice and the Process of Development." *Journal of Political Economy* 101 (2): 274–98.

Bunkanwanicha, P., and Y. Wiwattanakantang. 2008. "Big Business Owners in Politics." *Review of Financial Studies* 22 (6): 2133–68.

Cai, F., ed. 2003. *Zhongguo Renkou Yu Laodong Wenti Baogao: Zhuangui Zhong Di Chengshi Pinkun Wenti* (Report on China's Population and Labor: Urban Poverty in Transitional China). Beijing: Shehui Kexue Wenxian Chubanshe (Social Sciences Documentation Press).

Carney, R. W., and T. B. Child. 2013. "Changes to the Ownership and Control of East Asian Corporations between 1996 and 2008: The Primacy of Politics." *Journal of Financial Economics* 107 (2): 494–513.

Chomik, R., and J. Piggott. 2015. "Population Ageing and Social Security in Asia." *Asian Economic Policy Review* 10 (2): 199–222.

Claessens, S., S. Djankov, and L. H. P. Lang. 2000. "The Separation of Ownership and Control in East Asian Corporations." *Journal of Financial Economics* 58 (1–2): 81–112.

Credit Suisse Research Institute. 2015. *Global Wealth Report 2015.* Zurich: Credit Suisse Research Institute.

Easterly, W. 2001. "The Middle Class Consensus and Economic Development." *Journal of Economic Growth* 6 (4): 317–35.

Fan, C. C. 2008. "Migration, Hukou, and the City." In *China Urbanizes: Consequences, Strategies, and Policies*, edited by S. Yusuf and T. Saich, 65–89. Washington, DC: World Bank. http://siteresources.worldbank.org/INTEAECOPRO/Resources/3087694-1206446474145/Chapter_3_China_Urbanizes.pdf.

Freund, C. 2016. *Rich People Poor Countries: The Rise of the Emerging-Market Tycoons and Their Mega Firms.* New York: Peterson Institute for International Economics.

Frijters, P., T. Kong, and X. Meng. 2011. "Migrant Entrepreneurs and Credit Constraints under Labour Market Discrimination." IZA Discussion Paper 5967, IZA (Institute for the Study of Labor), Bonn. http://ftp.iza.org/dp5967.pdf.

Galor, O., and J. Zeira. 1993. "Income Distribution and Macroeconomics." *Review of Economic Studies* 60 (1): 35–52.

Gao, Q., and C. Riskin. 2009. "Market versus Social Benefits: Explaining China's Changing Income Inequality." In *Creating Wealth and Poverty in Postsocialist China*, edited by D. S. Davis and W. Feng, 18–34. Stanford, CA: Stanford University Press.

Giles, J., and Y. Huang. 2015. "Are the Elderly Left behind in a Time of Rapid Demographic and Economic Change? A Comparative Study of Poverty and Well-Being of East Asia's Elderly." Background paper for the East Asia and Pacific regional report on aging, World Bank, Washington, DC.

Gill, I. S., and H. Kharas. 2015. "The Middle-Income Trap Turns Ten." Policy Research

Working Paper 7403, World Bank, Washington, DC.

Gimpelson, V., and D. Treisman. 2015. "Misperceiving Inequality." NBER Working Paper 21174, National Bureau of Economic Research, Cambridge, MA.

Graham, C. 2017. *Happiness for All? Unequal Hopes and Lives in Pursuit of the American Dream*. Princeton, NJ: Princeton University Press.

Graham, C., S. Chattopadhyay, and J. Zhang. 2016. "Perceptions of Inequality in Southeast Asia: Some Novel Insights from Metrics of Well-Being." Unpublished background paper for this report, Brookings Insitution, Washington, DC.

Graham, C., and S. Pettinato. 2002. "Frustrated Achievers: Winners, Losers, and Subjective Well-Being in New Market Economies." *Journal of Development Studies* 38 (4): 100–40.

Hoff, K., and P. Pandey. 2004. "Belief Systems and Durable Inequalities: An Experimental Investigation of Indian Caste." Policy Research Working Paper 3351, World Bank, Washington, DC.

Indonesia Ministry of Finance and World Bank. Forthcoming. "Estimating Top Incomes in Indonesia." World Bank, Jakarta.

Jha, A. K., and Z. Stanton-Geddes, eds. 2013. *Strong, Safe, and Resilient: A Strategic Policy Guide for Disaster Risk Management in East Asia and the Pacific*. Washington, DC: World Bank.

Jirasavetakul, L.-B. F., and C. Lakner. 2017. "Distribution of Consumption Expenditure in East Asia." Policy Research Working Paper 7968, World Bank, Washington, DC.

Kanbur, R., C. Rhee, and J. Zhuang, eds. 2014. *Inequality in Asia and the Pacific: Trends, Drivers, and Policy Implications*. New York: Asian Development Bank and Routledge.

Khan, A. R., and C. Riskin. 2005. "China's Household Income and Its Distribution, 1995 and 2002." *China Quarterly* 182 (June): 356–84.

Lakner, C., and B. Milanovic. 2016. "Global Income Distribution: From the Fall of the Berlin Wall to the Great Recession." *World Bank Economic Review* 30 (2): 203–32.

Lakner, C., and C. Ruggeri Laderchi. 2016. "What Do We Know about the Super-Rich in East Asia?" Background paper for *Riding the Wave: An East Asian Miracle for the 21st Century*. Washington, DC: World Bank.

Li, L., S. Li, and Y. Chen. 2010. "Better City, Better Life, But for Whom?: The *Hukou* and Resident Card System and the Consequential Citizenship Stratification in Shanghai." *City, Culture and Society* 1 (3): 145–54.

Lozano-Gracia, N., D. Walker, and S. E. Antos. 2016. "Spatial Disparities in EAP." Background paper for *Riding the Wave: An East Asian Miracle for the 21st Century*. Washington, DC: World Bank.

Marmot, M. 2015. *The Health Gap. The Challenge of an Unequal World*. London and New York: Bloomsbury Publishing.

National Bureau of Statistics of China. 2010. "National Economy Maintained Stable Performance and Progress with Good Momentum for Growth in August." Retrieved December 10, 2015 from http://www.stats.gov.cn/english/.

Ravallion, M., and Q. Wodon. 1999. "Poor Areas, or Only Poor People?" *Journal of Regional Science* 39 (4): 689–711.

Rodrik, D. 2015. "Premature Deindustrialization." NBER Working Paper 20935, National Bureau of Economic Research, Cambridge, MA.

Tiongson, E. R., and M. Weise. 2016. "The Misperception of Inequality and Political Participation: Summary of Emerging Findings." Unpublished background note for this report, Georgetown University School of Foreign Service, Washington, DC.

UN-Habitat. 2013. *State of the World's Cities 2012/2013: Prosperity of Cities*. Nairobi: UN-Habitat.

United Nations, United Nations Department of Economic and Social Affairs, Population Division. 2014. *World Urbanization Prospects: The 2014 Revision*. New York: United Nations.

Wai-Poi, M., M. Wihardja, M. Mervisiano, and I. Setiawan. Forthcoming. *Estimating Top Incomes in Indonesia*. Jakarta: World Bank.

Wang, H., and Y. Chen. 2010. "An Analysis on the Work Welfare Discrimination against Migrants." *Chinese Journal of Population Science* 2: 47–54.

Weise, M. 2016. "Key Trends in Perceptions of Income Inequality in WVS and ISSP." Unpublished background report for this report, World Bank, Washington, DC.

Wong, L., and H. Wai-po. 1998. "Reforming the Household Registration System: A Preliminary Glimpse of the Blue Chop Household Registration System in Shanghai and Shenzhen." *International Migration Review* 32 (4): 974–94.

World Bank. 2006. *World Development Report 2006: Equity and Development*. Washington, DC: World Bank and Oxford University Press.

———. 2009. *World Development Report 2009: Reshaping Economic Geography*. Washington, DC: World Bank.

———. 2014a. *East Asia Pacific at Work: Employment, Enterprise, and Well-Being*. Washington, DC: World Bank.

———. 2014b. Taking stock: an update on Vietnam's recent economic development. Washington, DC: World Bank. http://documents.worldbank.org/curated/en/64124146813354445 1/Taking-stock-an-update-on-Vietnams-recent-economic-development.

———. 2015a. *East Asia's Changing Urban Landscape: Measuring a Decade of Spatial Growth*. Washington, DC: World Bank.

———. 2015b. *East Asia and Pacific Economic Update, April 2015: Adjusting to a Changing World*. Washington, DC: World Bank.

———. 2016a. *Indonesia's Rising Divide: Why Inequality Is Rising, Why It Matters, and What Can Be Done*. Washington, DC: World Bank.

———. 2016b. *Live Long and Prosper: Aging in East Asia and Pacific*. Washington, DC: World Bank.

———. 2016c. *Poverty and Shared Prosperity 2016: Taking on Inequality*. Washington, DC: World Bank.

———. 2017. *Global Economic Prospects, January 2017: Weak Investment in Uncertain Times*. Washington, DC: World Bank.

World Bank and Development Research Center of the State Council, People's Republic of China. 2014. *Urban China: Toward Efficient, Inclusive, and Sustainable Urbanization*. Washington, DC: World Bank.

World Bank and Ministry of Planning and Investment of Vietnam. 2016. *Vietnam 2035: Toward Prosperity, Creativity, Equity, and Democracy*. Washington, DC: World Bank. doi:10.1596/978-1-4648-0824-1.

Zeng, J., A. Shang, and S. Chishty. 2015. "The Evolution of China's Private Wealth Market." Business Insights, Bain & Company, Washington, DC. http://www.bain.com/publications/articles/the-evolution-of-chinas-private-wealth-market.aspx.

Looking beyond the Poverty Line: Economic Class in Developing East Asia and Pacific

3

Introduction

The rapid economic growth in developing East Asia and Pacific[1] over the past few decades has brought an unprecedented reduction in poverty. To ensure that growth is inclusive in the face of emerging challenges, however, it is vital to move beyond the simple poor–nonpoor dichotomy and to obtain a richer understanding of the region's transformation. Doing so requires taking a closer look at trends across the income distribution through the lens of economic class. As poverty decreased dramatically in East Asia and Pacific, a significant middle class emerged, although a sizable proportion of the region's population remains vulnerable to falling back into poverty as a result of shocks. Meanwhile, gaps in the delivery of services, such as higher education, housing, and water and sanitation, result in limited access and poor quality even for those in higher economic classes. The lens of economic class highlights how, over the past few decades, developing East Asia and Pacific has been transformed from a region of mostly poor people in low-income countries to a region of middle-income countries with a diversity of economic classes. Such economic diversity implies that efforts to deliver inclusive growth must take into account a range of specific needs and circumstances.

A picture of the income distribution by economic class

This report divides the income distribution into five economic classes based on levels of consumption per capita. The thresholds are derived from a combination of well-established international norms and country-specific evidence (box 3.1):

- The extreme poor, living on less than US$1.90 a day
- The moderate poor, living on US$1.90 to US$3.10 a day
- The economically vulnerable, living on US$3.10 to US$5.50 a day
- The economically secure, living on US$5.50 to US$15.00 a day
- The middle class, living on more than US$15.00 a day.

In 2015, the extreme poor accounted for 2.5 percent of the region's population, the moderate poor for almost 10 percent, and the economically vulnerable for approximately one-quarter (figure 3.1). The economically secure were the largest group in the region, with almost half of the population. The middle class accounted for 17 percent.

Not surprisingly, households in higher economic classes do better according to

BOX 3.1   Partitioning the income distribution into classes

A key theme of this report is that the challenges standing in the way of more inclusive growth in developing East Asia and Pacific are different for each income group. The relevant groups may be defined in two ways. First, one can define economic classes on the basis of some distinguishing characteristic that emerges from an empirical analysis—for instance, calculating the probability of different parts of the income distribution to fall into poverty over time, on the basis of panel data (also known as longitudinal data—observations obtained over several time periods for the same individuals). This was the approach followed for Latin America and the Caribbean in a recent report (Ferreira and others 2013). Second, one can identify economic class with reference to well-understood and widely supported thresholds that capture some broadly held views on discontinuities across classes. This report strikes a balance between these two approaches, integrating detailed country evidence and adopting preexisting lines, reflecting also the limited availability of panel data across the region. Specifically, the report focuses on the following segments of the expenditure distribution, where all expenditure cutoffs are expressed in terms of 2011 U.S. dollars (purchasing power parity [PPP]):

- **The extreme poor,** living on less than US$1.90 a day. This threshold is the World Bank's international poverty line.
- **The moderate poor,** living on US$1.90 to US$3.10 a day. The upper threshold is the moderate poverty line traditionally used by the World Bank in analyzing trends in developing East Asia and Pacific.
- **The economically vulnerable,** living on US$3.10 to US$5.50 a day. The cutoff to assess vulnerability is based on a 10 percent or higher chance of falling into poverty in the next measurement period, using panel data (following the methodology of Lopez-Calva and Ortiz-Juarez 2011).[a]

- **The economically secure,** living on US$5.50 to US$15.00 a day. These households are not at significant risk of falling into poverty (see above) but cannot yet be considered middle class (see below).
- **The middle class,** living on more than US$15.00 a day. This threshold is broadly consistent with the values used by other studies.[b] In principle, another class could be identified at the top end of the distribution—for instance, those living on more than US$50.00 a day, following Lopez-Calva and Ortiz-Juarez (2011). However, the household survey data are not well suited for measuring this group (see chapter 2).

In practice, this report is not dogmatic about the definition of classes per se, and it doesn't shy away from identifying common challenges across classes. This report also recognizes that although qualitative differences are clearly identifiable between the two ends of the distribution, a considerable degree of continuity exists between classes. In particular, strong continuities exist across the poverty line, with a lot of movement between the moderate poor and the economically vulnerable classes. Such continuities are highly relevant from a policy perspective.

a. The mean estimate of this expenditure level, across countries with available data and using alternative methodologies, is adopted. Specifically, the probability of falling into poverty is less than 10 percent, based on panel estimates using a Lowess (locally weighted scatterplot smoothing) or a logistic model, for incomes above the following levels in the following countries: Indonesia, US$8.25 (Lowess) or US$6.01 (logistic); the Philippines, US$6.20 (Lowess) or US$5.40 (logistic); and Vietnam, US$4.40 (Lowess) or US$4.20 (logistic). Data availability does not allow for the reliable estimation of country-specific vulnerability lines.
b. For instance, Wilson and Dragusanu (2008) define members of the middle class as those who earn an income of US$6,000 a year to US$30,000 a year (2007 PPP), and Kharas (2010) uses US$10 a day to US$100 a day (2005 PPP). Focusing on Latin America, Ferreira and others (2013) adopt a minimum threshold of US$10 a day (2005 PPP); likewise, respondents to the Latinobarómetro perception survey become more likely to self-identify as middle class than as poor at an income level of US$10 a day (2005 PPP). Adjusting for the intervening inflation and adopting a mean value yield a lower threshold of approximately US$15 a day (2011 PPP). Similarly, Pritchett (2003, 2006) argues that the upper bound for the global poverty line should be based on the lowest poverty line in the wealthy OECD (Organisation for Economic Co-operation and Development) countries; the United States has the lowest poverty line, equivalent to US$15.80 a day (2011 PPP).

several indicators that go beyond income and consumption, including access to services (appendix D, table D.1), asset ownership, and employment. Members of these households are less likely to be employed in agriculture and more likely to be employed in formal sector salaried jobs, thereby highlighting the importance of structural transformation and of better jobs in supporting higher living standards. For instance, a large majority of the middle class are civil servants, are professional or technical workers, or are in service and sales jobs.

Some patterns are less obvious because they go beyond a simple association with greater expenditure as economic class improves. Three stand out:

- The extreme poor are a heterogeneous group along several dimensions, including location and ethnicity.
- Groups that are more well off, including the economically secure and the middle class, still have limited access to some basic services, including good-quality housing.
- Large differences exist in female labor force participation rates across economic classes, as measured by household surveys.[2] These rates are very low for the two poor classes: less than 40 percent for the extreme poor and about 43 percent for the moderate poor, compared with 55 percent for the economically vulnerable and more than 68 percent for each of the higher economic classes.

The distribution of economic classes across countries

The distribution of economic classes across the countries of the region looks very different today than it did three decades ago. Most of the extreme poor are now spread across the three larger middle-income countries: Indonesia, China, and the Philippines together account for more than 80 percent of the total (figure 3.2). Indonesia accounts for two-fifths of the extreme poor in East Asia and Pacific. In contrast, in 1981, China alone accounted for more than 80 percent of the extreme poor in East Asia and Pacific.

The incidence of extreme poverty is very heterogeneous and remains high in a few countries. Rates of extreme poverty as a share of the population are highest in Papua New Guinea; the Lao People's Democratic Republic; Timor-Leste; and the Pacific Island countries of Kiribati, the Federated States of Micronesia, the Solomon Islands, and

FIGURE 3.1 Population distribution by economic class in developing East Asia and Pacific, 2002–15
Percentage of total population

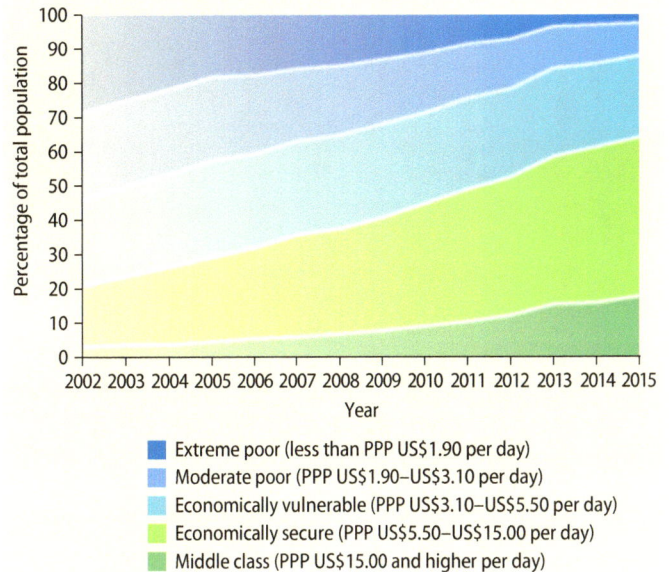

Source: World Bank EAP Team for Statistical Development.
Note: PPP = purchasing power parity. Appendix B provides details on the methodology underlying this figure.

FIGURE 3.2 Distribution of extreme poverty across developing East Asia and Pacific, 2015
Percentage of region's extreme poor

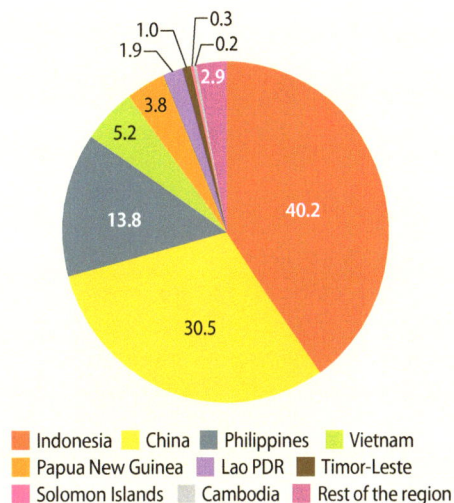

Source: World Bank EAP Team for Statistical Development.

TABLE 3.1   Population distribution by economic class and country in developing East Asia and Pacific, 2015

	Extreme poor (%)	Moderate poor (%)	Economically vulnerable (%)	Economically secure (%)	Middle class (%)
Cambodia	0.7	14.0	49.6	34.9	0.7
China	1.1	6.7	21.8	51.0	19.4
Indonesia	7.5	24.6	35.9	27.7	4.3
Lao PDR	13.8	27.9	36.0	20.1	2.2
Malaysia	0.0	0.3	2.6	31.3	65.7
Mongolia	0.2	2.4	15.9	64.8	16.6
Papua New Guinea	24.0	22.5	28.7	22.3	2.5
Philippines	6.6	18.7	30.8	34.7	9.2
Thailand	0.0	0.8	10.1	53.6	35.4
Timor-Leste	40.3	15.3	29.0	14.3	1.1
Vietnam	2.7	7.1	23.7	57.0	9.5
Pacific Island countries					
Fiji	1.0	5.4	36.4	46.1	11.2
Kiribati	13.3	19.7	36.8	27.5	2.6
Micronesia, Fed. Sts.	15.4	20.1	33.0	28.4	3.0
Samoa	0.8	8.3	28.0	49.0	13.9
Solomon Islands	24.4	31.7	28.4	14.1	1.4
Tonga	1.0	5.4	22.4	54.8	16.4
Tuvalu	1.6	9.4	27.9	49.1	12.0
Vanuatu	15.0	25.0	34.1	23.9	2.0

Source: EAP Team for Statistical Development.
Note: Population shares within any given country may not add exactly to 100 because of rounding errors.

Vanuatu (all above 10 percent; see table 3.1). Conversely, the incidence of extreme poverty is negligible in Malaysia and Thailand, both upper middle-income countries.

The extreme poor are also unequally distributed within countries along the rural-urban spectrum, with rural areas having much higher rates of extreme poverty. People living in remote areas that lack connective infrastructure or services, or that are agro-ecologically or otherwise geographically disadvantaged, also lack the services available to their more urban counterparts (see appendix C, table C.4), as well as access to jobs and markets. This means that people in remote areas either have a low asset base to begin with (because of low education and poor health care) or cannot use their assets effectively (because of lack of access to jobs and markets). Conversely, poverty rates are generally lower in larger cities than in smaller towns.[3] Poverty rates have also decreased faster in larger cities (with the exception of

cities in Indonesia, where poverty alleviation programs have led to especially sharp poverty reduction in smaller towns and rural areas). As a result, in most countries in East Asia and Pacific, including the Philippines and Vietnam, the vast majority of the poor live in smaller towns and rural areas. As urbanization proceeds, however, the share of poor people living in cities, particularly in megacities, is rising.

In several countries, extreme poverty is concentrated among ethnic minorities, particularly when it is associated with geographical remoteness. In Vietnam, although only 3 percent of the ethnic majority Viet population live below the extreme poverty line, 37 percent of those belonging to ethnic minorities live below that same threshold, accounting for 69 percent of the remaining extreme poor population (World Bank 2012). The differential poverty incidence across ethnic groups, which has been increasing over time, is strongly correlated with location:

ethnic minorities are concentrated in rural, remote, and mountainous areas. In China, ethnic minorities, which account for approximately 10 percent of the population, have lower incomes and are more likely to be poor than are members of the Han ethnic majority (Gradín 2015; Gustafsson and Sai 2014).[4] This statement generally holds even at the level of individual provinces, although ethnic minorities fare better in provinces where ethnicity is more heterogeneous (such as Guizhou or Yunnan). These differences largely reflect disadvantaged, including mountainous, locations with inadequate services.

Substantial variation exists across East Asia and Pacific in the incidence of moderate poverty and economic vulnerability, two groups that largely overlap in their characteristics and that experience a high degree of churning between categories. The moderate poor and the economically vulnerable account for 64 percent of the population in Cambodia and Lao PDR, and for more than half in Indonesia; Papua New Guinea; and the Pacific Island countries of Kiribati, the Federated States of Micronesia, the Solomon Islands, and Vanuatu; however, these groups account for less than 3 percent of the population in Malaysia. Again, there are significant rural-urban disparities.[5] The economically vulnerable are larger in number than the moderate poor across the region, with the exception of the Solomon Islands.

The size of the economically secure and middle classes also varies sharply across the region. In absolute terms, China accounts for approximately three-quarters of both groups (and of the region's total population). Almost all the remainder of these economic classes live in four countries with large populations—Indonesia, the Philippines, Thailand, and Vietnam—and in smaller but wealthier Malaysia. Indonesia accounts for one-quarter of the non-China economically secure in East Asia and Pacific. Of the non-China middle class, Malaysia accounts for more than one-third, Thailand for more than one-quarter, Indonesia for 13 percent (despite having 4 times the population of Thailand

and nearly 10 times that of Malaysia), and the Philippines and Vietnam for approximately 10 percent each.

Dramatic income gains across economic classes

Adopting the lens of economic class helps underscore how the income distribution at the regional level in East Asia and Pacific has changed dramatically. The incidence of extreme poverty has fallen sharply since the early 2000s (figure 3.1). Adopting a longer perspective, East Asia and Pacific has experienced an unprecedented decline in extreme poverty over the last three decades, steeper than in all other developing regions of the world—from 81.0 percent of the population in 1981 to 2.5 percent in 2015. The number of extreme poor has decreased by more than 1 billion over the same period, although there are still more than 50 million people in extreme poverty.

The share of the population classified as moderate poor has also fallen sharply, from 26 percent in 2002 to less than 10 percent in 2015. This decline has been particularly pronounced in rural areas, where the number of moderate poor declined by 92 million people between 2002 and 2012, and by 20 million excluding China. In contrast, the share of the economically vulnerable has remained stable, at around one-quarter of the population.

Almost two-thirds of all households in East Asia and Pacific now either are economically secure or have joined the middle class, reflecting the sustained growth that most of East Asia and Pacific has seen since 2002.[6] The expansion of these classes has been checked only by the end of the commodities boom. The economically secure grew from approximately 350 million in 2002 to 975 million in 2015, or by 8.2 percent per year. Over the same period, more than 300 million people joined the middle class, an increase of nearly 17 percent per year. The economically secure were heavily affected by the Asian financial crisis of 1997–98; the middle class in the region is almost entirely a phenomenon of the 2000s.

Different countries' pathways to prosperity

Regional growth trends have led the distribution of people across classes to change in different ways in different countries. Between 2002 and 2015, the majority of East Asian countries reduced extreme poverty rates to single digits, with the notable exceptions of Papua New Guinea and Lao PDR (figure 3.3). However, the relative sizes of other classes varied significantly from country to country. While the Philippines' economic class structure remained roughly the same over this period, Indonesia has reduced sharply the incidence of both extreme and moderate poverty since 2002 (see also box 3.2).

These trends have changed not only the concentration of classes across countries but also the distribution of economic classes within countries, particularly across the rural-urban spectrum. As urbanization advances, the share of the poor living in urban areas also increases. However, in East Asia and Pacific, as elsewhere, the incidence of poverty remains higher in rural settings. A less-expected finding is that, whereas in most countries it is cities that bring greater economic security, in several countries (including Lao PDR, Thailand, and Vietnam), economic security has also been rising sharply in rural areas. In part, such economic security is attributable to urbanization, which has reduced the supply of rural labor and thus raised rural wages while also increasing the remittances that rural areas receive from urban migrants.

An analysis of the changes in the economic class structure at the country level, combined with the current differences across countries, suggests the following broad typology of pathways to prosperity that East Asia and Pacific countries have followed:

• **Progressive prosperity:** Malaysia and Thailand, the richer countries in the region, have eliminated extreme poverty. Much of the population (approximately two-thirds

FIGURE 3.3   **Population distribution by economic class and country in developing East Asia and Pacific, 2002 and 2015**

Percentage of country's population

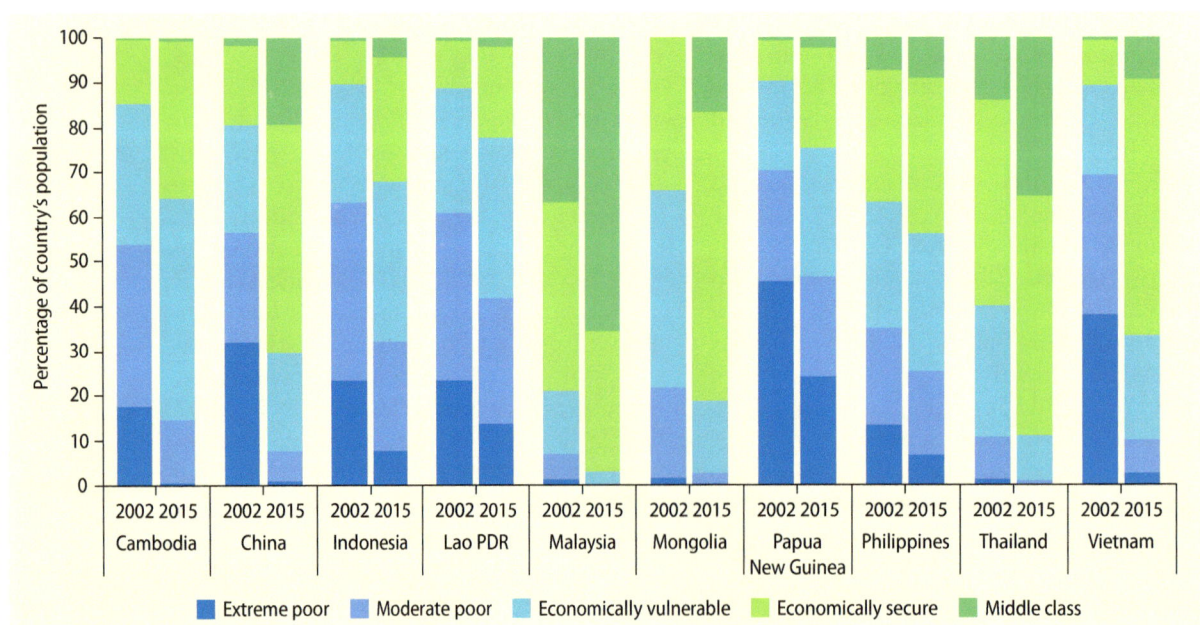

Source: EAP Team for Statistical Development.

in Malaysia and one-third in Thailand) now belongs to the middle class.

- **Out of poverty into prosperity:** In China, Mongolia, and Vietnam, as a result of sustained poverty reduction, most people are at least economically secure, and the middle class is growing. Overall, the income distributions of these countries now resemble Malaysia and Thailand back in 2002.
- **Out of extreme poverty:** Cambodia, Indonesia, and the Philippines enjoy low levels of extreme poverty, but the middle class in these countries is also small. A sizable share of the population is still either moderately poor or vulnerable to falling back into poverty.
- **Lagging progress:** Lao PDR and Papua New Guinea face more serious challenges, although each has distinctive features. These countries have made progress in reducing extreme poverty but still experience much higher incidence of extreme poverty than most other countries in the region. Put differently, the elasticity of extreme poverty in Lao PDR and Papua

New Guinea with respect to growth has proved relatively low. As a result, the income distributions of these countries resemble Indonesia back in 2002.

- **The Pacific Island countries:** These are a heterogeneous group. In terms of current composition of economic classes, Samoa, Tonga, and Tuvalu resemble the Out-of-poverty-into-prosperity group; Kiribati, the Federated States of Micronesia, and Vanuatu look similar to the Philippines, and the Solomon Islands are poorer even than Lao PDR (table 3.1). In terms of changes over time, most of these countries have performed poorly, though some modest progress has been made in reducing extreme poverty in the Solomon Islands, Tuvalu, and Vanuatu.

Looking ahead: extrapolating past trends

Projections based on a simple mechanical extrapolation of past trends would suggest that the goal of eradicating extreme poverty is well within reach for the region (figure 3.4);

FIGURE 3.4 **Poverty projections, developing East Asia and Pacific, US$1.90 a day and US$3.10 a day PPP**

Source: World Bank EAP Team for Statistical Development.
Note: The numbers in the figures represent millions of poor people according to the different poverty lines. PPP = purchasing power parity. Appendix B provides details on the methodology underlying this figure.

FIGURE 3.5 Population distribution by economic class in developing East Asia and Pacific, 2015–30

Percentage of total population

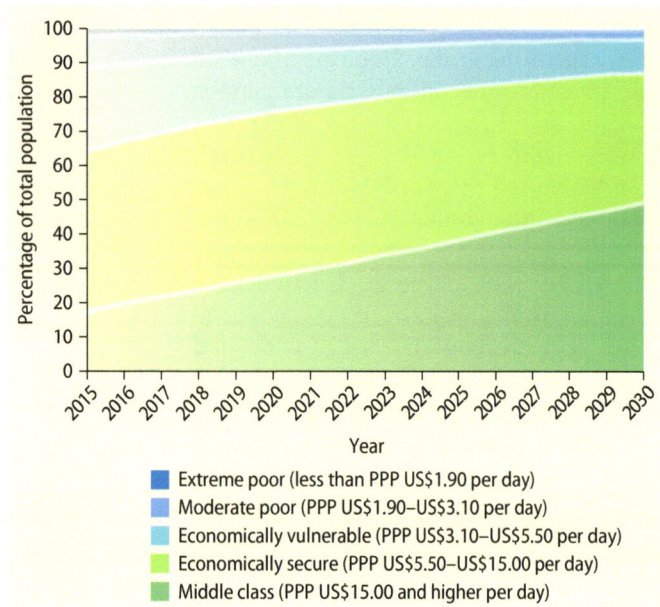

Year

- ■ Extreme poor (less than PPP US$1.90 per day)
- ■ Moderate poor (PPP US$1.90–US$3.10 per day)
- ■ Economically vulnerable (PPP US$3.10–US$5.50 per day)
- ■ Economically secure (PPP US$5.50–US$15.00 per day)
- ■ Middle class (PPP US$15.00 and higher per day)

Source: World Bank EAP Team for Statistical Development.
Note: PPP = purchasing power parity. Appendix B provides details on the methodology underlying this figure.

in such a framework, more than 40 percent of the region's population would be part of the middle class by 2030 (figure 3.5). Even if such projections were to come about, however, more than 60 million people would still be living in poverty (extreme and moderate) in this increasingly upper-middle-income region, and more than 200 million would remain highly vulnerable to falling into poverty.

More fundamentally, recent trends show growth becoming less inclusive, as captured by indicators of growing real and perceived inequality. Regional and global trends suggest that sustaining high levels of inclusive growth will become more difficult. Different challenges to inclusiveness are likely to emerge for different parts of the income distribution; partitioning the income distribution by classes allows us to characterize these challenges more fully, as discussed in chapter 4.

BOX 3.2 Country-level economic class dynamics: some examples

The aggregate class dynamics shown in figure 3.1 have been shaped by country-specific patterns. This box presents evidence from four large countries in East Asia and Pacific for which, despite some problems with comparability of surveys over time (see appendix A), long-term evidence appears to be reliable.

Figure B3.2.1 highlights some interesting contrasts in country-level economic class dynamics. First, the Philippines stands out for having shown very little dynamism until recently; now there appears to

be some movement here both at the low end (elimination of poverty) and at the top (rise in economic security). Second, Indonesia and even more China and Vietnam in the past several years have seen slowing progress in eliminating extreme poverty (as the target has been virtually reached) and more progress in moving households over the threshold of economic security. China and Vietnam also stand out as having made a serious dent in the extent of economic vulnerability.

box continues next page

BOX 3.2   Country-level economic class dynamics: some examples *(continued)*

FIGURE B3.2.1   Population distribution by economic class in China, Indonesia, the Philippines, and Vietnam, 2002–15
Percentage of total population

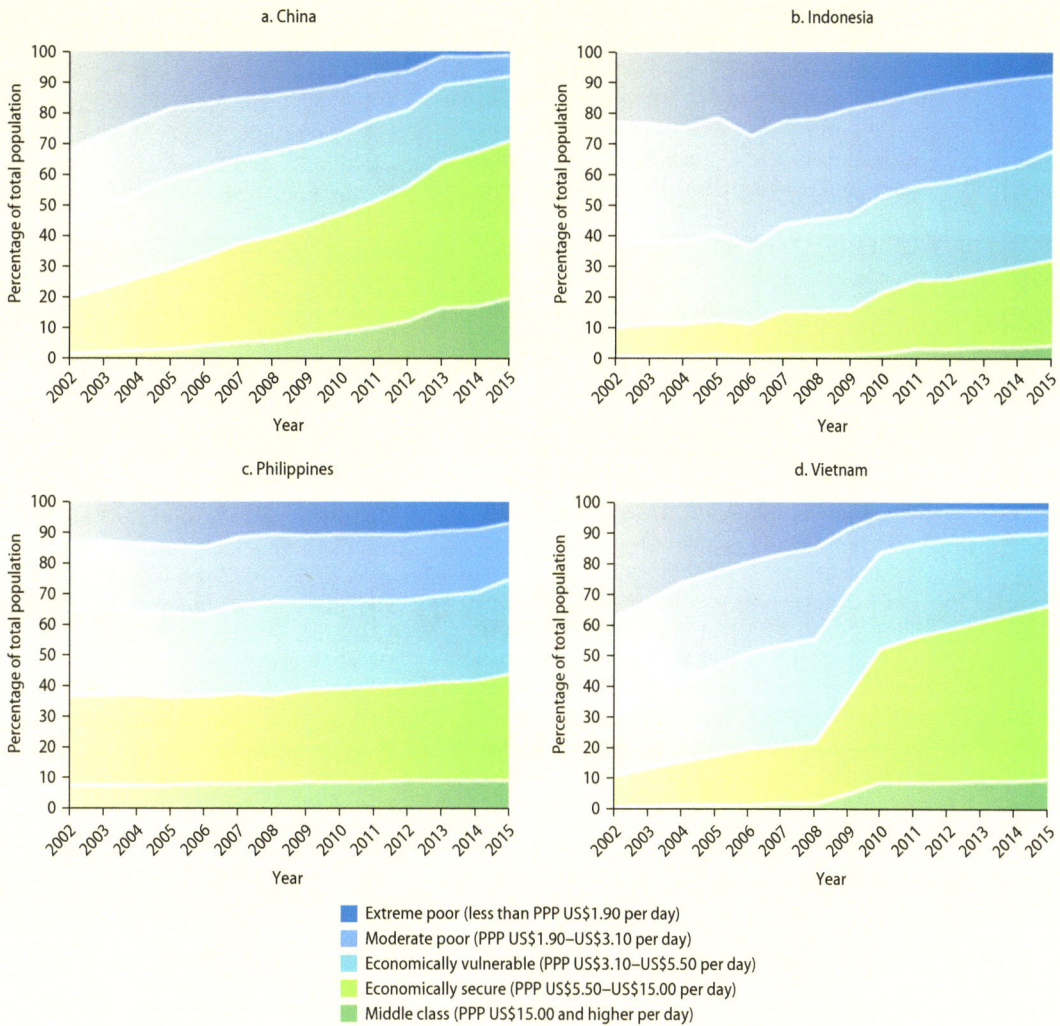

a. China

b. Indonesia

c. Philippines

d. Vietnam

- Extreme poor (less than PPP US$1.90 per day)
- Moderate poor (PPP US$1.90–US$3.10 per day)
- Economically vulnerable (PPP US$3.10–US$5.50 per day)
- Economically secure (PPP US$5.50–US$15.00 per day)
- Middle class (PPP US$15.00 and higher per day)

Source: World Bank EAP Team for Statistical Development.
Note: PPP = purchasing power parity. Country series might include breaks in comparability, though overall trends are deemed to be robust; see appendix A for details. Appendix B provides details on the methodology underlying this figure.

Notes

1. Developing East Asia and Pacific is defined as Cambodia, China, Indonesia, Lao PDR, Malaysia, Mongolia, Myanmar, Papua New Guinea, the Philippines, Thailand, Timor-Leste, Vietnam, and the Pacific Island countries.
2. Typically, respondents appear to underestimate women's unpaid work both in the care economy and in family businesses, as those are not seen as real "jobs" as captured by time-use surveys. Although a shift to paid employment often does not lead to a parallel decline in time spent in unpaid activities, the data show that participation in jobs that are defined as such (most likely "paid jobs") sets apart the poor from the rest of the distribution.
3. This pattern is not unique to East Asia and Pacific. Poverty map data for eight countries in six developing regions also find an inverse relationship between poverty rates and city size (Ferré, Ferreira, and Lanjouw 2012).
4. This does not apply to the Manchu minority and applies relatively less to the Hui minority.
5. In China in 2015, the rate of moderate poverty was only 2.2 percent in urban areas but 15.0 percent in rural areas.
6. The economically secure increased from 18 percent of the population in 2002 to 47 percent in 2015. The middle class increased from 3 percent of the population in 2002 to 17 percent in 2015; this is likely an underestimate given the difficulties for household surveys to capture the top tail of the distribution (see chapter 2).

References

Ferré, C., F. H. Ferreira, and P. Lanjouw. 2012. "Is There a Metropolitan Bias? The Relationship between Poverty and City Size in a Selection of Developing Countries." World Bank, Washington, DC. doi:10.1093/wber/lhs007.

Ferreira, F. H., J. Messina, J. Rigolini, L. F. Lopez-Calva, M. A. Lugo, and R. Vakis. 2013. *Economic Mobility and the Rise of the Latin American Middle Class.* Washington, DC: World Bank.

Gradín, C. 2015. "Rural Poverty and Ethnicity in China." In *Measurement of Poverty, Deprivation, and Economic Mobility,* edited by T. I. Garner and K. S. Short, 221–47. Bingley, U.K.: Emerald Group Publishing.

Gustafsson, B., and D. Sai. 2014. "Why Is There No Income Gap between the Hui Muslim Minority and the Han Majority in Rural Ningxia, China?" *The China Quarterly* 220: 968–87.

Kharas, H. 2010. *The Emerging Middle Class in Developing Countries.* Paris: OECD Publishing.

Lopez-Calva, L. F., and E. Ortiz-Juarez. 2011. "A Vulnerability Approach to the Definition of the Middle Class." Policy Research Working Paper No. WPS 5902, World Bank, Washington, DC. https://openknowledge.worldbank.org/handle/10986/3669.

Pritchett, L. 2003. "Who Is Not Poor? Proposing a Higher International Standard for Poverty." Working Paper 33, Center for Global Development, London, U.K.

———. 2006. *Who Is Not Poor? Dreaming of a World Truly Free of Poverty.* Oxford, U.K.: Oxford University Press.

Wilson, D., and R. Dragusanu. 2008. *The Expanding Middle: The Exploding World Middle Class and Falling Global Inequality.* New York: Goldman Sachs.

World Bank. 2012. *Malaysia Economic Monitor 2012: Unlocking Women's Potential.* Washington, DC: World Bank.

Economic Class and the Challenges of Inclusive Growth | 4

Introduction

Inclusive growth involves reducing poverty, fostering upward economic mobility, and providing economic security for all income groups. Since the beginning of the century, countries in developing East Asia and Pacific[1] have experienced unprecedented poverty reduction. Yet perceptions of rising inequality and of shrinking opportunities for upward mobility, together with a high exposure to shocks, suggest the need for scaled-up public policy actions to secure upward mobility throughout the income distribution. Such actions might involve a focus on different constraints for each segment of the income distribution, as discussed in this chapter. For some residents of the region, such as people trapped in extreme poverty, the challenge is very much about upward mobility, whereas for other people, such as the economically vulnerable, being able to secure what they have is as important as public policy designed to reduce barriers to upward mobility.

Securing upward mobility: removing constraints to inclusive growth

In this report, the concept of inclusive growth, where poverty is reduced and no one is left behind, involves two elements in addition to poverty reduction: (a) economic mobility, defined as the ability to improve one's lot in life and move to a higher economic class, and (b) economic security, which enables an individual to hold on to his or her gains. Comprehensive evidence on these dimensions is hard to come by for the East Asia and Pacific region, but such evidence provides an important complement to the familiar story of the region's success in reducing extreme poverty (box 4.1).

Given the East Asia and Pacific region's recent high growth and significant reduction in poverty, it would be expected that a longitudinal analysis would show that most households experienced increases in income and that much upward mobility had occurred across classes. The analysis here confirms those hypotheses, with some nuances. First, in each class other than the middle class, a majority of people experienced a positive increase in consumption over a two-year period,[2] and the increases were proportionally larger for poorer classes. Second, although at least one in five people moved to a higher economic class, some people from all economic classes experienced downward transitions. Despite those movements, the largest share of households remained in the same class

BOX 4.1   Sources used to analyze mobility

TABLE B4.1.1   Data used to analyze short- and long-term mobility

Country	Analysis	Survey instrument	Survey years
Cambodia	Long run		2004–12
Indonesia	Short run	National Socio-Economic Survey	2008–10
	Long run		2000–10
Lao PDR	Short run	Lao Consumption and Expenditure Survey	2008–12/13
Philippines	Short run	Philippine Family Income and Expenditure Survey	2006–09
Vietnam	Short run	Vietnam Household Living Standards Survey	2010–12
	Long run		2004–12

This chapter's analysis of mobility relies on several sources of data. To discuss short-term regional trends in mobility, data were used for Indonesia, the Lao People's Democratic Republic, the Philippines, and Vietnam. These four countries were selected because of the availability of panel—or longitudinal—data for each, which allow for individual households to be followed over time. These four countries are sufficiently different from each other in economic development, class composition, and growth rates that it is possible to begin to sketch a picture of class dynamics for the region as a whole. The most recent sample years available were selected for use here, with a two-year minimum break between observations. Whereas Lao PDR, the Philippines, and Vietnam have followed the same households for many years, Indonesia has a very short panel. To facilitate comparisons of countries, two-year trends were extrapolated from the longer panel periods.[a] The data are drawn from expenditure surveys, which serve as a proxy for consumption (table B4.1.1).

The analysis of long-term trends does not use true household panels and instead relies on a methodology of matching households by time-invariant characteristics and their distributions across cross-sectional data sets.[b] The methodology required choosing countries for which there are cross-sectional comparable data spanning a long period, defined as at least eight years. In addition, an attempt was made to compare long- and short-term mobility to understand the extent to which short-term trends represent permanent transitions. Using these criteria, the long-term analysis was conducted on Indonesia and Vietnam, for which short-term mobility estimates also were available, and on Cambodia.

a. All transitions have been adjusted to the shortest period for which true transitions can be measured for the greatest number of countries (that is, two years). Vietnam has a two-year panel, and the annual Indonesia data can also be explored in a two-year panel. The three-year Philippines data and the five-year Lao PDR data are extrapolated to two-year periods. These adjustments to estimate two-year transitions rates allow comparison of mobility across countries, although at the cost of strong assumptions about household income growing linearly. By definition, therefore, short-term volatility cannot be captured. Similarly, such comparisons cannot take into account the possibility that different countries might be at different points in their economic cycle in the periods for which they are observed. However serious, such constraints could be addressed only by relying on higher-frequency (for example, yearly) nationally representative panel data for all countries that are to be compared—data that are currently unavailable.
b. See Dang and others (2014) for a discussion of the construction of synthetic panels.

(figure 4.1). Third, upward mobility appears to be higher over the long run than the short run, with more households moving up and fewer staying in the same class or experiencing negative transitions. The share of households that stayed in the same class over a 10-year period was also significantly less than in Latin America over a 15-year period (Ferreira and others 2013). Overall, therefore, it seems the net result of the region's high reduction in poverty, supported by high growth, has been mapped by very different household-level trajectories. And it is important to remember that mobility patterns are very country specific, partly reflecting the different country situations over the period of analysis.[3]

A close look at the characteristics of the households that experienced different trajectories helps explain what has enabled upward mobility for different income groups:

- *Climbers*—those who improved their class—accounted for one-fifth (in the Philippines) to one-third (in Indonesia and Lao People's Democratic Republic) of households. Households in poorer classes were more likely to improve their class (figure 4.2) than were their richer counterparts. Country patterns differed, with economically secure households being the big winners in Indonesia, whereas extreme poor households experienced the largest gains in Lao PDR. Households that climbed out of moderate poverty or economic vulnerability tended to have better access to public services (education, health, and so forth) and more physical and financial assets, as well as a broader social network than other households in the same economic class. People who moved out of economic security into the middle class had more education, were living in an urban area, had access to better jobs and, if women, were more likely to be in paid employment.

- *Stayers*—those who did not change economic class—accounted for between 45 percent of the population (in Indonesia) and 69 percent (in the Philippines). The class composition of this group varied by country, with households in extreme poverty being more likely not to have changed class in Lao PDR and the Philippines and economically secure households more likely not to have changed class in Indonesia and Vietnam. In Vietnam, those who did not change class tended to be older, more urban, and more educated, compared with those who did change class. In contrast, stayers in the Philippines tended to be younger and have greater household assets than those who moved.[4]

- *Sliders*—those who moved to a lower economic class—represented about one-sixth of all samples. Profiles of the backsliders—those who moved to a lower class—varied by country, with less-educated people, those

FIGURE 4.1   **Short-run class mobility, aggregate**

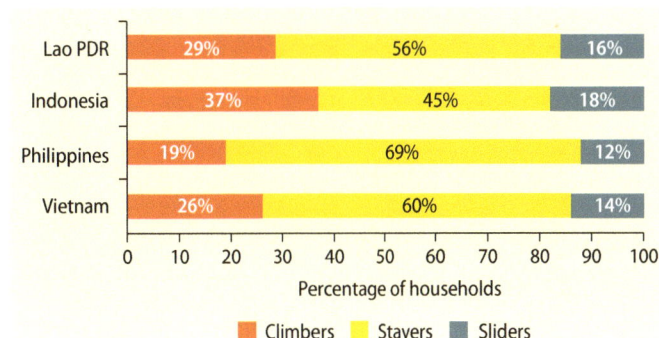

Source: Cunningham 2016.
Note: "Climbers" denotes households that moved up in economic status, "stayers" are those that remained in the same economic class, and "sliders" are those that moved to a lower economic class. Analysis for different countries covers different years, as detailed in box 4.1.

who received fewer transfers, those who lived in more rural settings, and asset-poor households being particularly likely to have slid in Vietnam. In the Philippines, sliders were older and held more formal jobs.

Downward mobility across classes reflects both an ex ante exposure to risks and a limited ex post ability to manage the impacts of adverse shocks by some people, despite significant resilience overall. Shocks include economic shocks that affect prices and assets, personal shocks such as illness, and natural shocks. It is challenging to learn more about the effects of exposure to shocks and their impacts by class because of the paucity of relevant data. Nevertheless, for Vietnam, some evidence is available from the country's nationally representative panel and from other sources (box 4.2). Negative shocks as reported by households[5] are associated with a greater probability of moving down the class ladder among the moderate poor and the economically vulnerable. Even the middle class faces risks. Conversely, moderate poor households that did not receive a shock were 50 percent more likely than those who did experience a shock to have moved up one class over a two-year period and were 34 percent more likely to move up two classes.[6] Although these findings underline the significance of shocks, they also show that even moderate poor households can

FIGURE 4.2   Class mobility, by initial income group, short run

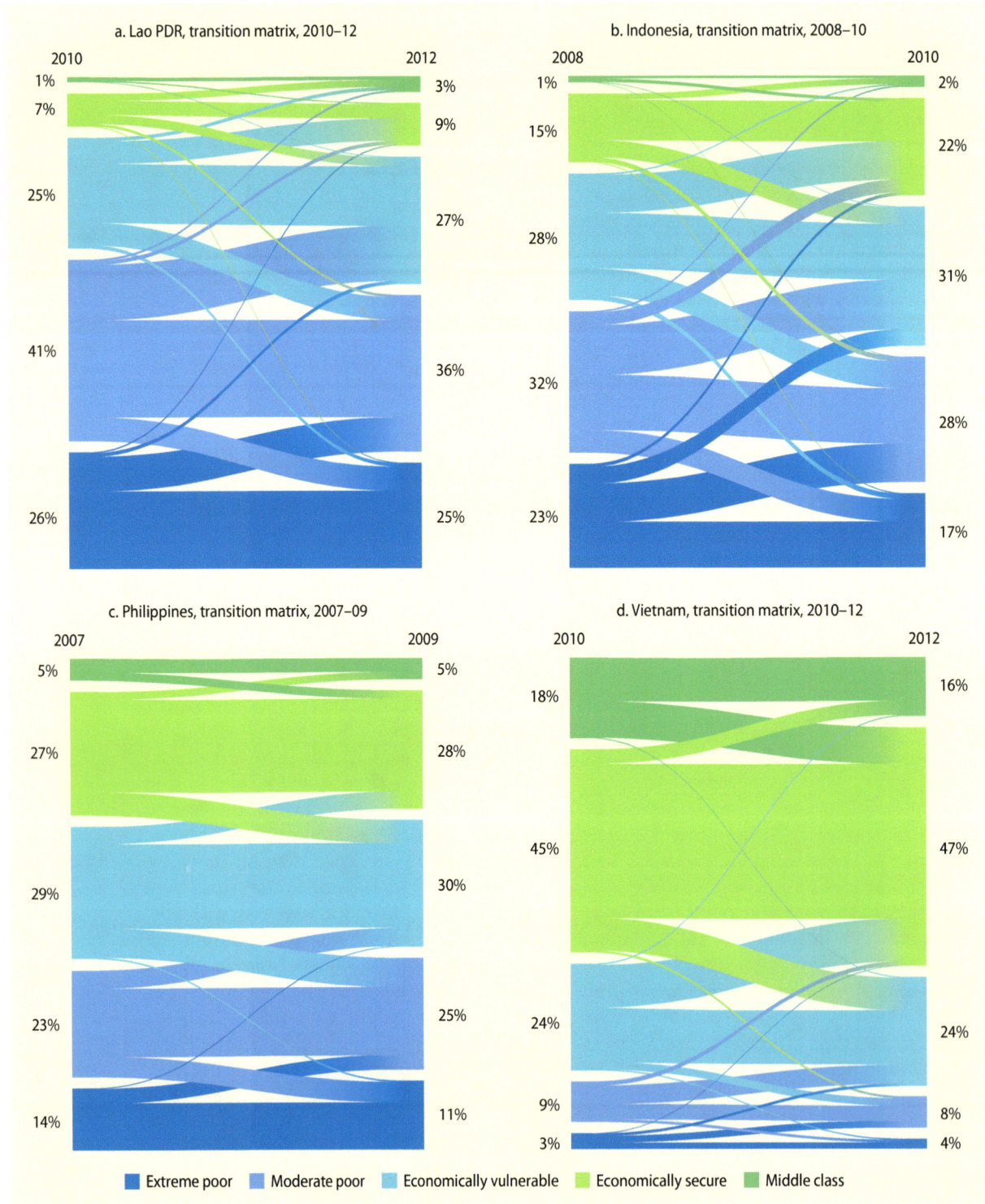

a. Lao PDR, transition matrix, 2010–12

2010	2012
1%	3%
7%	9%
25%	27%
41%	36%
26%	25%

b. Indonesia, transition matrix, 2008–10

2008	2010
1%	2%
15%	22%
28%	31%
32%	28%
23%	17%

c. Philippines, transition matrix, 2007–09

2007	2009
5%	5%
27%	28%
29%	30%
23%	25%
14%	11%

d. Vietnam, transition matrix, 2010–12

2010	2012
18%	16%
45%	47%
24%	24%
9%	8%
3%	4%

■ Extreme poor   ■ Moderate poor   ■ Economically vulnerable   ■ Economically secure   ■ Middle class

Source: Cunningham 2016.

BOX 4.2 Shocks in developing East Asia and Pacific

According to Vietnam's nationally representative panel, moderate poor households are particularly susceptible to shocks, although the risk is rather similar across classes. Approximately 10 percent of a sample of urban and rural moderate poor in the region experienced a shock within the previous two years, whereas 8 percent of economically vulnerable households were hit by a shock.[a] The type of shock did not appear to differ by class. A grouping of the available information into four broad categories—natural shocks that encompass all nature-related shocks, economic shocks that include prices and use of assets, personal shocks such as illness or family structure, and other shocks such as crime—shows that more than 40 percent of households that experienced a shock in the previous two years named an economic shock, with low income and high food prices being the primary shocks. The second most common shock among all classes was a personal shock, typically sickness or death of a household member. Natural disasters emerged strongly for the poorer classes, although natural shocks constituted less than 10 percent of all shocks experienced by economically secure households and were not listed at all by middle-class households.[b] The time period covered by these data (2010–12) had a low incidence of negative impacts from natural disasters. For example, the number of people killed, the number of houses destroyed, and the cumulative damage from tropical cyclones (as a share of gross domestic product [GDP]) during 2010–12 was among the lowest in the time period 1990–2013. Similar results emerged for a sample of rural households as for the reported national sample.[c]

Data collected by small panels in marginalized rural regions of Cambodia, Lao PDR, and Thailand provide complementary insights, despite not being strictly comparable with the findings for Vietnam. As in Vietnam, the propensity to experience a shock was similar across classes in rural areas of Cambodia, Lao PDR, and Thailand. This last finding is less surprising in a rural setting than in the nationally representative Vietnam case because aggregate shocks—those that affect entire communities—are very common in agricultural settings. More than 80 percent of moderate poor households in Cambodia and more than 60 percent in Lao PDR and Thailand experienced a shock in the year of the survey. Similarly, 70 percent of economically vulnerable households in rural Cambodia and around 60 percent in rural Lao PDR and Thailand were hit by at least one shock in the previous year. Those percentages compare with 68 percent of economically secure households in Cambodia having experienced at least one shock in the previous year, although the difference in probabilities between classes is not statistically significant (at the 5 percent level) and there was no difference with the middle classes in Lao PDR and Thailand.

In Cambodia, Lao PDR, and Thailand, illness of a household member was by far the most frequent personal shock. The majority of shocks reported by moderate poor households and economically vulnerable households in rural areas of the three countries were natural shocks and personal shocks. The difference in the propensity of having experienced one kind of shock or the other was not statistically significant. Livestock disease was the most commonly cited natural shock, followed by floods (and droughts in Lao PDR). These trends did not differ by economic class, with the exception of the middle class in rural Thailand, where personal shocks far outweighed the others.

a. The Vietnam Household Living Standards Survey asks households about the shocks they had experienced, up to three. Among households that experienced a shock, a high number of households reported the maximum number (for an average of 2.6 shocks).
b. Recent evidence using new high-resolution flood hazard maps and spatial socioeconomic data found that, although poor households overall in Vietnam were not particularly exposed to flooding, poor households living in slums in Ho Chi Minh City faced much higher chances of flooding than the rest of the population (Bangalore, Smith, and Veldkamp 2016).
c. The time period covered by these data (2010–12) had a low incidence of negative impacts from natural disasters. For example, the number of people killed, the number of houses destroyed, and the cumulative damage from tropical cyclones (as a share of GDP) during 2010–12 was among the lowest in the time period 1990–2013.

overcome negative circumstances if they have the appropriate assets base, because lack of assets rather than lack of shocks appears to explain slides into poverty.

Social protection programs and insurance play an important role in reducing households' exposure to shocks and in helping households cope with the consequences of shocks without eroding the future profitability of their assets. The effectiveness of those programs and insurance varies greatly, however, depending on the nature of the shocks experienced. Shocks are often classified as aggregate shocks, which affect entire communities (such as financial crises, natural disasters, global epidemics, or spikes in food prices) or idiosyncratic shocks, which affect individuals (such as bad health, job loss, unexpected family event). Aggregate shocks limit people's ability to pool risks and tend to result in large losses.

In developing East Asia and Pacific, aggregate shocks are common. In the past couple of decades, different parts of the region have been affected by two major financial crises, several spikes in food prices, natural disasters ranging from earthquakes to tsunamis, and repeated hits by massive cyclones.[7] In addition, millions of people in the region are exposed to the severe consequences of large natural shocks because populations are concentrated in vulnerable low-lying coastal areas or on marginal and hazardous lands in cities. In such areas, insecurity of tenure provides little incentive for households to invest in risk management, and poor provision of services such as health care compounds the effects of disasters such as flooding (Baker and Gadgil 2017). Therefore, any public policy strategy aimed at supporting inclusive growth in the region must address the overall risk management agenda by covering both idiosyncratic and aggregate shocks and including both ex post and ex ante measures.

Eliminating extreme poverty

The extreme poor accounted for 2.5 percent of the region's population in 2015, down sharply from 18 percent a decade earlier and significantly lower than the 13 percent average extreme poverty rate across the developing world. This remarkable success means the East Asia and Pacific region as a whole has already met the World Bank Group's 2030 target for the reduction of extreme poverty. Yet the incidence of extreme poverty remains high in some countries, while in others the rate is still significant for small pockets of the population, particularly ethnic minorities and people who live in remote areas. The implied "last mile" challenge of eliminating extreme poverty means very different things in these different contexts (box 4.3).

In Lao PDR, Papua New Guinea, and several Pacific Island countries where the

---

BOX 4.3   Diverse barriers make escaping extreme poverty difficult

Recent research among poor, marginalized communities in Lao PDR and the Philippines illustrates the challenges of eradicating extreme poverty in the region. In these communities, people living in extreme poverty found it extraordinarily difficult to escape poverty—but for different reasons. Examining the specific, localized, and heterogeneous nature of the living circumstances of those people highlights why it is difficult to design policies that reach such groups effectively.

The research in Lao PDR was conducted mostly in poor, ethnic minority villages in the highlands. The extreme poor in these villages faced almost insurmountable barriers to upward mobility. The most prominent barrier is location. Villages are remote and often accessible by only a single dirt road and thus are difficult, expensive, and time consuming to reach. Villagers lack access to markets, jobs, and public services. Although most villages have a primary school, few have a secondary school, health center, sufficient electricity, or adequate sanitation. Residents can seldom afford to travel outside their villages to obtain needed services or to pay the costs for services. Children tend to drop out of school early, and dirt, disease, and ill health are common. Geographical remoteness thus places clear limits on the ability of poor families to live healthy lives, acquire skills and education, and invest in their futures.

box continues next page

BOX 4.3   **Diverse barriers make escaping extreme poverty difficult** (continued)

The locations of such villages also curtail residents' livelihoods. Nonfarm job opportunities are too far away, so poor people depend on agricultural work to survive. Yet markets are also distant, so it is not worthwhile for villagers to diversify into cash crops that could enable them to earn a better living. In some villages, poor families whose diets consist mainly of rice and cassava reported not having enough food for several months a year and that they suffered from poor nutrition and bad health.

Families living in extreme poverty have little capacity to manage risk. Their livelihoods are highly susceptible to drought, bad weather, natural disasters, and other shocks, such as livestock epidemics and disease. Health shocks were almost always catastrophic and were one of the commonly reported causes of impoverishment. To cope with such shocks, families borrowed beyond their means, leading to cycles of indebtedness and sometimes bankruptcy.

Ethnicity, language, and gender also are deeply connected to poverty in these villages. Most villagers belong to ethnic minorities, and they usually speak a language that differs from the country's dominant language (as in Lao PDR). The language barrier limits villagers' uptake of services and reduces their confidence to seek work in other parts of the country. Cultural norms regarding gender also significantly limit the ability of girls to continue their schooling and lead poor families to avoid investing in girls, thus significantly exacerbating intrahousehold inequality. In one remote village, only 4 of 44 students in the primary school were girls.

Research in urban slums in Manila identified a set of different—and yet similarly almost insurmountable—barriers to escaping poverty. The poorest people in Manila were homeless or were squatters living in informal settlements. They reported

difficulties in getting jobs, because they had arrived in the city from rural areas without any skills. In Manila, they lived in poor-quality, makeshift housing or lacked housing altogether and thus were exposed to crime, natural disasters, floods, dirt, and disease. Like their rural counterparts, these city dwellers are extremely vulnerable to shocks and have limited capacity to manage risk. Finally, their lack of identity documents is a key barrier to escaping poverty. In the Philippines, those born to extreme poor families sometimes lack a birth certificate, which is needed to get a job, to receive government benefits, and to go to school, but the only way for them to get a birth certificate is to return to the town of their birth, which is not something that they can afford to do. Thus, they are stuck in the informal economy, often scavenging.

The contrasting examples of remote villages of Lao PDR and urban slums in the Philippines illustrate the disparate characteristics of the remaining pockets of extreme poor households in the East Asia and Pacific region. In both settings, those households face difficulties in their ability to benefit from investments in job growth, agriculture, health, education, and other public services—from efforts to grow and invest—but for different reasons. In rural villages of Lao PDR, extreme poor households are constrained by location, agroecological disadvantage, lack of public services, ethnicity, and gender. In the slums of the Philippines, extreme poor households are constrained by lack of appropriate skills, insecure housing, and lack of identity documents. In both settings, extreme poor residents find it hard to manage risk. These differences highlight the specific challenges that governments around the region face in fostering upward mobility for the remaining groups living in extreme poverty.

Source: Beath, Parker, and Woodhouse 2016.

incidence of extreme poverty still reaches double digits, the policy priority is to provide plenty of opportunities for unskilled workers, following the path of the successful countries in the region. Lao PDR has created opportunities for poor people by improving human capital and access to land (Pimhidzai 2015).

Yet over the decade to 2013, household consumption grew at a rate almost 4 percentage points lower than overall gross domestic product per capita. Had growth been more broadly shared, rather than led by the exploitation of natural resources, even greater progress would have been achieved.

The example of Lao PDR also underscores the role that risk management plays in fostering truly inclusive growth. Because most of the poor work in agriculture, they remain very vulnerable to shocks to that sector of the economy, as well as to idiosyncratic shocks such as catastrophic health expenditures. Such unmitigated shocks erode the improvements that households are able to make in good years.

Extreme poverty is deeply interconnected with ethnicity and location in ways that are difficult to identify, measure, and tackle. These complex interactions exist in all countries, including those with a high overall poverty incidence such as Lao PDR (box 4.3). But the interactions are particularly relevant in countries with a lower overall incidence of poverty, where extreme poverty is concentrated in small pockets of the general population. In Vietnam, for instance, ethnic minorities account for 15 percent of the total population but constitute a majority of the country's extreme poor. Ethnic minorities have experienced gains in welfare since the early 1990s, but progress toward reducing poverty and child mortality has stalled in recent years. Poor education, malnutrition, and low access to sanitation exert mutually reinforcing adverse effects on equality of opportunity for ethnic-minority children.

The influence of ethnicity on people's livelihoods, barring situations of outright discrimination, tends to manifest itself in either specific cultural practices or language, which affect what people do or what they can access. The way ethnicity shapes the livelihoods of households living in extreme poverty can therefore be both positive and negative. Whereas a strong sense of identity and reliance on local support networks can be strengths, for example, traditional agricultural practices can lead to very low productivity for communities of people living on marginal lands. Similarly, ethnic minorities can find themselves excluded by dominant ethnicities when the use of certain services or markets requires knowledge of the mainstream language. Also, the specific

challenges or vulnerabilities of ethnic minorities tend to vary significantly across groups. In Lao PDR, for example, minority groups (the non Lao-Thai) are more likely overall to be poor, but the Chine-Tibet group has done significantly better than other minorities. Such differences between ethnic minorities apply to both the incidence of poverty and the likelihood of moving into or out of poverty (Pimhidzai 2015).

Location can similarly define much of what ethnic minorities have access to, including basic rights such as being registered at birth, lack of which may seriously hinder a person's ability to access social services such as education (Beath, Parker, and Woodhouse 2016). Birth registration is particularly low among the poor in Cambodia, Indonesia, and Myanmar.

Location also defines the "last mile" challenge of eradicating extreme poverty in urban areas, particularly in sprawling urban slums of several large cities in the East Asia and Pacific region (Baker and Gadgil 2017). Although slums can be places of opportunity for their inhabitants if there is access to jobs, that opportunity may come at the cost of safety if slum dwellers live in precarious dwellings on land at high risk of natural disasters, such as coastal flooding. In addition, although many people migrate to cities for new economic opportunities, those who do so to flee desperate or threatening circumstances may not be able to take advantage of such opportunities if they lack the right skills, identification documents, or basic assets (such as savings or housing) that would help them settle in and start anew (Beath, Parker, and Woodhouse 2016). Similarly, for all the opportunities that urban areas offer, slum dwellers may have to rely on the expensive private provision of services that are normally available publicly, such as water and electricity, which in turn erodes the prosperity that living in a city would otherwise bring.

As with extreme poor households in remote Lao PDR, great heterogeneity can be found, even in the relatively homogeneous definition of *slum*. In metro Manila, where an estimated 3 million people, or 1 in 4 of the population, live informally, a recent study (World Bank forthcoming b) identified 2,500 different informal settlements. The settlements were grouped into five different categories. Each group faced very different challenges in terms of access to jobs and services and vulnerability to risks, so the policy solutions required to improve the livelihoods of their inhabitants would be very different.

From a policy perspective, the heterogeneity of extreme poor households is a challenge in at least two ways. First, although growth patterns that produce large numbers of unskilled job opportunities can be trusted to improve the lives of many extreme poor, specific groups may face sources of exclusion or may be located in areas too remote or underserved to benefit from such opportunities. Second, countries that have already seen the benefits of broad-based growth in reducing extreme poverty now face the task of tailoring policies to meet the specific needs of the remaining small pockets of extreme poverty. Although those countries may already have the necessary resources and institutional capacity, the fragmentation of target groups, as well as their specific needs and constraints, may pose significant challenges in designing and implementing programs.

Transitioning to economic security

Headline figures on the East Asia and Pacific region's extraordinary improvement in living standards focus on the virtual eradication of extreme poverty. Yet the mobility analysis previously presented, and the panel analysis that has informed the identification of the economic classes adopted in this report indicate that those who live just above the poverty line face a large risk of falling back into poverty. In addition, statistical analysis of the characteristics of those living in moderate poverty and of those one class above—the economically vulnerable—highlights significant overlap in the characteristics of the two groups, suggesting that the group a household falls into may be significantly influenced by chance.

In other words, above the extreme poverty line, there is a large gray area of households that struggle to make ends meet and achieve economic security, especially in the short term. For example, in Indonesia, 21 percent of households considered economically vulnerable in 2008 were found in 2010 to have fallen into moderate poverty, whereas 35 percent of moderate poor households had climbed to the economically vulnerable class. In the Philippines, between 2007 and 2009, 22 percent of economically vulnerable households fell into moderate poverty, whereas 17 percent of moderate poor households rose to become economically vulnerable. In Vietnam, between 2010 and 2012, only 7 percent of economically vulnerable households slid into moderate poverty, and 46 percent of moderate poor households moved up to the economically vulnerable class (Cunningham 2016). In Indonesia and Vietnam, where estimates of long-term mobility using synthetic panels are available, the backward movement in class from economically vulnerable to moderate poor was more muted over 10 years.

The dynamism of both moderate poor and economically vulnerable households is shown by their ability to save to purchase small assets, such as cell phones or motorcycles. They appear to lack mechanisms to save for larger productive assets, however. In some contexts, they have been able to make up for the deficiencies in what is provided to them—for example, by organizing their own early-warning system for flooding in one of Indonesia's slums (Baker and Gadgil 2017). But ad hoc solutions, however valuable, cannot replace systematic mechanisms to manage risks ex ante and to help households deal with shocks. Moderately poor households are also significantly likely to fall into extreme poverty or to enjoy only limited income growth that does not allow them to rise above their initial class.

In many ways, both moderate poor and economically vulnerable households face challenges that are similar to, if smaller than, those faced by extreme poor households. They may struggle with a low asset base, limited education, poor health owing to a lack of quality health care services, scarce large assets, and limited access to public infrastructure. Many work on small farms, at low-value jobs, or not at all, particularly many women in these classes. Because of their low asset base, negative shocks are likely to hit them harder, often resulting in a slide into moderate or extreme poverty.

The primary shocks likely to affect moderate poor and economically vulnerable households relate to loss of income, as a result of drought or livestock disease, personal shocks (including illness and death), and price shocks. Furthermore, the largely rural locations where these people reside and their limited links to the formal sector make it difficult to establish effective social protection networks. For instance, both the limited availability of, and coverage for, health insurance magnify the impact of illnesses, putting households at risk of impoverishment because of the out-of-pocket payments for health care.

Other factors, such as insecure tenure or limited access to finance, make it difficult for people in these classes to pursue better opportunities and thus diversify the risks to their livelihood by engaging in additional, more productive activities. Skills are also a constraint; many people in these classes have limited education. Because the majority are employed in agriculture or fishing, or are otherwise self-employed, there is a need to strengthen their skills to make them more productive in their present activities and to give them access to other opportunities. Also, their children have little access to early childhood development services and experience significant barriers to progression through the formal education system, reinforcing the intergenerational transmission of inequality.[8]

Another characteristic that distinguishes moderate poor and economically vulnerable households from economically secure ones is that they are less likely to be in paid employment. Only 60 percent of the moderate poor and 72 percent of the economically vulnerable are employed, in contrast to 80 percent of the economically secure. That is largely because female labor market participation

in jobs as defined by household surveys is low.[9] In addition, a large number of young people are not in school, are not employed, or are not receiving job training. High inactivity rates suggest that there is limited demand for these groups' skills. Even when employed, these young people have low returns to their human capital. Their participation in the formal sector is also low, reducing policy makers' scope for using formal labor market payment systems to deliver cash transfers that might strengthen their livelihoods.

For moderate poor and economically vulnerable households, most employment opportunities are with small and medium-sized enterprises. Weaknesses in the business climate constrain these businesses from expanding employment opportunities, including for the moderate poor and economically vulnerable households, and from making investments that would increase labor productivity. A particular challenge lies in labor market policies that distort employer incentives in an effort to protect workers (World Bank 2014a). The East Asia and Pacific region has some of the strictest (although some of the weakest) employment protection legislation in the world, as well as extremely high minimum wages.[10] The outcome is weaker incentives to hire workers, particularly women, youth, and less-skilled individuals. In several countries, women's labor force participation is further discouraged by nonlabor constraints: moderate poor and economically vulnerable households have particularly low female labor force participation rates, at least in the formal jobs captured by household surveys, which reflects traditional gender-based household roles and social norms, as well as limited availability of clean water, childcare, and eldercare.

In many countries, moderate poor and economically vulnerable households are concentrated in rural areas. Thus, they are particularly affected by official limitations to geographical mobility, where such restrictions are in force (particularly China and Vietnam) and by disparities in the provision of services across the rural-urban spectrum and across different zones in the same city. As discussed, de facto and de jure barriers to migration (chapter 2, box 2.5), together with limited support services to match migrants with city jobs, all reduce the reallocation of labor across space and sectors and depress productivity. Also, many people in these classes have limited access to public infrastructure, including electricity, clean water, and sanitation. Some of these limitations, such as low access to electricity and poor mobility within cities, are closely related to residents' low productivity and lack of employment opportunities.

Matching economic security with high-quality public services

Economically secure and middle-class households are identified by their low risk of sliding back into poverty. In most of the region, however, risk management tools are underprovided,[11] so even the middle classes are at risk of suffering significant downward mobility. Although the middle class especially can benefit from good jobs and the social protection measures that often come with such jobs, the middle class is not immune from aggregate shocks. For example, in Thailand, in 2011, 70 percent of the estimated US$47 billion in damage and losses resulting from natural disasters affected the manufacturing subsector (Global Facility for Disaster Reduction and Recovery, World Bank, and Rockefeller Foundation 2016), which tends to be a source of "good jobs."

In addition, in many countries in East Asia and Pacific, economic security has not been accompanied by an appropriate provision of public services, in contrast with countries elsewhere at similar income levels. This lack of services brings the risk that the middle classes could turn to an insular world of private service provision and could disengage from the national policy dialogue on service delivery and developmental outcomes. In turn, the failure of the economically secure and the middle class to keep government accountable risks making everyone less likely to receive quality services.

Access to high-quality services, including housing, clean water, sanitation, electricity, health care, and education, remains a challenge for many economically secure households in the region. One-third of economically secure households and 15 percent of the region's middle class (outside China) lack access to good-quality housing, clean water, and (to a lesser degree) sanitation (figure 4.3). These nonmonetary deprivations reflect geographical divides in service delivery, particularly between urban and rural areas.[12] Education quality, defined by learning outcomes, varies significantly by country. In fact, the region has some of the world's best-performing and some of the world's worst-performing education systems. In particular, education quality is a challenge in Indonesia, Mongolia, and the Philippines, as well as in lower-income countries such as Cambodia and Lao PDR. Other countries, such as Malaysia and Thailand, have recently been losing ground on internationally comparable tests of student performance.[13]

FIGURE 4.3 **Nonmonetary poverty by class, developing East Asia and Pacific 2012**

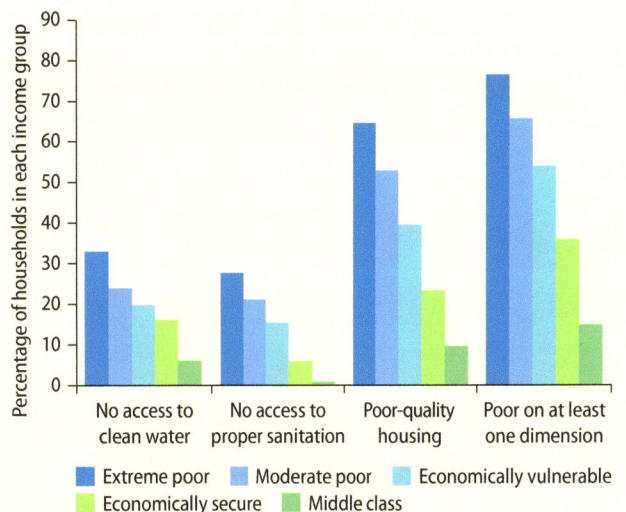

Source: Wai-Poi and others 2016.
Note: Access to clean water means piped water, protected well water, or water sold by a vendor. Access to proper sanitation means flush toilets or improved pit latrines. Good-quality housing means a roof that is made of concrete, cement, brick, stone, wood, or tiles; walls that are made of concrete, cement, brick, or stone; and a floor that is nonsoil. The countries sampled here are Cambodia, Indonesia, Lao PDR, Mongolia, the Philippines, Thailand, and Vietnam. Poor on at least one dimension means suffering from at least one deprivation among no access to clean water, no access to proper sanitation, or poor-quality housing.

The growing size and incomes of those living in economic security and of the middle class have increased their political influence particularly in upper-middle-income countries and in some lower-middle-income countries. A key question is whether this growing economic and political clout will benefit only these groups or whether it will make them successful advocates for a service delivery agenda that benefits the broader population.

Given their high aspirations, there is a risk that the people who make up these classes will increasingly opt out of public services that are of low quality and instead turn to privately provided services for health care, education, clean water, and transportation. Some may even choose to live in gated communities

that provide residents with private sanitation, electricity, and security service. That would reduce demand and accountability for higher-quality public services, as well as reinforce and perpetuate inequalities of opportunity. Across countries at different levels of development, there are already signs that opting out of publicly provided services may have begun, especially regarding significant use of private health care services (figure 4.4) and, to a lesser extent, private education at the primary and lower secondary levels, particularly among the middle class (figure 4.5).[14]

Surveys also indicate that economically secure households in Malaysia, the Philippines, and Thailand are already less engaged in a range of civic organizations, such as political parties and labor unions

FIGURE 4.4 **Public and private health care facility use by economic class, developing East Asia and Pacific, 2012**

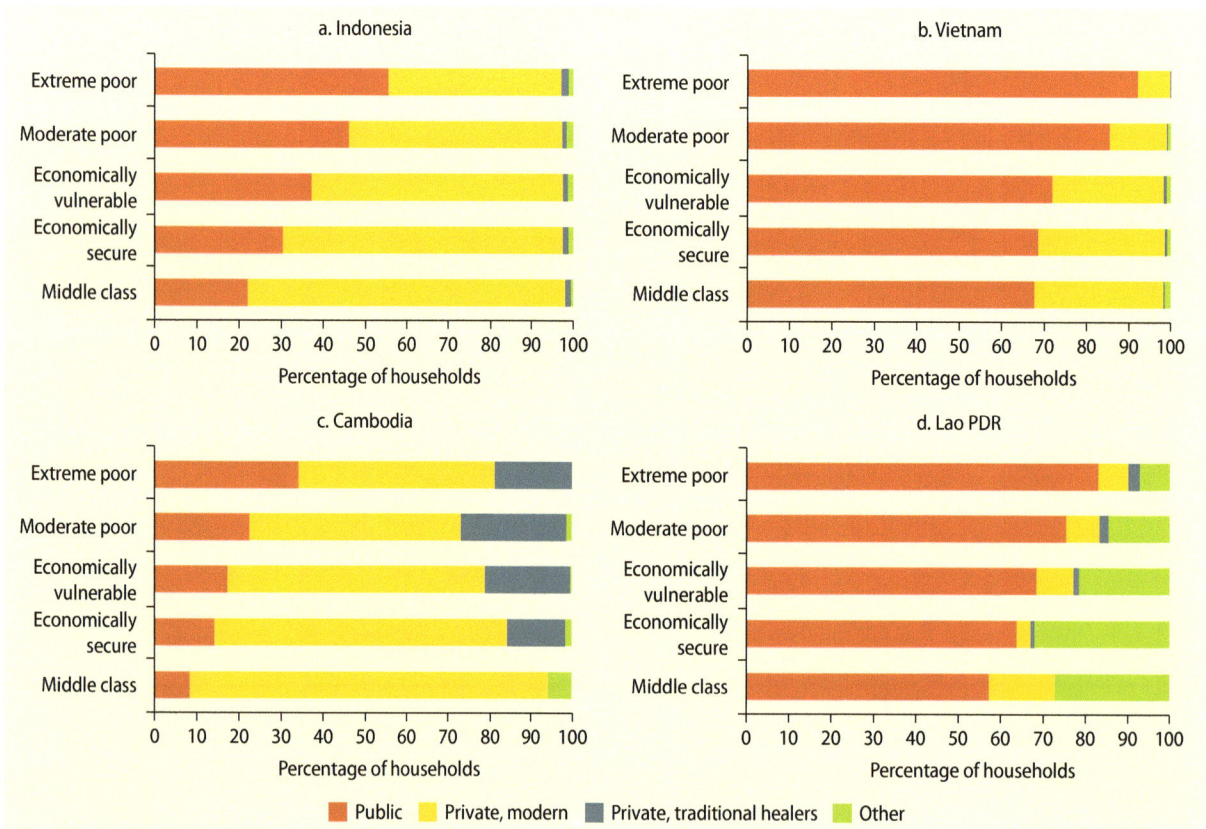

Source: Wai-Poi and others 2016.

and religious, sporting, cultural, educational, environmental, professional, humanitarian, consumer, and self-help groups (appendix C, table C.5). In the Philippines and Thailand, residents have less faith in public institutions, including the church, army, press, television, unions, police, courts, political parties, parliament, civil service, universities, corporations, and banks (appendix C, table C.6), although the opposite is true in China and Malaysia.[15] Similarly, the middle class may push for some problems to be simply moved to places with poorer populations and whose residents have less voice. For example, in China, middle-class protests against factories that pollute and that are dangerous have resulted in stricter enforcement of environmental protections and in plants being moved to poorer areas.[16]

The dangers are heightened by two factors. First, any expansion of public services and social protection would have to be funded through increased tax revenue, including higher personal income taxes. Those taxes would be paid mostly by economically secure and middle-class households, and those households might be reluctant to support public spending that brings them no returns. Second, because of the greater investment these two classes make in their children, as well as the tendency of people to marry others from the same class, the middle class will become increasingly disconnected from the rest of society. In turn, any growth of inequality and an opting out of public services would weaken social cohesion and possibly lead to a political impasse.

At the same time, as middle-class households care increasingly more about such issues as consumer safety, they can push for better regulations and better goods and services, which would benefit all households. For instance, recent food safety scandals in China have led to stronger regulations and better products for all residents. In addition, given these middle-class households' own vulnerability to shocks, they could have a stake in developing an appropriate system for managing risks.

FIGURE 4.5 Private education by economic class, developing East Asia and Pacific, 2012

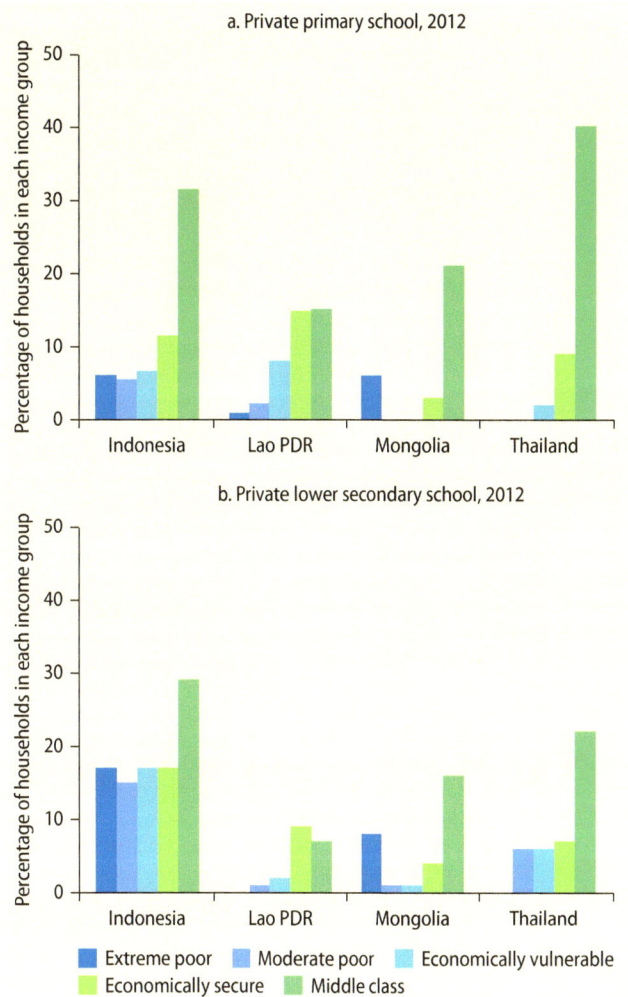

a. Private primary school, 2012

b. Private lower secondary school, 2012

Extreme poor   Moderate poor   Economically vulnerable
Economically secure   Middle class

Source: Wai-Poi and others 2016.

Notes

1. Developing East Asia and the Pacific is defined as Cambodia, China, Indonesia, the Lao People's Democratic Republic, Malaysia, Mongolia, Myanmar, Papua New Guinea, the Philippines, Thailand, Timor-Leste, Vietnam, and the Pacific Island countries

2. Economically secure households in Indonesia are the exception. In Indonesia, fewer than 50 percent experienced a positive increase.

3. For example, in the Philippines, most people did not move, but the chances of backsliding were also the least. This pattern is striking

because the Philippines panel data cover a period that includes both growth and crisis (2006–09). The lack of overall economic dynamism seems to also have implied greater resilience (lack of backsliding) during the period of economic stagnation.

4. Receipt of transfers, degree of job formality, and household wealth do not seem to affect the likelihood of being a so-called stayer in the household samples used here.

5. Note that shocks are not identified endogenously in the survey data as drops in incomes but are self-reported (through questions such as "Did you experience a shock?" and "What kind?"). Their identification, therefore, is not linked to income gains or losses or to a specific magnitude of a shock (for example, a drop of more than 10 percent in income) or to the specific duration of a shock.

6. The qualitative results are broadly similar across countries. For instance, in rural marginalized Cambodia, 32 percent of the moderate poor who do not experience a shock move up one or two classes over a two-year period, compared with 26 percent of those who experience a shock. Conversely, the moderate poor who do experience a shock are more likely than those who do not to become extreme poor; the probabilities are 32 percent and 3 percent, respectively.

7. More rigorous analysis shows how seriously East Asia and Pacific has been hit in the past decade. For example, in the first 9 months of 2011, the region experienced 80 percent of global losses that were due to natural disasters (Jha and Stanton-Geddes 2013).

8. A few countries, such as Vietnam, are approaching universal access to early childhood development opportunities, but this is a new endeavor for many other countries.

9. This tends to exclude unpaid family labor in households' entrepreneurial activities, often because they are combined, interspersed, or both throughout the day with domestic work or with caring for children or elderly relatives. As is the case with those care-giving activities, their economic contribution tends to be underestimated.

10. For an analysis of minimum wages in member countries of the Association of Southeast Asian Nations (ASEAN), see Del Carpio and Pabon (2014).

11. Following a year of major natural disasters globally, estimates by commercial insurers in 2012 found that several East Asia and Pacific countries, including China and Thailand, were underinsured for natural disasters (Centre for Economic and Business Research 2012).

12. Only one-half of rural economically secure households but three-quarters of urban economically secure households are free of nonmonetary poverty, defined as suffering from at least one of lack of access to clean water, lack of access to proper sanitation, or poor-quality housing.

These rural constraints are particularly pronounced in Cambodia and Lao PDR, where most rural economically secure households are deprived with respect to at least one nonmonetary dimension. In contrast, the share of rural economically secure households that experience nonmonetary poverty is two-thirds in Indonesia, 56 percent in Thailand, 40 percent in Vietnam, and only 19 percent in the Philippines.

13. For instance, in Indonesia and Malaysia, more than 50 percent of 15-year-olds reportedly had less than limited proficiency in reading (OECD 2012). In Lao PDR, two-thirds of rural test takers and one-third of urban test takers could not comprehend basic text (World Bank 2014b; see also World Bank forthcoming, a).

14. In Indonesia, health care and education account for 8 percent of total spending by economically secure households and 12 percent of spending by the middle class. Fully two-thirds of economically secure households and three-quarters of the middle class use private health facilities. On average, across developing East Asia and Pacific countries for which data were available, one-third of middle-class households use private primary schools.

15. Wai-Poi and others (2016) used the World Values Surveys to examine these attitudes in China, Malaysia, the Philippines, and Thailand. Because data on income are not available from the surveys, these researchers define "secure" households as those that never go without food, those that never or only rarely go without needed medical treatment, and those that never have to dip into savings to support themselves. The proportions of secure and nonsecure households using that definition are largely consistent with those of economically secure and middle-class households in each country. There is little difference in civic engagement in China between secure and nonsecure

households, where civic engagement is very low to begin with.

16. Protests in Chinese cities have been found to be associated with increased government imposition of fines for pollution, of plant closures, and of suspensions of activities of polluting factories (Ekman 2015). However, there are also examples of urban middle-class protests that resulted in a new chemical factory being relocated from a wealthy coastal city to a poorer, smaller city (Forbes 2015).

References

Baker, J., and G. Gadgil, eds. 2017. *East Asia and Pacific Cities: Expanding Opportunities for the Urban Poor.* Urban Development Series. Washington, DC: World Bank.

Bangalore, M., A. Smith, and T. Veldkamp. 2016. "Exposure to Floods, Climate Change, and Poverty in Vietnam." Policy Research Working Paper 7765, World Bank, Washington, DC.

Beath, A., B. Parker, and A. Woodhouse. 2016. "Heterogeneity and Marginalization among the Extreme Poor in East Asia and the Pacific." Background paper for *Riding the Wave: An East Asian Miracle for the 21st Century.* Washington, DC: World Bank.

Centre for Economic and Business Research. 2012. "Lloyd's Global Underinsurance Report." Lloyd's, London.

Cunningham, W. 2016. "Class Mobility." Background paper for *Riding the Wave: An East Asian Miracle for the 21st Century* Washington, DC: World Bank.

Dang, H.-A., P. Lanjouw, J. Luoto, and D. McKenzie. 2014. "Using Repeated Cross-Sections to Explore Movements into and out of Poverty." *Journal of Development Economics* 107 (C): 112–28.

Del Carpio, X., and L. Pabon. 2014. "Minimum Wage Policy: Lessons with a Focus on the ASEAN Region." 87864-EAP, World Bank, Washington, DC.

Ekman, A. 2015. "China's Emerging Middle Class: What Political Impact?" Institut français des relations internationales, Center for Asian Studies, Paris.

Ferreira, F. H. G., J. Messina, J. Rigolini, L.-F. López-Calva, M. A. Lugo, and R. Vakis. 2013. *Economic Mobility and the Rise of the Latin American Middle Class.* Washington, DC: World Bank.

Forbes. 2015. "Environmental Protests Expose Weakness in China's Leadership." http://www.forbes.com/sites/forbesasia/2015/06/22/environmental-protests-expose-weakness-in-chinas-leadership.

Global Facility for Disaster Reduction and Recovery, World Bank Group, and Rockefeller Foundation. 2016. "Toward a Regional Approach to Disaster Risk Finance in Asia." http://pubdocs.worldbank.org/en/622001465500604140/DRF-Rockefeller-FINAL-002.pdf.

Jha, A. K., and Z. Stanton-Geddes, eds. 2013. *Strong, Safe, and Resilient: A Strategic Policy Guide for Disaster Risk Management in East Asia and the Pacific.* Washington, DC: World Bank.

OECD (Organisation for Economic Co-operation and Development). 2012. Program for International Student Assessment database. http://www.oecd.org/pisa/pisaproducts/pisa2012database-downloadabledata.htm

Pimhidzai, O. 2015. "Drivers of Poverty Reduction in Lao PDR." Lao PDR Poverty Policy Notes, World Bank, Washington, DC.

Wai-Poi, M., R. Purnamasari, T. Indrakesuma, I. Uochi, and L. Wijaya. 2016. "East Asia's Rising Middle Classes." Background paper for *Riding the Wave: An East Asian Miracle for the 21st Century.* Washington, DC: World Bank.

World Bank. 2014a. *East Asia Pacific at Work: Employment, Enterprise, and Well-being.* Washington, DC: World Bank.

———. 2014b. *Lao Development Report 2014: Expanding Productive Employment for Broad-Based Growth.* Washington, DC: World Bank.

———. Forthcoming a. *Education Quality and Economic Prosperity in East Asia and Pacific.* Washington, DC: World Bank.

———. Forthcoming b. "Navigating Informality: Perils and Prospects in Metro Manila's Slums, Metro Manila Slum Study." World Bank, Washington, DC.

A Policy Agenda for Inclusive Growth | 5

Introduction

Despite the huge economic progress in developing East Asia and Pacific, some groups run the risk of being left behind in extreme poverty. Other groups enjoy only limited economic security and are finding that they cannot hold on to their gains for long. At the same time, the rapid pace of development is changing the needs and aspirations of the population, generating demand for higher-quality public services. And inequalities (real or perceived) are growing or remain high.

To address the needs of the different economic classes, this report identifies three policy priorities, or pillars: fostering economic mobility, increasing economic security, and underlying those priorities, strengthening the institutions required for inclusive growth. Within each area, the different needs of the various classes may be best served by different types of policy or program designs, so this chapter focuses selectively on those that appear to be a binding constraint for specific classes.

This chapter summarizes key areas for action under each pillar, then translates those areas into priorities across different country conditions (box 5.1). Finally, it describes specific measures that might help achieve those priorities. By addressing the priorities most relevant to their conditions, governments can lay the foundations for a new social contract, which will adapt the region's development model to the challenges ahead.

The three pillars: economic mobility, economic security, and institutions for inclusive growth

Economic mobility

Despite the remarkable economic dynamism in the region, many households find it difficult to improve their economic status. For all groups, short- and long-term income gains are not always sufficient to lift households into higher economic classes (chapter 4). In Indonesia, for example, 36 percent of the extreme poor and 29 percent of the moderate poor did not improve their class over a 10-year period. Although broad-based employment creation has been central to the region's ability to increase opportunities in the past, ensuring that everybody can access jobs and that the quality of those jobs improves should be fundamental elements of a strategy for fostering economic mobility. Such an agenda is very broad, but key priorities include the following:

- *Bridging gaps in access to jobs and services.* Although overall levels of labor

---

BOX 5.1   Diverse countries, different challenges

This report adopts a classification of countries into five groupings, based on their common characteristics in terms of class structures and their evolution. Such groupings are not expected to do justice to all country-level specificities but rather to introduce more nuanced messages than could emerge from a simple regional overview, especially with regard to policies. The five groupings are as follows:

Progressive prosperity countries (Malaysia and Thailand), which have eliminated income poverty while substantially increasing the share of middle-class households

Out-of-poverty-into-prosperity countries (China, Mongolia, and Vietnam), where most people are at least economically secure and the middle class is growing

Out-of-extreme-poverty countries (Cambodia, Indonesia, and the Philippines), where extreme poverty levels are low but the shares of the middle class are also low

Lagging-progress countries (Lao People's Democratic Republic and Papua New Guinea), which still have high levels of extreme poverty

Pacific Island countries, which are a heterogeneous group and are distinct from the rest of the region

market participation are high in the region, women experience large gaps in participation across all income classes. Another barrier that prevents people from accessing jobs includes cumbersome regulations for obtaining identity documents. Those barriers may compound the difficulties lower-income households face in accessing services or government programs, which include language and high implicit costs, both for themselves and for their children.

- *Improving the quality of jobs.* Although agricultural employment has declined, the pace of change has differed by country and income level. Lower-income households constitute the majority of those engaged in agriculture, with many trapped there by insecure or ill-defined property rights that prevent investment or mobility to urban areas. Regulatory barriers to mobility and low connectivity of remote rural areas also thwart moves to more productive jobs. In addition, those who do move out of agriculture are unlikely to join the salaried sector; they generally resort to working as microentrepreneurs, with barriers to formalization that make it too onerous to leave the informal sector. Removing these constraints and securing property rights

are therefore key interventions to improve the quality of jobs.

- *Furthering financial inclusion.* Given the region's employment profile and the role played by micro and small firms as key sources of jobs (World Bank 2014a), improving the quality and productivity of the employment opportunities they offer is another important priority. Furthering financial inclusion can be very effective in this respect. It calls for developing sound legal and regulatory frameworks that balance financial stability, integrity, and inclusion; supporting the information environment needed for the financial sector to assess creditworthiness; and educating and protecting the users of financial services to enable them to make financially sound decisions. Such an agenda has benefits that extend well beyond those recipients who have no option but to become microentrepreneurs, because it supports a financial sector that is more efficient and transparent for all income classes.

Economic security

Social protection systems have historically played a limited role in East Asia's development model, despite the fast pace of innovation over the past decade. Poverty reduction has been mostly fueled by job creation and growing productivity rather than redistribution, while risk management, both at the household and at the country level, has not been a priority. To provide greater economic security for all groups, governments need to focus on at least three priorities:

- *Strengthening social assistance.* Over the past decade, several cash transfer programs (conditional or not) have been introduced in the region, although they remain absent in a few lower-income and lower-capacity countries. Such programs can play a key role in improving the economic opportunities of the poorest and thus reducing poverty more quickly, particularly in the pockets of the population where extreme poverty remains high.
- *Strengthening social insurance.* Although most countries have put in place measures to help households insure against idiosyncratic risks, such as pensions, their coverage tends to be limited. This area has seen the large-scale adoption of innovative measures, such as social pensions in China, but the programs are fragmented, hindering mobility within the labor market. Population aging and urbanization are likely to exacerbate demands for the public sector to provide social protection more systematically across the income spectrum. The blurring of the distinction between contributory and noncontributory programs offers a way forward toward universal coverage, provided such coverage follows a fiscally responsible growth path. Many countries in the region have made progress by moving away from universal but de facto regressive measures such as food and fuel transfers. Yet expanding the system in a fiscally sustainable manner is likely to require expanding the revenue base.
- *Increasing resilience to large systemic shocks, such as natural disasters.* To complement risk management measures at the household level, country-level measures are needed that increase resilience to large systemic shocks, particularly

natural disasters. Such measures would involve both managing risks ex ante—for example, by developing market-based crop insurance mechanisms or by investing in early warning systems—and setting up ex post mechanisms for coping with negative shocks when they materialize, such as adaptive (that is, scalable) safety nets.

Delivering inclusive growth

To create an environment that fosters inclusive growth, governments need to increase their capacity to mobilize resources. They also need to level the playing field to allow different economic actors to compete fairly. Supportive institutional and policy reforms are required to deal with the two key regional trends highlighted earlier: aging and urbanization. Key areas for action include the following:

- *Mobilizing resources through progressive taxation* by strengthening personal income taxation, including by broadening the tax base, reviewing marginal tax rates, and eliminating the preferential treatment of capital income; establishing effective property taxes; and enhancing tax administration
- *Increasing the effectiveness of pro-inclusion spending programs* through better management tools, including social registries (databases of individuals and their socioeconomic situations) and improved targeting mechanisms
- *Leveling the playing field* by boosting competition, reducing opportunities for capture in the more regulated sectors of the economy, and tackling nepotism and corruption
- *Adapting to population aging* by supporting lifelong learning to upgrade workers' skills throughout their lives, eliminating incentives for older workers to retire too early, opening up aging labor markets to greater inflows of young immigrants, and adapting the health sector to the challenges of aging, including the increased incidence of noncommunicable diseases

• *Promoting efficient urbanization* by supporting efficient land use in cities of all sizes, including by clarifying property rights; strengthening title registration; creating institutions that allow for transparent, market-based land valuation; establishing effective urban planning to reduce red tape and to facilitate changing land-use allocations; and strengthening urban governance to improve the delivery of services and provision of urban infrastructure, including by improving coordination between different levels of government and different jurisdictions.

A new social contract: priorities across different country groups

This report proposes a selective policy agenda to address the needs of the different economic classes, with a focus on three pillars: fostering economic mobility, increasing economic security, and strengthening the institutions required for inclusive growth. The assignment of priorities within this policy framework can be adapted to the region's heterogeneous country and policy contexts and level of economic progress. The following priorities are proposed based on the country typology used in this report.

For the *lagging-progress countries*, the priority is to accelerate poverty reduction. In the Lao People's Democratic Republic and Papua New Guinea, the incidence of poverty is still more than 40 percent, although progress has moved some of the population up into higher economic classes. Key policy actions should center, first, on accelerating poverty reduction by strengthening basic education and financial inclusion; removing barriers to labor reallocation from agriculture to more productive sectors; and tackling obstacles that prevent the marginalized population from accessing public services. Second, policies should help the vulnerable manage the impact of shocks by strengthening social assistance and making economies more resilient to disasters.

For the *out-of-extreme-poverty countries*, the priorities are securing progress and fostering upward mobility, while tackling the remaining pockets of extreme poverty. The incidence of extreme poverty in Cambodia, Indonesia, and the Philippines is now in the single digits. Unlike other countries in the region that have low levels of extreme poverty, however, the three countries also have a percentage of the middle class that is in the single digits. Policy priorities for this group therefore need to reflect the needs and aspirations of a diverse population, spanning those in moderate poverty, the vulnerable, and those who are economically secure. Integrating existing social assistance programs to provide greater economic security is a key priority, with strengthening mobility a close second. Strengthening mobility will be particularly important in the Philippines, where the distribution has been mostly static until recently. Given the size of their populations, however, Indonesia and the Philippines are still home to large numbers of extreme poor. Having such large numbers calls for identifying and removing the very specific constraints those groups face in accessing economic opportunities and service delivery.

For the *out-of-poverty-into-prosperity countries*, the priority is reducing the remaining vulnerabilities while meeting the needs and aspirations of the middle class. In China, Mongolia, and Vietnam, sustained poverty reduction has led to the emergence of a middle class. The priorities are, first, to reduce residual vulnerabilities, including among rural households and groups with special needs (in China, this includes the elderly and children left behind when their parents migrate; in Mongolia, those living in the *ger* areas;[1] and in Vietnam, ethnic minorities); and second, to meet the needs and aspirations of the middle class while preparing for rapid aging. That second priority will require improving migrants' access to public services; enhancing pension systems in a sustainable manner; and ensuring good-quality and cost-effective health care and education. In China, reforming urban planning to promote efficient land use and environmental sustainability is also critical.

For the *progressive prosperity countries*, the priorities are to satisfy the middle class's growing aspirations while mobilizing resources to address remaining disparities. These richer countries, which include Malaysia and Thailand, have continued to move large numbers of the economically vulnerable into economic security, and they now have large middle (and rich) classes. A first priority is to satisfy the middle class's growing aspirations and demands for quality public services, including health and education, which will support continued upward mobility. Second, reforms should help narrow Malaysia's and Thailand's rural-urban and cross-regional disparities in economic and social development. In turn, such reforms will require increased resource mobilization.

For the *Pacific Island countries*, the inclusive growth agenda needs to be tailored to their idiosyncratic circumstances (see box 5.2). Because human resources will remain their principal asset, priorities to foster economic mobility include using existing opportunities more effectively, seeking access to international job markets, supporting managed urbanization, and improving agricultural productivity. Priorities to strengthen economic security include investing in disaster loss prevention, mitigation, and management, and improving health and other social programs. Finally, delivering on inclusive growth will not be possible without improving the effectiveness of public expenditures and service provision, addressing the challenges of remoteness, and mobilizing development aid.

Addressing such issues simultaneously can form the basis for a new social contract that will offer something to all groups. The lowest-income groups will be given the opportunity to escape poverty. The vulnerable will be protected from shocks that could push them back into poverty. The economically secure and the middle class will enjoy access to the improved services they need to continue raising their incomes and standard of living.

BOX 5.2   A policy agenda for the Pacific Island countries

Their combination of extreme remoteness, small size, geographic dispersion, and environmental fragility means that Pacific Island countries (PICs) face a considerably diminished set of opportunities compared with most other countries. PICs, for example, are unlikely to experience export-driven growth and associated employment creation on the scale seen in the broader East Asia and Pacific region. The policy agenda for PICs, in the context of the three pillars used in this report, will have to recognize those special constraints.

Fostering economic mobility

Investing in people. In both the short and long term, human resources will remain the PICs' principal resource. Using existing opportunities in tourism and international job markets, as well as creating fresh opportunities in new areas such as information and communication technology, fisheries, and deep sea mining, will greatly depend on the extent to which PICs invest in overarching and market-responsive improvements in basic education. To those ends, the PICs need to invest in solid foundational education that rests on early childhood development and quality schooling, as well as in higher-end technical and managerial skills.

Improving access to international jobs markets. Given current rates of population growth, it is likely that domestic formal job markets will not be able to absorb the growing number of job seekers in the PICs, even in the most optimistic scenario. Therefore, a policy to aggressively seek and expand access to international job markets would be highly advantageous. Not only can PICs seek to expand ongoing low-skill seasonal employment arrangements with Australia and New Zealand, but they also can implement policies that help workers climb the skills ladder and effectively compete with other international workers who are drawn by the emerging skill gaps in advanced and bigger economies in the area.

box continues next page

BOX 5.2   A policy agenda for the Pacific Island countries *(continued)*

Supporting managed urbanization in the PICs. By consolidating populations living in far-flung and hard-to-service remote locations, urbanization will allow PICs to harness some economies of scale, create "thicker" markets, and increased specialization. This objective will require investments in connective infrastructure and improved urban planning and administration to prevent congestion, conflict, and urban unemployment.

Improving agricultural productivity. Most people in the PICs rely on subsistence agriculture for their livelihood. Especially in the short run, programs and policies that improve agricultural productivity, including the introduction and production of new and healthier foods, can go a long way in improving livelihoods of agricultural households. Improved value chains that link urban and rural areas will benefit both urban dwellers and agricultural producers.

Improving economic security

Managing shocks. Several PICs are among the countries in the world most vulnerable to natural disasters, which leads to frequent and significant reversals of economic gains. Hence, significant investments in disaster loss prevention, mitigation, and management are needed. Tackling aggregate shocks will mean further expanding and strengthening regional risk-sharing initiatives such as the Pacific Catastrophe Risk Assessment and Financing Initiative. It will also mean pursuing prudent macroeconomic policies that build up savings in good times to invest in disaster prevention and management. Such measures need to be paired with cost-effective and well-targeted safety net programs that protect the poorest and the most vulnerable.

Improving health and other social programs. In spite of strong traditional systems of self-help, the growing epidemic of noncommunicable diseases and unwanted pregnancies have increased vulnerability across the PICs. More investments are needed for social programs that complement traditional systems in helping people reduce exposure to these types of shocks. Measures include strengthening tobacco controls and increasing excise duties; reducing consumption of unhealthy foods through targeted preventive measures, taxes, and better regulation; and improving the efficiency and impact of the health budget.

Delivering inclusive growth

Improving the effectiveness of public expenditures and services to improve development outcomes. Human development indicators remain low in several PICs, in part because of low levels of public spending on basic human services. The scope for further revenue mobilization is limited, however, so improving public services has to rest on improving the quality of expenditure. By setting priorities for improvements in public financial management and for the quality of service provision, the PICs can do more with less.

Addressing challenges of remoteness. Meeting the needs and aspirations of population groups living in remote islands will continue to be highly challenging. Although orderly urbanization provides a potential solution, innovative thinking, including the use of appropriate information and communication technology systems, will be required to extend basic health, education, and social services to such groups in a sustainable manner.

Mobilizing development aid. Even assuming best-case outcomes for revenues and expenditures, the Pacific Island countries will continue to need development aid to maintain sustainable fiscal positions while addressing development needs. It will therefore be important for PICs to pursue both bilateral and multilateral engagement to mobilize international assistance.

Sources: Haque and Packard 2014; World Bank 2017a, 2017b.

And the rich will benefit from a stable social and political environment. All classes will therefore have an incentive to contribute to and support reforms, which in turn will position the region to respond effectively to the challenges ahead.

Fostering economic mobility

Broad-based employment creation has been central to the ability of developing East Asia and Pacific to increase opportunities. Yet the region cannot take for granted continued productivity gains of the kind it experienced in the past (World Bank 2014a) at a time when inequalities in access to jobs, and especially good jobs, are becoming more salient. Although "qualitative accounts from Cambodia, Indonesia, the Philippines, and Thailand indicate that finding employment and starting new businesses are the most frequently offered explanations for households moving out of poverty" (Narayan, Pritchett, and Kapoor 2009, as quoted in World Bank 2014a, 50), many still living in extreme poverty might not be able to access these opportunities. Barriers to accessing services might further compound their challenges by diminishing human capital or limiting mobility. And unless existing and new jobs result in growing productivity, those who can access them will not experience rising living standards. Therefore, the central elements of a strategy for fostering economic mobility must be ensuring that everyone has opportunities for paid employment, that people can move to better opportunities if available, and that the quality of jobs improves over time.

Addressing existing gaps in access to jobs, particularly better jobs

This section focuses first on some of the most glaring gaps in access to jobs that are revealed in the analysis of economic classes and then on the regulatory barriers that appear to contribute to those gaps.

Female labor market participation
Although women's participation in the labor market is high overall in the region, it differs according to economic class (see chapter 4). Lower-income households' economic potential remains partly unexploited because women face a range of nonmarket constraints, reflecting gender-specific household roles and social norms. Although the situation varies by country and economic class, alleviating such constraints can increase labor market participation for women,[2] and thus can facilitate the transition of households into the middle class.

Public provision of services that women are expected to provide, such as caring for children and the elderly, could make it possible for women to engage in paid work. However, care for the elderly is not widely provided currently, and childcare provision could be expanded to cover urban areas more fully (Baker and Gadgil 2017). In rural areas, nontraditional delivery mechanisms could be explored, such as training local women to provide childcare in their homes. Fetching water also consumes a significant amount of poorer women's (and children's) time,[3] so strengthening access to water could play an important role in improving female labor market participation. Where electrification is not yet universal, such as in Cambodia and Lao PDR, improving access can allow women from moderately poor and economically vulnerable households to use labor-saving appliances to reduce time spent in unpaid work (Goldin 2006); such appliances appear to be within the range of items that their families can save up to buy.

High shares of young people not in education, employment, or training
Youth who are not in employment, education, or training represent a large share of the moderate poor and economically vulnerable. Much policy innovation has been devoted to assisting them, as learned from experiences from other parts of the world. For example, the Urban Youth Employment Program in Papua New Guinea provides behavioral and socioemotional skills training, financial literacy training, and public works opportunities to low-skilled youth. The program also provides more skilled youth a more professionally oriented, longer-term module of behavioral and socioemotional training, technical skills training, and internship opportunities. Although the program has yet to complete an impact evaluation, the second module (for the more skilled) has been frequently evaluated in the Latin American context, with consistently positive results for employment, wages, and formal sector employment, particularly for women (Ibarraran and Rosas 2009; Vezza and others 2014).

Regulatory barriers

Several regulatory requirements might make it difficult for certain groups to access jobs, services, and government programs, beyond the difficulties that migrants face in accessing services (see chapter 2, box 2.5). Examples include cumbersome procedures to obtain identity documents, such as in Lao PDR, where birth registration processes and charges and other regulations make it difficult for those in extreme poverty to register their children. Appropriate responses could include incentives for birth registration (such as small cash or in-kind incentives to cover transport and other costs) and the waiving of registration fees. In addition, procedures should be established for births to be registered late and for replacement documents to be available without obliging parents to return to the municipality of birth. Central governments should conduct one-time outreach campaigns in every community (perhaps connected with censuses) to ensure that households or individuals who lack documents acquire them. Administrative fees should be waived during the campaign (World Bank and World Health Organization 2014).

Although barriers such as registration requirements are easy to identify, other types of hurdles are more elusive, such as cultural and linguistic barriers. In countries where extreme poverty is increasingly concentrated among ethnic minorities, such as Vietnam, the low status of such minorities and the difficulty in reaching them with antipoverty programs reinforce traditional stereotypes of the marginalized (Wells-Dang 2012). Specific factors that limit ethnic minorities' access to jobs in urban areas, to social assistance programs, and to other basic services are therefore overlooked. Language barriers and access to information play a key role, particularly where service delivery is concerned. In Vietnam, current initiatives to use teaching assistants who know the local mother language in the first few years of primary school hold promise for boosting learning among children who do not learn Vietnamese at home.

Specific barriers to accessing services, especially education

Access to some services can be limited for some groups, especially lower-income groups, by the way provision of those services is organized. Access is particularly important in the case of education. However, both access and quality[4] of education at the preschool, primary, secondary, and higher levels vary greatly within countries and, in general, are lower in rural areas (World Bank, forthcoming a). In Vietnam, for example, upper secondary education is not universal. Compulsory education ends after the ninth grade, and access to the upper secondary level is allocated through entrance exams in many provinces. In larger urban areas, children are likely to find a place in an academic secondary school if they are interested in pursuing an academic rather than a vocational education. However, in smaller urban areas, the rationing is more binding. Larger numbers of students, typically from a poorer background, are barred from secondary school and are streamed toward vocational education or simply left without any options for further schooling. Vocational education is typically considered to be of lower quality and carries some social stigma. To identify alternatives to this type of early streaming, the government is currently experimenting with a greater variety of courses, including vocational courses, in academic secondary schools.

Early childhood development (ECD) programs are among the most cost-effective strategies for improving learning and increasing equity of outcomes because they improve school readiness and significantly increase children's chances of enrolling in and successfully completing primary education (Belfield and others 2006; Heckman and others 2010). ECD programs are also a critical component of any coordinated strategy to tackle malnutrition, which has severe, detrimental effects on educational and labor market outcomes (World Bank 2016a, 72–95). Malnourishment is particularly prevalent among ethnic minorities and poorer households. However, participation in ECD programs is very low in most of the region, particularly among the poorer economic classes, thereby putting young children at a social and cognitive disadvantage even before starting school. Fortunately, there is a growing consensus about the elements of a high-quality ECD program for the poor. A good example of the implementation of such principles is Indonesia's early childhood education and development (ECED) program, which has successfully reached less affluent children living in villages across the geographically dispersed nation by using community-defined and -operated ECD services (box 5.3). Relatedly, measures to improve parents' attitudes toward the education of their children and to improve parent-teacher relationships can have a significant effect on students' literacy.[5]

Going beyond ECD, policy efforts should include incentives for extremely poor households to invest in primary and secondary education, although those alone might not be enough. In Vietnam, financial support is provided to ethnic minorities to attend upper secondary schools, including cash transfers conditional on school attendance, although coverage could be expanded. In the Philippines, where the *Pantawid Pamilya* program provides educational subsidies, identity documents are one of the constraints that prevent the extreme poor from enrolling. In general, countries with large or concentrated groups of the extreme poor should consider school feeding programs, along the lines of India's Mid-Day Meals Scheme. Efforts are also needed to address the constraints that result in low tertiary education enrollment rates among poorer, rural, and ethnic minority students. For instance, in China, measures have been implemented since 2012 to promote equal access to higher education, with some success.[6]

Improving the quality of jobs available

Much of the productivity growth experienced by the region over the past couple of decades has been driven by labor reallocation and structural transformation. China's case is well known, but Indonesia, Mongolia, and

---

BOX 5.3 Starting off strong through community-focused early childhood development in Indonesia

In 2008, the government of Indonesia began implementing a community-driven early childhood education and development (ECED) program to increase the supply of ECED services in poor communities. The program capitalized on the country's strong tradition of community-driven development. At the time, only 33 percent of children ages 0–6 from the wealthiest quartile of families were receiving ECED services, and only 8 percent of children from the poorest quartile of families accessed such services.

The program targeted poor communities. Trained local facilitators helped village members identify their ECED needs and prepare proposals for small grants to finance up to two services per village for three years. Up to two teachers per service received an intensive 200 hours of training. Most communities used their resources to establish center-based playgroups primarily serving children ages 3 to 6. Centers typically operated at least three days a week, usually in sessions of two hours a day.

Data collected in 2009, 2010, and 2013 showed how the program performed:

- The program increased enrollment in ECED services by 7 to 22 percent.
- It increased social competence by 0.25 of a standard deviation (s.d.), language and cognitive development by 0.13 s.d., and emotional maturity by 0.24 s.d. for the poorest children.
- It reduced emotional symptoms of children from the poorest households by –0.17 s.d.
- The program's effects were larger for children from the poorest households and for children from households with poor parenting skills.

As of 2013, the ECED program had reached 3,000 villages across 50 districts in the country. To date, more than 600,000 children have been reached.

Sources: Brinkman and others 2015; Hasan, Hyson, and Chang 2013; Jung and Hasan 2014.

Vietnam have similarly benefited (World Bank 2014a). Those processes have meant that the quality of jobs has improved and that people have been able to move to take up jobs. For such reallocation to occur, policies must improve the regulation of property rights on agricultural land. That regulation not only favors investment in agriculture, which raises productivity, but also allows people to move out of agriculture if they see better opportunities elsewhere. Similarly, addressing gaps in infrastructure provision, particularly for broad connectivity, is crucial to raise productivity of jobs in both rural and urban areas and to favor mobility. Finally, addressing the constraints to formalization that many micro and small enterprises face can help reduce the pervasive informality in the economy and raise productivity.

Investing in agricultural development and removing uncertainty from property rights to land

With three-quarters of the extreme poor and two-thirds of the economically vulnerable employed in agriculture, agricultural development remains a central priority for the region, even if the goal is to invest in agriculture to foster the kind of structural transformation that moves workers out of the sector. Agricultural development directly benefits some of the poorest segments of society, attenuates pressures for rising inequality, and lays the foundations for the success of other reforms.

The way land is regulated is central to efforts to improve agricultural productivity. In many areas in China, for example, uncertainty about the security and duration of land-use rights deters farm investment by both reducing incentives and preventing land from being used as collateral for loans. It also hampers agricultural consolidation, dulls incentives for off-farm work and entrepreneurship, and discourages both migration and the productive use of land left behind by migrants. The result is lower agricultural productivity and increased rural-urban inequalities (Hou and Huo 2016; Tan, Heerink,

and Qu 2006; Yan 2013). Similarly, in the Philippines, despite a protracted program of agrarian reform (de los Reyes, Librojo, and Capacio 2016), land-related investment remains hampered by a complicated and sometimes contradictory legal framework governing property rights and by weak land records based on inaccurate information. Property holders are discouraged from registering their claims by high transaction costs. The priority is to secure property rights for the majority of the population through land governance reforms, which include improvements in land information systems and the removal of bias against rural titles.

Addressing poor connectivity

Connectivity is a particularly significant constraint to mobility and market access in remote rural agricultural areas, including in Indonesia, the Philippines, and Vietnam. The lack of access can be tackled in the short term by enhancing the cost-effectiveness of transport, which includes increasing transport capacity using the existing level of infrastructure, for instance, by disseminating adapted vehicles through specific investment financing schemes. Longer-term improvements can address rural road or track conditions, especially by strengthening all-weather road connections between poorer areas and potential growth poles. Improvements in physical infrastructure must be complemented by enhanced value-chain services, including transport services, input provision, and access to credit, including credit for agricultural inputs.

Removing barriers to formalization

Workers who move out of agriculture are unlikely to move to the salaried sector. They generally resort to work as microentrepreneurs, because barriers to formalization make moving out of the informal sector too onerous. Although such informal sector jobs could be the springboard to better opportunities in an urban setting, they rarely are. Evidence from Indonesia, for example, shows that few individuals see their businesses grow from petty self-employment activities to businesses that hire workers. Furthermore, some groups of workers, such as young people, receive negative returns from time they spend in petty business activities, thus reducing their human capital (Naidoo, Packard, and Auwalin 2015). Many regulatory factors also help sustain the labor market segmentation that results in pervasive informality. Those factors include, for example, rules on access to credit that might exclude the self-employed; different treatment of different types of workers by the labor code; and rules on how social protection benefits are designed, particularly those that tie coverage of social insurance to certain types of work and that are financed by mandatory contributions from employers. As discussed later in this chapter, some of the innovations in the area of social protection are starting to address some of these constraints, but much remains to be done in this area.

Furthering financial inclusion to foster savings

Developing countries in East Asia and Pacific have the highest levels of financial inclusion compared with other developing regions, as measured by the share of adults who have an account at a financial institution or use mobile banking. That percentage reflects a great increase over the past few years, particularly among lower-income groups.[7] Yet an estimated 490 million people remain "unbanked"—without access to the services of a bank or similar financial organization (Demirguc-Kunt and others 2015). Prohibitive transaction costs, distance from financial providers, or legal and regulatory barriers, including onerous documentation requirements, help explain this finding. Poor, rural or geographically remote, unemployed, less educated, elderly, and young households are especially likely not to hold accounts at formal financial institutions.[8] Limited financial literacy among households reduces the benefits from whatever financial services are available.[9] Small and medium-size enterprises,

agricultural and rural enterprises, and young firms—which account for a majority of the region's employment—are particularly constrained in their access to finance.[10]

Supporting greater financial inclusion requires three broad, complementary policies (World Bank 2014b): developing sound legal and regulatory frameworks that balance financial stability, integrity, and inclusion; supporting the information environment needed for the financial sector to assess creditworthiness; and educating and protecting the users of financial services to enable them to make financially sound decisions. Beyond these high-level interventions, new insights from the behavioral economics literature are also contributing to the design of schemes that effectively promote savings at low cost, without requiring matching funds or other expensive incentives. In general, such schemes rely on easy deposits to encourage frequent saving behavior, somewhat difficult withdrawal to discourage impulse buying, and clear savings goals for larger assets. For instance, with commitment savings accounts, individuals make deposits and relinquish access to the funds for a given period or until a goal has been reached (box 5.4). Such accounts can both shield funds from family or social network pressures and mitigate self-control issues.

Increasing economic security

To increase economic security, governments not only need to invest in measures that help accelerate poverty reduction but also need to help households and countries become more resilient. At the household level, such social protection systems would ideally both help close the poverty gap and offer all income groups a way of managing risks. At the country level, investment would focus on putting in place both ex ante mitigation measures and ex post coping measures.

Social protection policies and programs vary widely. Yet all countries have some form of social insurance covering at least some segments of the formal sector (notably the civil service), and most have some form of targeted

BOX 5.4   Creativity plus a little behavioral economics: rural savings in Mindanao

A small rural bank in the Philippines has shown that a combination of nontraditional savings mechanisms and behavioral economics can induce and increase personal savings. The Green Bank of Caraga in Mindanao offered women the SEED (Save, Earn, and Enjoy Deposits) program. Program clients were offered the same interest rates and deposited their money in the same way as anyone else, with a few adjustments. First, the clients signed a contract with the bank that allowed withdrawal of funds only when a trigger, set by the client herself, was met. The client could specify a date, an expenditure type, or a sum of savings, and the bank was committed to release the money only when such a goal was met. Nearly half the clients opted for a date when expenses would be incurred, such as Christmas, a birthday, or a graduation. Others selected specific expenditures such as

education expenses or capital for business. Second, participants took home a piggy bank that had a slot for depositing money. The key to open the bank and access the money was held by the bank. The participants would take the piggy bank to the Green Bank periodically for the latter to transfer the savings into the formal account. The clients were not required to make deposits into their account.

By outsourcing to the bank the enforcement of the savings goal and providing a mechanism for small savings to be easy to deposit but hard to access, the program participants saved 81 percent more over a year than a randomly selected group of bank clients who had been assigned to the traditional bank savings mechanism.

Sources: Ashraf, Karlan, and Yin 2006; Ashraf, Karlan, and Yin 2010.

program for the poorest. Programs that blur the line between these two systems—and particularly between contributory and noncontributory schemes—appear to offer a way to extend coverage to the "missing middle" of the distribution. Having started late to put in place a modern social protection system, countries in the region have an opportunity to learn from international experience, avoiding pitfalls such as the creation of welfare traps and excessive labor taxation. Two main challenges are to avoid the fragmentation of schemes for different types of workers, which limits mobility and results in uneven treatment, and to ensure that systems are expanded in a fiscally sustainable manner by expanding the revenue base (see also "Increasing the Redistributive Capacity of the State", below).

Strengthening social assistance

Although most countries in the region have placed limited emphasis on investing in social protection, several social assistance and social insurance schemes have recently been

introduced or scaled up, albeit with significant variations from country to country and with gaps in coverage. Since the introduction in 2008 of the *Pantawid Pamilya* program in the Philippines—a geographically targeted conditional cash transfer program aimed at poor families with children or pregnant women—several cash transfers have been introduced, both conditional (such as in Cambodia and Indonesia) and unconditional. The largest such program is China's *dibao* or minimum living standard guarantee, which was first introduced in urban areas and then in rural areas and currently covers about 70 million people. The program tops up household incomes and provides several noncash benefits to beneficiaries, such as exemptions or reductions in school fees and subsidies on housing or utilities.

Such programs are increasingly targeted based on needs or poverty, partly in order to better respond to the changing nature of poverty in those countries. In China, for example, the *dibao* approach reflects a growing concern that although rural incomes were growing, transitory poverty was on the rise and its geographical dispersion was increasing (Golan, Sicular, and Umapathi 2014). Other countries, such as Fiji, are consolidating their programs to improve targeting and effectiveness. Technology is also facilitating the targeting and administration of such programs, for example by allowing the creation of large national social registries in the Philippines (box 5.5) and in Indonesia (the Unified Database). Smart card technology is also offering new opportunities for program delivery.

Despite these positive developments, several lower-income or lower-capacity countries still lack a fundamental social assistance program (Cambodia, Lao PDR, Myanmar, and most of the Pacific Island countries). Thailand and Vietnam, which lack such programs despite their income levels, remain anomalies.

Strengthening social insurance

As far as social insurance is concerned, pension systems exist in all countries, covering at least part of the formal sector. Their focus therefore tends to be mostly urban. Faced with the prospects of an aging population, persistently high levels of informal sector workers, and the rarity of the long-term employer-employee bond that characterized the early experience of the newly industrialized countries, developing East Asia and Pacific countries have resorted to a plurality of social pensions (noncontributory and old-age transfers). Such pensions take differing forms: several Pacific Island countries and Timor-Leste have introduced universal schemes; Thailand has introduced a pensions-tested scheme available to all those without

---

BOX 5.5 **National household targeting system in the Philippines (*Listahanan*)**

The Philippines is one of the few large developing countries in the world with a complete, nationwide database of the poor that is used by a large number of social programs to target interventions. This remarkable instrument, known as the *Listahanan*, was constructed over six years starting in 2010. The government has formally adopted it as a targeting database, meaning that all nationally implemented programs, including the country's core social assistance programs, use it to identify potential beneficiaries, provided that they meet program-specific eligibility criteria. The data collection effort to build the *Listahanan* took place in 2009–10, when data were collected on about 11 million households (almost 60 percent of the Filipino households). Of those, 5.2 million were identified as poor and were targeted for government assistance. The process involved three stages:

- The geographic identification of areas to be surveyed, on the basis of earlier poverty estimates
- The survey itself, which yielded information to develop proxy means tested models to identify the poor in the absence of income information
- A community validation process to allow communities to challenge the list of poor once the

preliminary results of targeting became available (and to build trust in the system by making it very transparent).

Since then, the *Listahanan* has become the backbone of the Philippines's antipoverty programs; it is now used to target 25 national programs, including the *Pantawid Pamilya*, the PhilHealth subsidized health insurance, and the social pension program. It is also used by policy makers to plan disaster relief assistance, by civil society to monitor government effectiveness, and by academics. The *Listahanan* was updated in 2015 to cover 75 percent of the population (15.8 million households), and a new set of proxy means tested models was developed. Those revisions significantly reduced errors in misclassifying poor and nonpoor households. Those methodological developments were accompanied by a communication effort to increase public awareness and understanding of the *Listahanan* and to broaden and deepen support for the instrument within the government and among other stakeholders.

Source: World Bank (forthcoming b).

formal sector pensions; and Malaysia and the Philippines have introduced more tightly targeted schemes. China has brought 350 million additional working-age people, rural and urban, into pension schemes in recent years. Although these schemes vary significantly by age threshold and generosity, many (particularly China's) have a high reliance on public subsidies. One of the design innovations of the China project is that the elderly automatically benefit from programs if their household members are making contributions, thereby providing strong incentives to enroll in this voluntary scheme.

Similar innovations aimed at increasing coverage are seen in relation to health risks, despite varying degrees of success in introducing subsidized schemes and keeping costs under control. In many of the lower-income countries, large segments of the population lack health insurance coverage because it is conditional on formal employment status.[11] Thailand provides a successful example of expanding health insurance coverage by relying on general revenues (box 5.6). Other countries, such as China, face greater challenges in this area, because of the complexities of health care provision. Wide-ranging reforms rapidly achieved near-universal health insurance coverage, accompanied by massive investments in the health insurance infrastructure and the supply of health services starting in the early 2000s,[12] but costs have escalated and health care gains have slowed after a period of rapid improvement.[13] Further, total household out-of-pocket health expenditures, and the incidence of impoverishing and catastrophic health expenditures, have not appreciably decreased with the introduction of health insurance (Zhang and Liu 2014).

These encouraging trends show that the elements of a comprehensive social protection system can be put in place over time. Countries with high shares of poor and vulnerable populations can give priority to putting in place or strengthening social assistance programs. Countries with higher shares of the economically secure and middle class can focus on expanding the coverage of social insurance. Recent experience shows that the key to expanding social insurance is to delink entitlement to social insurance from employment and from users'

BOX 5.6   Guarding against health risks: Thailand's success

In 2001, the Thai government introduced the Universal Coverage Health Scheme (UCS) for those who were not funded under the employer insurance programs (roughly three-quarters of the population). Under the scheme, all Thai citizens were eligible for health care that was low cost (in the years that a minimal copayment was charged) or free. The UCS was funded out of general revenues, rather than through employer contributions. Several cost-containment measures were simultaneously implemented, including a single purchaser model; incentives for providers to contain costs; and a quality control system for providers. Although these efforts contained costs, overall health costs to the state nearly doubled during the 10 years of implementation.

Within a year after the UCS was implemented, health insurance coverage increased from 25 percent to 100 percent of the Thai population. The insurance improved health care: infant mortality rates fell to 11 per 1,000, eliminating the infant mortality gap between rich and poor provinces, and access to medical care increased for the poor (more than for the nonpoor). But the program also closed the gap in out-of-pocket health care payments between classes. Before the scheme, 33 percent of the total health expenditure was paid by the patient or family, with payments highest among those near the poverty line. Under the scheme, the full cost was covered (minus a small copayment in some years, but collection was irregular). Impoverishment caused by health care expenses decreased from 2.7 percent in 2000 to 0.5 percent by 2009.

Source: Hanvoravongchai 2013.

direct contributions in order to increase coverage of informal sector workers, the poor, and the economically vulnerable. To achieve that expansion, it will be critical to increase general revenue financing, for instance, through publicly financed contribution subsidies. Expanding the system in a fiscally sustainable manner will require increasing fiscal space by expanding the revenue base, whether taxes are earmarked—as in Japan, which funds half its basic pension from sales tax—or not.

Increasing resilience to large aggregate shocks

Social protection measures can help households deal with idiosyncratic shocks, but large aggregate shocks such as natural disasters call for different types of measures. First, ex ante risk-mitigation strategies can reduce households' exposure to certain risks. Investments in infrastructure can minimize the impact of natural disasters, for example, and investments in human capital can help households diversify their sources of livelihood. Such measures are most effective, however, in the case of well-defined, sufficiently large-scale sources of risk.

In addition, ex post measures can help people cope with shocks that materialize. International evidence suggests that a package of interventions would be most effective, especially for poorer households (Hallegatte and others 2017). Those interventions would include the following:

- *Fostering financial inclusion* helps people build up savings beyond physical assets that might be affected by the shock, as well as facilitates access to credit that allows people to cope with the consequences of the shock. The experience of Cyclone Nargis in Myanmar in 2008, however, illustrates the potential pitfalls of increasing debt as a coping strategy for those at the bottom of the distribution. In areas where farming was badly affected, up to 50 percent of farmers lost their collateral, particularly land, after increasing

their borrowing when trying to cope with the impact of the storm.
- *Market insurance* (applied to either crops or livestock) can mitigate risks through pooling and diversification. Traditional insurance products often suffer from high transaction costs and might prove unaffordable for poorer groups.[14] Across East Asia and Pacific there is significant scope to expand insurance take-up,[15] including by strengthening regulatory frameworks. Examples of innovation include public-private partnerships such as the Mongolian Livestock Insurance Pool, which covers more than 10,000 herders. But increasing coverage of poorer groups remains a challenge: in the Mongolian example, only about 15 percent of herders in the relevant areas are covered. Index-based insurance helps to minimize the limitations of traditional contracts, but it might still require large subsidies to ensure that sufficient numbers enroll. In indexed-based insurance, policies are linked to the amount of rainfall over a given time, for instance, or commodity prices at a given date. Thus, indexing can mitigate weather-related and price risks in agricultural production and promote agricultural investment and productivity. Similarly, policies can use clearly defined, exogenous disaster triggers to activate ex post income support and eventually to end disbursements (Acevedo 2015).
- *Adaptive safety nets* "can protect poor households from climate and other shocks before they occur through predictable transfers, building community assets, and other programs that help them build resilience; and can be scaled up to respond to extreme events when they hit" (Acosta 2016, 12)
- *Targeted safety nets*, in general, provide support to households by increasing their coverage when a large-scale disaster strikes, even if they are not designed with such disasters in mind. Such benefits can be designed to be adaptive, so programs can be scaled up when assistance is most needed.

BOX 5.7   (Almost) Ready for Winston

On February 20, 2016, Tropical Cyclone Winston, the most powerful storm on record in the Southern Hemisphere, cut a path of devastation across Fiji. The storm killed more than 40 people and caused widespread destruction, which was particularly severe for the housing and agriculture sectors. Some of the worst-hit areas were the largely rural provinces and outlying islands that had a high concentration of households living below the poverty line. Total damage and losses were estimated at 22 percent of gross domestic product (GDP) (US$957 million).

In the aftermath, the government of Fiji drew on its existing social program registries to provide cash transfers to affected citizens. Four weeks after Winston, the government transferred US$9.4 million to 43,524 beneficiaries covered under the three core social protection programs (the Poverty Benefits Scheme, the Care and Protection Scheme, and the Social Pension Scheme). The benefit levels were set to the equivalent of approximately three months of ordinary benefits, to enable households to meet their immediate food needs without resorting to negative coping strategies like selling productive assets.

The initial results from a comprehensive impact evaluation suggest that both poor and near-poor households did suffer severe losses in the wake of Winston and that adaptive safety nets were effective in assisting the poor to cope. Of all surveyed households in affected areas that received additional cash assistance, 37 percent lost their entire dwelling, 74 percent sustained damage to their roofing, and 49 percent lost their crops or harvest. Within four weeks, the majority of households had spent their entire additional social assistance, with 99 percent of expenditure on essential items. Food and materials to repair damaged dwellings formed the two most important categories of expenditure, followed by clothing and school supplies. Less than 1 percent of the assistance was spent on kava, alcohol, or cigarettes, addressing a common concern that additional social assistance would be used unwisely for nonessential items.

Three months after the cyclone, beneficiaries under the Poverty Benefits Scheme were more likely to have recovered from the shocks they faced than comparable households that did not receive the additional assistance. The recovery includes having recovered from sickness or injury; repaired their dwelling; replenished their food stocks; remedied the damage to their agricultural land; repaired village or neighborhood infrastructure; and resolved problems of conflict, violence, or insecurity. Following these positive results, the government is expected to consider ways to build a broader social registry that has the ability to target not just existing beneficiaries, but also the near poor and others excluded from current programs.

Sources: Doyle and others 2016; Erdman 2016; World Bank 2011.

As the example of the relief effort in Fiji shows (box 5.7), having invested in creating social registries for existing targeted programs meant that when disaster struck in 2016 following Cyclone Winston, the information base for delivering programs to some of the most vulnerable groups was readily available.

- *Disaster risk financing* is also required to support the scaling up of social assistance and other reconstruction needs. Several measures offer protection against the fiscal implications of possible shocks, including reserves, contingency credit lines, regional risk pools, and bonds transferring part of the risk to global capital markets or reinsurance (Hallegatte and others 2017).

- *Early warning systems* may also prove useful in reducing exposure to risks and enabling timely ex post assistance. Providing information about possibly disruptive weather events such as cyclones can enable households to take protective measures, ranging from moving assets to higher or safer ground to evacuating. At the policy level, an early warning system that considers a broader set of shocks would rely on a predefined and frequently monitored set of indicators across several domains (for example, macroeconomic, weather-related, firm-sector, and household behaviors). Such indicators would signal an impending crisis and predict who would be affected and how they would be affected. Trigger levels that categorize shock-related situations as normal, alarming, or crisis would be matched to national or local policies to manage the response and alleviate the impacts (for example, evacuation plans). Indonesia, for example, is developing a Crisis Monitoring and Response System, retrofitted to the data availability and country-specific behaviors that signal an impending economic crisis.

Strengthening the institutions for inclusive growth

Increasing the redistributive capacity of the state

To remove the constraints to inclusive growth experienced by different groups in the population, governments need to implement a tailored package of policies. Financing such packages will prove expensive, so it will be vital not only to mobilize more resources in a more progressive way (which in itself would contribute to making growth more inclusive), but also to adopt tools that can target resources more effectively.

Mobilizing resources through progressive taxation
Developing East Asia and Pacific's tax systems mobilize few resources. In 2010, the region raised only around 15 percent of gross domestic product (GDP) in tax revenues, compared with 20 percent in Latin America and 35 percent in advanced economies (Bastagli, Coady, and Gupta 2015).[16] Besides generally low tax revenues, reliance on indirect taxes is high, intake from personal income tax and property tax is limited, and tax administration is poor. A reliance on indirect taxation and low (effective) rates on higher incomes are making the system more regressive, and

capacity limitations on the administration side limit the extent to which the system can be made more progressive (Park 2012). Given these challenges, strengthening personal income taxation, increasing reliance on property taxes, and improving tax administration are priorities to mobilize additional revenues and increase tax fairness.

To strengthen personal income taxation, governments may have to broaden the tax base, review marginal tax rates, and eliminate differential treatment of labor income versus capital income (after allowing for corporate taxes).[17]

Broadening the tax base is an option to consider in the many East Asia and Pacific countries characterized by high basic exemption limits or high threshold levels at which the top income rate is applied. In Fiji, income tax is applied at an exemption threshold of nearly 1.7 times per capita income, and in Myanmar and Papua New Guinea the exemption is up to 1.2 times per capita income. Such high exemption thresholds clearly limit the coverage of the tax system. For example, in China, according to household survey data, 80 percent of workers are not liable to pay personal income taxes (Lam and Wingender 2015). Similarly, the very high levels at which top tax rates start to apply constrain revenue mobilization potential. Papua New Guinea stands out, with an applicability at 45 times per capita income, whereas in Organisation for Economic Co-operation and Development (OECD) countries, the highest threshold is 8 times per capita income. In China, the highest marginal tax rate applies at about 35 times the national average wage, compared with four times the average in OECD countries (de Mooij, Lam, and Wingender 2017).

Reviewing marginal tax rates, especially for the top income bracket, is an option that raises concerns because of the expected trade-off between equity and potential efficiency costs, for example, a reduction in labor supply following an increase in the tax rate. At an average of 32 percent, however, top rates in the region are lower than in OECD countries. A wide range of estimates exist for the magnitude of efficiency costs in OECD countries, commonly expressed as the elasticity of taxable income.[18] Estimates are even more limited in East Asia, so the optimal top marginal tax rate is difficult to assess. A higher reform priority appears to be the level at which the top tax rate is applied, rather than the top tax rate itself. Simulations for China suggest that shortening personal income tax brackets could raise revenues of around 2 percent of GDP (Lam and Wingender 2015).[19] Marginal tax rates for low-income workers are also an important concern. The system of social security contributions in China creates a very high tax burden for the poorest workers because it includes a minimum employee contribution.

Eliminating the differential treatment of capital income versus personal income is a third option to increase the revenue base. Capital incomes, including capital gains, are typically taxed at a lower rate than ordinary income, which has been identified as one reason for the limited redistributive effect of taxation in developing countries (Bastagli, Coady, and Gupta 2015). Although a consolidated tax with a single tax base (including both capital and labor income) is often considered at the theoretical ideal, most advanced economies have moved toward a dual income tax, with capital incomes taxed separately (de Mooij, Lam, and Wingender 2017).[20] Similarly, in Indonesia, dividends are taxed at 10 percent and interest at 20 percent, which is substantially lower than the 30 percent top marginal tax rate that many dividend earners face for their salary incomes. Differences in treatment make it possible for business owners to move income into categories taxed at lower rates. That tax treatment does not recognize the reality of compensation packages such as stock options or equity stakes, which blur the line between capital and labor incomes. In China, after accounting for taxes on corporate profits, a 15 percent tax on dividends would be broadly consistent with a 35 percent top marginal tax rate on labor income (de Mooij, Lam, and Wingender 2017).

Another option to mobilize resources through progressive taxation is provided by *increasing reliance on property taxes*. Such an option, however, might be feasible only in the medium term, because it requires building an effective administrative infrastructure. But property taxes could significantly support revenue mobilization, with expected progressive results and little inefficiency (unlike other forms of wealth, property is both visible and immobile). In East Asia and Pacific as in other developing regions, however, recurrent property taxes on immovable property are underused, mobilizing a lower share of GDP than in OECD countries. Property tax revenues are low in Indonesia at 0.35 percent of GDP, Mongolia at 0.15 percent, and Thailand at 0.20 percent (Norregaard 2015). By contrast, in China, property taxes account for 1.6 percent of GDP, which is comparable with the levels observed in OECD countries (de Mooij, Lam, and Wingender 2017).[21] Best practice suggests that existing property tax regimes in the region could be shifted from a focus on transaction-based taxation (which reduces spatial mobility) to recurrent (annual) taxes on immovable property. That regime would provide a more stable income stream (especially for local governments) and avoid opportunities for collusion between buyer and seller in understating the transaction (Norregaard 2015). Property taxes should also adopt a progressive rate structure with special arrangements for poor, large families and asset-rich, income-poor households.[22]

Finally, *strengthening tax administration* can have substantial payoffs for efficiency and equity, and it should be set as a priority (Bastagli, Coady, and Gupta 2015).[23] Concentrating enforcement efforts on large taxpayers—for example, by establishing large-taxpayer offices—is likely to result in the biggest payoffs for both revenue and equity. Improving compliance, including through increased withholding of income taxes on capital and use of third-party reporting, could remedy one of the most striking features of tax systems in the region, namely, the extremely low share of the population that pays taxes (as proxied by the share of registered taxpayers). In a sample of eight countries, an estimated 14 percent of households are registered taxpayers, blunting the effectiveness of income taxes in mobilizing and redistributing resources. Although many countries withhold taxes for capital incomes (Thailand is a notable exception), which significantly improves compliance, gaps remain with capital gains. That result contrasts with labor incomes, which are largely subject to withholding and thus face a higher effective tax burden. In Indonesia, capital gains (for example, on stocks or real estate) are subject to the standard personal income tax, but there is no withholding, so compliance is limited (World Bank 2016b). As a result, only 5 percent of personal income tax revenues in Indonesia are from capital incomes, with the rest coming from withholdings on salaries. Finally, because compliance is weaker for taxes that are bureaucratically more cumbersome, are harder to understand, or are easier for taxpayers to bribe their way out of (Usui 2011), efforts to simplify the tax system and increase transparency are also likely to pay off.

Leveling the playing field for different economic actors to compete fairly

Perceptions of growing inequalities and unequal opportunities, along with high or growing concentrations of income, wealth, and economic power, are all signals that governments could do more to allow fairer competition among different actors. Priorities in this area include boosting competition, reducing opportunities for revenue capture in the more regulated sectors of the economy, tackling nepotism and corruption, and more generally strengthening and enforcing the rule of law.

Given the historical role that large companies, especially family-owned companies, have played in the development of the region, policies need to increase scrutiny of their role and of the potential for mutually reinforcing links with the concentration of political power. Regulatory agencies could play a vital role in ensuring that East Asia's large firms do not end up stifling competition. In particular, family firms often consolidate their holdings through pyramidal holding structures, which guarantee a disproportionate share of votes relative to the owners' capital (Kandel and others 2015). Another example is the use of dual-class shares, which separate control rights and cash flow rights and which have recently become popular with tech companies, including some in East Asia and Pacific. Although many of these practices are legal, they stifle competition. Countries such as Israel and the United States have fought these pyramidal structures; Israel, for example, has banned companies with more than two levels of subsidiaries (Bebchuk 2012). Measures are also needed to strengthen asset disclosure and corporate transparency, and to reduce the opacity of ownership structures, which are particularly prevalent in family-controlled firms.

Coping with aging

Populations in developing East Asia and Pacific are aging more rapidly than any region in history, a trend driven by sharp declines in fertility and steady increases in life expectancy. In many countries, aging is occurring at low-income levels—people are "getting old before getting rich" (World Bank 2016c, 9). Significant differences can be seen across countries. Populations in some middle-income countries (including China, Indonesia, Malaysia, Mongolia, Thailand, and Vietnam), which are already relatively old, are aging rapidly. In poorer countries (including Cambodia, Lao PDR, Myanmar, Papua New Guinea, and the Pacific Island countries), populations are relatively young and still have decades of potential demographic dividends to realize. In all countries, however, aging raises policy challenges and poses economic and social risks, with the speed of change heightening the urgency of policy action.

When the labor forces of a country age, economic growth tends to slow. More immediately, countries face the fiscal challenges of providing sustainable health, pension, and long-term care systems. Relatedly, poverty rates are higher among the elderly, not only because health and pension insurance is insufficient, but also because traditional family- and community-based support networks are being undermined by declining fertility. Rapid urbanization and migration are also leading to the dispersion of extended families.[24] That said, the region starts from a favorable position. People already have long working lives. Entitlements to pensions, health care, and long-term care are still modest, so this is an opportunity to put in place systems now that can be sustainable in the future. Household savings in the region are already high, and people tend to save until later in life. Finally, people in developing East Asia and Pacific have in recent decades seen a steady increase in the number of years lived in good health.

In addition to putting in place comprehensive social protection systems, older or rapidly aging countries need to implement several complementary policy reforms to adapt to changing demographics (World Bank 2016c):

- *Fertility and childcare policies.* Although several countries, including Mongolia and Vietnam, have introduced direct monetary incentives to support fertility, international evidence suggests that those measures are not very effective or cost-effective. Other measures have more potential to change the trade-offs between women's fertility and labor market decisions, such as longer maternity and paternity leave, which in the region are typically short and available only to the minority of workers in the formal sector. Subsidized childcare has the same potential, whether delivered as subsidies to households, as in the Republic of Korea, or to employers, as in Malaysia.
- *Upgrading of education and skills systems.* Countries need to support lifelong learning to upgrade workers' skills throughout the life cycle. Some countries in the region

are already following this path, such as Korea and Singapore, which have dedicated programs for training older workers. However, use of these programs remains limited.

- *Adaptation of the health sector.* The health challenges of aging are seen in the increased incidence of noncommunicable diseases such as cardiovascular diseases, cancer, chronic respiratory diseases, and diabetes, which reinforces the need to transform health delivery systems. Priorities include strengthening primary care, reducing overprovision of services, improving coordination among providers, and instituting transparent and evidence-based processes for prioritizing new technologies and drugs. The aim is to manage the treatment of older patients with chronic conditions affordably and at the right levels of the system. Such reforms would be important without aging, but the aging population makes them even more important. Aging is also creating a rapidly growing demand for and market for elder- and long-term care, as traditional family networks become increasingly stretched. Innovation is urgently needed here, including with respect to home- and community-based care ("aging in place"), which can provide more positive experiences for older people at a lower cost than residential care. Although the state may provide financing for elder- and long-term care (with copayments for all but the poor and the disabled), the private sector will likely play an important role in providing such care.
- *Extension of productive working lives.* Many policies extend productive working lives by eliminating incentives for older workers in the formal sector to retire too early or by simplifying the return to work for women who have had children. Longer productive lives can also be supported by specific reforms—for example, by targeting labor market institutions that discourage employment of older workers, such as seniority wage systems,

and by using incentives to adjust workplaces to accommodate older workers (for instance, through greater use of flexible and part-time work arrangements).

- *Opening up of aging labor markets to greater inflows of young immigrants.* Opening labor markets will also help stave off countries' declining working-age populations. Singapore and Hong Kong SAR, China, offer examples of the economic benefits of more open immigration benefits.

Countries with younger populations, meanwhile, need to prepare now for rapid aging in the future. Such preparation requires setting up pension and health systems that can achieve significant coverage and are also sustainable. Countries also can maximize the demographic dividend from their still-expanding labor forces through investments that raise productivity and maximize youth employment.

Institutions for efficient urbanization

The structural transformation in East Asia and Pacific is changing the distribution of the population along the rural-urban spectrum. In countries with low urbanization rates, urban expansion is still dominated by the largest cities; in more urban countries, urban expansion is happening rapidly in cities of all sizes. In China and Vietnam, however, inefficient constraints on land allocation are suppressing potential productivity gains from urban agglomeration, both in large metropolitan areas and in secondary cities. Further, impressive reductions in monetary poverty have not always been matched by improvements in urban infrastructure, including access to water, sanitation, and good-quality housing. That lagging investment harms welfare. It can exclude the poorest, especially new rural-to-urban migrants, and it can lead to high levels of nonmonetary poverty among those who have reached economic security, and to a lesser extent among the middle class.

For countries where most of the urbanization has yet to happen, it is essential to lay the institutional foundations for efficient urban expansion. Such foresight will enable countries to take advantage of urbanization's potential to boost productivity, reduce service delivery costs (through economies of density in serving more compact locations), and, more generally, deliver inclusive growth (Baker and Gadgil 2017). Urbanization intersects with a variety of institutional arrangements at the local level, from centralized to decentralized administrations, often varying by sector as well as by country. Ensuring that this evolving landscape becomes an effective environment for the delivery of key services and contributes to inclusive growth will require a set of coordinated interventions along two dimensions.

First, it is vital to support urban development and efficient land use along the entire rural-urban spectrum. The focus of spatial policies should not be to create spatial equality; rather, the focus should be on promoting growth and long-run convergence in living standards, building on the specific characteristics and economic strengths of different environments. Cities along the rural-urban spectrum can play different roles and functions. Primary cities can lead in innovation and technology. Secondary cities can provide the manufacturing backbone of the country. And smaller cities can act as the interface between urban and rural areas. Spatially aware policies can promote such development patterns by doing the following:

- *Encouraging efficient urban agglomeration,* which requires developing fluid, transparent land markets, including clarifying property rights, strengthening title registration, and creating institutions that will allow for transparent, market-based land valuation. It also requires effective urban planning, with master plans linked to the budget process.
- *Providing incentives to cluster service and knowledge-based sectors in large cities and relocating land-intensive industry to smaller cities and towns.* For such a spatial reallocation of economic activities to

occur, red tape needs to be reduced and changes in land-use allocations need to be facilitated.

- *Investing in connections between small cities/market towns and the rural areas they serve* both as markets and as centers for the delivery of services.

Within cities, spatially aware policies can foster efficient land use through transit-oriented development (TOD) or smart growth that prioritizes new developments along established public transport routes. Such policies would also favor more inclusive urbanization by ensuring a better spatial match between jobs, public transport, affordable housing, service provision, and urban amenities such as recreational areas. In addition, efforts to incorporate risk reduction into land-use and infrastructure planning could boost growth and ultimately save lives.

A second priority is strengthening urban governance to improve the delivery of services and provision of urban infrastructure (box 5.8). Many East Asian countries have strongly centralized systems for service delivery. However, the delivery of core urban services (including public transport, road, water supply and sewerage, solid waste management, and drainage) is often better managed at the local level. Cities can be given more responsibility for service delivery, provided that local authorities have the necessary resources, including technical capacity. In addition, land-use policies must reserve rights of way, so that basic services and connective infrastructure can be extended as cities expand. Finally, policies must consider the needs of and constraints faced by rural-to-urban migrants to prevent new forms of exclusion as they continue to be the engine of urbanization.

In creating more efficient institutions for urbanization, metropolitan areas face a conundrum. Their governance structures are often fragmented, which hampers integrated urban planning and investment and results in a failure to realize economies of scale or

---

BOX 5.8   Institutions for effective urban governance: lessons from Malaysia

Many problems related to urban planning, development, and service delivery may at first glance appear to be technical or financial. As a recent study in Malaysia found, however, the underlying causes tend to be institutional, and they can significantly hamper cities' competitiveness. Among the key challenges identified were the centralization or federalization of urban service delivery, constraints in urban and spatial planning, and financial and technical constraints facing local authorities. In the case of Malaysia, the following are recommended priorities for strengthening institutions for effective urban governance.

The first priority is to deliver selected urban services by shifting more management and decision making to the local level and to enhance the system of local performance indicators. Creating indicators involves identifying services to be delivered locally using criteria such as economies of scale, externality effects, equity, and local responsiveness and accountability. Such services could include intraurban highways and federal intraurban roads, urban public transport including buses and rail, drainage and flood mitigation, solid waste management and disposal, and emergency services. This priority also involves strengthening metropolitan governance for some functions and services, particularly planning, and investing in city performance indicators, which are essential for tracking improvements in urban service delivery.

The second priority is to increase the capacities of local authorities in specific financial and technical areas and ensure adequate local agency staffing. Areas such as property assessments are weak and would benefit from updated systems. The system of fiscal transfers also needs to be revised to be more transparent, predictable, and formula based.

Source: World Bank 2015a.

agglomeration. Those structures also lead to unequal coverage and quality of services and infrastructure. Such inefficiencies and inequalities are likely to be deepened by further decentralization in service delivery. The inequalities may particularly affect vulnerable groups such as internal migrants, who may face limitations in choosing to settle in a particular jurisdiction. Regional government authorities and other mechanisms (voluntary or mandated by law) can help coordinate service provision across administrative boundaries and improve the efficiency and equity of service delivery, while continuing to be responsive to local needs.

Countries should develop effective systems of property tax assessment and collection as quickly as possible. Such systems, which are mostly lacking, can help mobilize the resources required to pay for local services, foster accountability for the delivery of such services, and encourage the development of land. Property taxation reforms are slow, incremental processes. Their technical credibility and political feasibility hinges on good land records and a valuation infrastructure (including standards, professional monitoring, access to market data, and automated valuation systems). To broaden the use of property taxation, therefore, governments must implement measures aimed at strengthening investments in urban areas, including improvements in land registration and increased transparency in the public information on parcel definition and land values.

Fiscal transfers are likely to remain the key source of financing for urban administrations over the medium term. Such transfers should be more transparent and predictable, and ideally should be based on a formula that at least partly reflects local needs. Incentive payments could also be introduced, based on solid performance indicators for the local level. The 1970 New Economic and Social Development Plan in Japan is an example of equitable funding for public services. It has been widely credited with first reducing disparities in living standards and then contributing to convergence in incomes between leading and lagging areas in Japan, through

investments in basic services and infrastructure. The central government provided both earmarked and non-earmarked transfers. The earmarked transfers were allocated mostly to investments in basic services (including rural roads) and social institutions (such as public utilities, medical facilities, and schools) and used cost-sharing agreements with local governments.

Greater coordination is needed between different levels of government and different jurisdictions, especially in the case of megacities. Uncoordinated actions by jurisdictions in a larger metropolitan area can lead to suboptimal investment in public goods, depletion of local resources (the "tragedy of the commons"), and a race to the bottom in taxes, hindering local finances. In large cities, intensive development and redevelopment of intracity areas can also help reduce the need for further expansion and the resulting extension of service networks.

Throughout this quest to reform institutions for more efficient urbanization, governments must adopt people-centered policies. This approach requires being aware of how individuals use services, their expectations for access and quality, and whether they fully appreciate the economic and health benefits of services (such as sanitation). An example of failing to incorporate the user perspective is that major roads are often designed in ways that do not respect (or they even disrupt) the nature of the settlements they cross, with deleterious consequences for road safety.

Notes

1. *Ger* is the name of Mongolian traditional tents, which in urban areas are used in peripheral and underserved areas (that is, slums).
2. See World Bank 2012, 2015b chapter 2.B, "Realizing the Economic Potential of Women," for an analysis of these issues in the case of Malaysia.
3. One-quarter of moderate poor and economically vulnerable women do not have access to potable water, and depending on the country, these shares rise significantly for the extreme poor.

4. In Lao PDR, 21 percent of rural children have never been to school (as of 2010), and the rural-urban gap in attainment of lower secondary education increased from 29 percentage points to 42 percentage points between 2000 and 2011. In Cambodia, Lao PDR, and the Solomon Islands, less than 70 percent of children who enter primary school actually complete it. In the Philippines, among adolescents who reached the end of primary school, 94 percent of those from the richest households, but only 69 percent of those from the poorest households, continued to lower secondary school (as of 2008). In Vietnam, ethnic minority students drop out in higher numbers at earlier ages than students from the Kinh majority, and are 10 times less likely to attend university. In Timor-Leste, the net secondary school enrollment rate was only 38 percent (as of 2012). In China, the gross tertiary enrollment rate reached 40 percent in 2015, but among rural and ethnic minority students, the rate is far lower and has increased slowly.

   The uneven quality of education is noticeable in achievement disparities, which start in the early grades. For example, early-grade reading assessments indicate that in Cambodia and Lao PDR, 13 percent of students in grade 3 were unable to read a single word. See World Bank (forthcoming a).
5. As shown by the Vanuatu Literacy Education Programme's Effective Literacy and Numeracy Practices Database (UNESCO 2009).
6. In 2015, 75,000 university students were enrolled through these special plans. Also, to address regional inequalities, the Collaborative Admission Plan for Supporting the Central and Western Regions arranges dedicated college matriculation quotas for universities in the eastern region to admit students from provinces of the central and western regions. This plan admitted 900,000 students during 2011–15, and the gap in college admission rates between the national average and the worst-performing provinces fell from 15 percentage points in 2010 to under 5 percentage points in 2015.
7. In China, account penetration among adults rose from 64 percent to 79 percent between 2011 and 2014, as 188 million people became first-time bank account holders. Bankcard-based rural cash withdrawal services were initiated in 2010 and subsequently expanded, with a rapid increase in debit-card issuance. In Vietnam, account penetration rose from 21 percent in 2011 to 31 percent in 2014, and the share of households that save with a formal financial institution rose from 8 percent to 15 percent.
8. For instance, significant rural-urban disparities persist with respect to the number of bank branches, ATMs, and point-of-sale terminals. In the Philippines, 36 percent of municipalities do not have a banking office, and 12 percent lack access to all financial service providers (including pawnshops, remittance agents, money changers, and mobile banking agents). These mainly remote provinces have a high concentration of poor and marginalized farmers and fishermen and are often vulnerable to natural and other disasters.
9. For instance, 68 percent of adults in Lao PDR thought they needed more information about managing money (Finmark Trust 2015).
10. In Indonesia, 48 percent of firms consider access to finance the top business environment constraint. Only about one-half of small and medium enterprises (SMEs) hold savings or checking accounts, and only 17 percent have a bank loan or line of credit (Indonesia—Enterprise Survey 2015, World Bank database, http://microdata.worldbank.org/index.php/catalog/2665). In China, the majority of SMEs consider access to finance to be the biggest obstacle to their operations and growth.
11. Health insurance covers 85 to 95 percent of the population in China, Mongolia, and the Philippines and 40 to 60 percent in Indonesia and Vietnam. Coverage is much lower in poorer countries such as Cambodia, Lao PDR, and Papua New Guinea, although efforts have been made to remove financial barriers for targeted subgroups, such as the poor, and specific services, such as maternal and child health.
12. Social health insurance was first introduced to cover formal sector workers in 1998. It expanded to the rural population in 2003 and to urban informal sector workers, the poor, children, and the elderly in 2007. As a result, the social health insurance system covered more than 95 percent of citizens in both urban and rural areas by 2011. The depth

of insurance coverage has expanded more gradually.

13. For instance, perverse provider incentives create a strong bias toward excessive treatment, including medically unnecessary high-technology services, irrational drug prescriptions (including, in particular, excessive use of antibiotics), and lengthy hospital stays (see China Joint Study Partnership 2016).

14. In China, the penetration of agricultural insurance remains extremely low despite significant fiscal subsidies, thus reflecting the high transaction costs associated with the fragmented smallholder farming system.

15. In China, only 7 percent of farming households and 6 percent of those in the poorest quintile hold any type of non–life insurance product. In Lao PDR, 77 percent of adults do not hold any kind of insurance product.

16. Across the region, tax revenues ranged from a low of 5 percent in the Federated States of Micronesia to 27 percent in Timor-Leste in 2012.

17. A recent reform proposal for China includes a comprehensive tax on capital income with a rate similar to the top marginal tax rate on labor income after allowing for corporate taxes (de Mooij, Lam, and Wingender 2017).

18. Cross-country evidence from OECD countries shows that cutting top rates did not result in higher growth, which suggests that the elasticity of labor supply in relation to income tax cannot be very high (Piketty, Saez, and Stantcheva 2014). Replicating this analysis for East Asia and Pacific also finds no relationship between growth and changes in top marginal income tax rates, although this result is difficult to interpret, because under the current schedules, the top tax rate applies to a very small number of taxpayers.

19. In the simulated schedule, more than half of workers would face a marginal tax rate of less than 5 percent, with three-quarters of workers paying an average tax rate of less than 20 percent. Under the new brackets, less than 10 percent of taxpayers face the top marginal tax rate of 45 percent, compared with 0.1 percent of taxpayers at the moment.

20. It has also been argued that a dual income tax might be easier to administer in low-capacity settings (Bird and Zolt 2011).

21. However, in China, property taxes are primarily transaction based, whereas recurrent taxes are more important in other countries.

22. For example, asset-rich, income-poor households include pensioners who live in large houses, but on relatively low incomes (pension). They could defer their tax liability until they die or sell their house—effectively this amounts to the tax being paid in the form of an equity stake in the house.

23. Note also that some East Asia and Pacific countries have quite low administration costs. For example, Indonesia has the seventh-lowest enforcement costs per unit of revenue, slightly above Norway and below the United States (Claus, Martinez-Vazquez, and Vulovic 2014).

24. For instance, see Cai and others (2012) for an analysis of poverty among the elderly in rural China.

References

Acevedo, M. C. 2015. "The Effectiveness of Ex-Ante Risk Management Strategies in Latin America and the Caribbean." Unpublished paper, World Bank, Washington, DC.

Acosta, P. 2016. *What Makes Social Protection Systems Adaptive?* https://unfccc.int/files/adaptation/application/pdf/presentation_3_pablo_acosta_-_ftc_standing_committee.pdf.

Ashraf, N., D. Karlan, and W. Yin. 2006. "Tying Odysseus to the Mast: Evidence from a Commitment Savings Product in the Philippines." *Quarterly Journal of Economics* 121 (2): 673–97.

———. 2010. "Female Empowerment: Impact of a Commitment Savings Product in the Philippines." *World Development* 38 (3): 333–44.

Baker, J., and G. Gadgil, eds. 2017. *East Asia and Pacific Cities: Expanding Opportunities for the Urban Poor.* Washington, DC: World Bank.

Bastagli, F., D. Coady, and S. Gupta. 2015. "Fiscal Redistribution in Developing Countries: Overview of Policy Issues and Options." In *Inequality and Fiscal Policy*, edited by B. Clements, R. de Mooij, S. Gupta, and M. Keen, 57–76. Washington, DC: International Monetary Fund.

Bebchuk, L. 2012. *Corporate Pyramids in the Israeli Economy: Problems and Policies.*

Report prepared for the Committee on Increasing Competitiveness in the Economy, May 2012. http://mof.gov.il/Committees /CompetitivenessCommittee/FinalReport _ExpertOpinion2.pdf.

Belfield, C. R., M. Nores, S. Barnett, and L. Schweinhart. 2006. "The High/Scope Perry Preschool Program Cost–Benefit Analysis Using Data from the Age-40 Followup." *Journal of Human Resources* 41 (1): 162–90.

Bird, R., and E. Zolt. 2011. "Dual Income Taxation: A Promising Path to Tax Reform for Developing Countries." *World Development* 39 (10): 1691–703.

Brinkman, S., A. Hasan, H. Jung, A. Kinnell, and M. P. Pradhan. 2015. "The Impact of Expanding Access to Early Childhood Services in Rural Indonesia: Evidence from Two Cohorts of Children." Policy Research Working Paper 7372, World Bank, Washington, DC.

Cai, F., J. Files, P. O'Keefe, and D. Wang. 2012. *The Elderly and Old Age Support in Rural China: Challenges and Prospects*. Washington, DC: World Bank.

China Joint Study Partnership. 2016. *Deepening Health Reform in China: Building High-Quality and Value-Based Service Delivery*. Policy summary. http://documents.worldbank. org/curated/en/800911469159433307 /Deepening-health-reform-in-China-building -high-quality-and-value-based-service-delivery -policy-summary. Washington, DC: World Bank Group.

Claus, I., J. Martinez-Vazquez, and V. Vulovic. 2014. "Government Fiscal Policies and Redistribution in Asian Countries." In *Inequality in Asia and the Pacific: Trends, Drivers, and Policy Implications*, edited by C. Rhee, J. Zhuang, and R. Kanbur. Manila: Asian Development Bank.

de los Reyes, V. R., R. Librojo, and J. L. Capacio. 2016. *Offering Guideposts for Reform Efforts: Lessons from the Agrarian Reform Program in the Philippines*. Manila: Department of Agrarian Reform.

Demirguc-Kunt, A., L. Klapper, D. Singer, and P. Van Oudheusden. 2015. *The Global Findex Database 2014: Measuring Financial Inclusion around the World*. Washington, DC: World Bank.

de Mooij, R., W. R. Lam, and P. Wingender. 2017. "Modernizing the Tax Policy Regime." In *Modernizing China: Investing in Soft Infrastructure*, edited by W. R. Lam, M. Rodlauer, and A Schipke. Washington, DC: International Monetary Fund.

Doyle, J., O. Ivaschenko, J. Kim, and J. Sibley. 2016. *Does Manna from Heaven Help? The Role of Cash Transfers in Disaster Recovery: Lessons from Tropical Cyclone Winston in Fiji*. Washington, DC: World Bank.

Erdman, J. 2016. "Tropical Cyclone Winston Makes Category 5 Landfall; Strongest on Record in Fiji." Weather Channel. February 22, 2016. https://weather.com/storms/hurricane /news/tropical-cyclone-winston-fiji-strongest -landfall.

Finmark Trust. 2015. "FinScope Consumer Survey 2014, Lao PDR." *Latest News* (blog), July 13. https://www.finmark.org.za /finscope-consumer-survey_laos-2014/.

Golan, J., T. Sicular, and N. Umapathi. 2014. *Any Guarantees? China's Rural Minimum Living Standard Guarantee Program*. Washington, DC: World Bank.

Goldin, C. 2006. "The Quiet Revolution That Transformed Women's Employment, Education, and Family." *American Economic Review: Papers and Proceedings* 96 (2): 1–21.

Hallegatte, S., A. Vogt-Schilb, M. Bangalore, and J. Rozenberg. 2017. *Unbreakable: Building the Resilience of the Poor in the Face of Natural Disasters*. Washington, DC: World Bank. doi: doi:10.1596/978-1-4648-1003-9.

Hanvoravongchai, P. 2013. "Health Financing Reform in Thailand: Toward Universal Coverage under Fiscal Constraints." Universal Health Coverage Studies Series 20. World Bank: Washington, DC.

Hasan, A., M. Hyson, and M. C. Chang, eds. 2013. *Early Childhood Education and Development in Poor Villages of Indonesia: Strong Foundations, Later Success*. Washington, DC: World Bank. http:// www-wds.worldbank.org/external/default /WDSContentServer/WDSP/IB/2013/06/17/00 0442464_20130617121704/Rendered/PDF/7 84840PUB0EPI0000PUBDATE06011020130 .pdf.

Haque, T. and T. Packard. 2014. "Well-being from Work in the Pacific Island Countries." World Bank East Asia and Pacific Regional Report. Washington, DC: World Bank.

Heckman, J. J., S. H. Moon, R. Pinto, P. A. Savelyev, and A. Yavitz. 2010. "The Rate of Return to

the High/Scope Perry Preschool Program."
Journal of Public Economics 94 (1): 114–28.

Hou, J., and X. Huo. 2016. "Property Rights Insecurity, Land Transaction Restrictions, and Welfare Loss: Empirical Evidence from Specialized Farmers in China." Paper prepared for the 17th Annual World Bank Conference on Land and Poverty, March 14–18, World Bank, Washington, DC.

Ibarraran, P., and D. Rosas. 2009. "Evaluating the Impact of Job Training Programmes in Latin America: Evidence from IDB Funded Operations." *Journal of Development Effectiveness* 1 (2): 195–216.

Indonesia—Enterprise Survey 2015, World Bank database, http://microdata.worldbank.org /index.php/catalog/2665.

Jung, H., and A. Hasan. 2014. "The Impact of Early Childhood Education on Early Achievement Gaps: Evidence from the Indonesia Early Childhood Education and Development (ECED) Project." Policy Research Working Paper 6794, World Bank, Washington, DC.

Kandel, E., K. Kosenko, R. Morck, and Y. Yafeh. 2015. "The Great Pyramids of America: A Revised History of US Business Groups, Corporate Ownership and Regulation, 1930–1950." Unpublished paper, May.

Lam, W. R., and P. Wingender. 2015. *China: How Can Revenue Reforms Contribute to Inclusive and Sustainable Growth.* Washington, DC: International Monetary Fund.

Naidoo, D., T. Packard, and I. Auwalin. 2015. *Mobility, Scarring and Job Quality in Indonesia's Labor Market.* Washington, DC: World Bank.

Narayan, D., L. Pritchett, and S. Kapoor. 2009. *Moving Out of Poverty.* Vol. 2 of *Success from the Bottom Up.* New York: Palgrave Macmillan.

Norregaard, J. 2015. "Taxing Immovable Property: Revenue Potential and Implementation Challenges." In *Inequality and Fiscal Policy*, edited by B. J. Clements, R. A. de Mooij, and S. Gupta. Washington, DC: International Monetary Fund.

Park, C.-Y. 2012. "Taxes, Social Transfers, and Inequality in Asia." Accessed June 27, 2017. https://www.imf.org/external/np/seminars /eng/2012/asiatax/pdf/park.pdf.

Piketty, T., E. Saez, and S. Stantcheva. 2014. "The Optimal Taxation of Top Labor Incomes: A

Tale of Three Elasticities." *American Economic Journal: Economic Policy* 6 (1): 230–71.

Tan, S., N. Heerink, and F. Qu. 2006. "Land Fragmention and Its Driving Forces in China." *Land Use Policy* 23: 272–85.

UNESCO (United Nations Educational, Scientific, and Cultural Organization). 2009. Vanuatu Literacy Education Programme's Effective Literacy and Numeracy Practices Database, accessed June 27, 2017. http://www.unesco .org/uil/litbase/?menu=8&programme=34.

Usui, N. 2011. "Tax Reforms toward Fiscal Consolidation: Policy Options for the Government of the Philippines." Policy note, Asian Development Bank, Manila.

Vezza, E., B. García, G. Cruces, and J. Amendolaggine. 2014. "Programa Juventud y Empleo, Ministerio de Trabajo, República Dominicana: Informe de Evaluación de Impacto Cohortes 2008–2009." Unpublished paper, World Bank, Washington, DC.

Wells-Dang, A. 2012. *Ethnic Minority Development in Vietnam: What Leads to Success?* Washington, DC: World Bank.

World Bank. 2011. *Assessment of the Social Protection System in Fiji and Recommendations for Policy Changes.* Washington, DC: World Bank.

———. 2012. *Malaysia Economic Monitor 2012: Unlocking Women's Potential.* Washington, DC: World Bank.

———. 2014a. *East Asia Pacific at Work: Employment, Enterprise, and Well-being.* Washington, DC: World Bank.

———. 2014b. *Global Financial Development Report 2014: Financial Inclusion.* Washington, DC: World Bank.

———. 2015a. *Achieving a System of Competitive Cities in Malaysia.* Washington, DC: World Bank.

———. 2015b. *Malaysia Economic Monitor 2015: Transforming Urban Transport.* Washington, DC: World Bank.

———. 2016a. *East Asia and Pacific Economic Update, October 2016: Reducing Vulnerabilities.* Washington, DC: World Bank.

———. 2016b. *Indonesia's Rising Divide.* Washington, DC: World Bank.

———. 2016c. *Live Long and Prosper: Aging in East Asia and Pacific.* Washington, DC: World Bank. doi:10.1596/978-1-4648-0469-4.

———. 2017a. *Pacific Possible: Long-term Economic Opportunities and Challenges for the Pacific Island Countries.* Washington, DC: World Bank.

———. 2017b. *Financing Pacific Governments for Pacific Development.* Washington, DC: World Bank.

———. Forthcoming a. "Growing Smarter: Learning and Growth in East Asia and the Pacific." Washington, DC: World Bank

———. Forthcoming b. *Breaking the Intergenerational Transmission of Poverty: The Philippines' Conditional Cash Transfer Program.* Washington, DC: World Bank.

World Bank and World Health Organization. 2014. *Global Civil Registration and Vital Statistics—Scaling Up Investment Plan 2015–2024.* Washington, DC: World Bank.

Yan, X. 2013. *Land Tenure Arrangements, Factor Market Development, and Agricultural Production in China: Evidence from Henan Province.* Weikersheim, Germany: Margraf.

Zhang, L., and N. Liu. 2014. "Health Reform and Out-of-Pocket Payments: Lessons from China." *Health Policy and Planning* 29 (2): 217–26.

Statistical Appendix: Poverty data availability for developing East Asia and Pacific

A

The East Asia and Pacific poverty repository hosts 75 household surveys from 19 countries (table A.1). These data are used for monitoring poverty and shared prosperity and, more broadly, can be used to identify economic class. In addition, 20-point grouped data for China are available for the following years: 2002, 2005, 2008, and 2010–13. This report relies on estimates based on the data available and approved for use by the respective National Statistical Offices as of June 2017.

The frequency with which household surveys are conducted varies across countries. National representative household surveys are conducted annually in Cambodia, Indonesia, and Thailand; every two years in Vietnam; and every three years in the Philippines. For other countries, the survey gap can be five years or more.

Country-specific notes

Cambodia

The Cambodia Socio-Economic Survey has been conducted since 1993/94. It collects information on households and individual household members.

In 2004, the survey adopted a more standardized methodology, including

survey design, questionnaire, fieldwork, and overall methodology in collecting and processing information.

Coverage of the surveys increased from 59 percent of villages in 1993/94 to 100 percent in 2004.

After the 2004 survey, Living Standards Measurement Study surveys were collected every year from 2007 through 2013. The sample sizes for the 2004 and 2009 surveys were close to 12,000 households; in other years, the sample sizes were about 3,600 households.

All of the surveys were collected over the entire year and are representative of the entire country.

China

China's population reached 1.37 billion in 2015. Between 2002 and 2015, China experienced low demographic growth of slightly above 0.5 percent per year, less than the average in the East Asia and Pacific region (0.7 percent). Given China's size, estimates of poverty and the number of poor in China greatly influence regional and global aggregates.

Estimates of poverty are typically based on analysis of household-level data from large-scale nationally representative surveys.

TABLE A.1   Available household surveys for countries in developing East Asia and Pacific

Country code	Survey name	1996	2000	2001	2002	2003	2004	2005	2006	2007	2008	2009	2010	2011	2012	2013	2014	2015
CHN*	HIES				X			X			X		X	X	X	X		
FJI	HIES				X						X			X	X	X		
FSM	HIES							X								X		
IDN	SUSENAS		X	X	X	X	X	X	X	X	X	X	X	X	X	X	X	X
KIR	HIES								X									
LAO	LECS				X					X					X			
MNG	HSES												X	X	X		X	
MYS	HIS						X			X		X			X		X	
PHL	FIES		X			X			X			X			X			X
PNG	HIES	X										X						
SLB	HIES							X								X		
THA	SES		X		X	X	X	X	X	X	X	X	X	X	X	X		
TLS	TLSS/TLSLS			X						X								
TON	HIES			X								X						
TUV	HIES												X					
VNM	VHLSS		X		X		X		X		X		X		X		X	
VUT	HIES												X					
WSM	HIES									X								

Note: * China is group data. From 2013, the survey name is Integrated Urban and Rural Household Survey; and prior to that there are two different surveys: Urban Household Survey and Rural Household Survey. HIES = Household Income and Expenditure Surveys; SUSENAS = National Socio-Economic Survey (Indonesia); LECS = Lao Expenditure and Consumption Surveys; HIS = Household Income Survey; HSES = Household Socio-Economic Surveys; FIES = Family Income and Expenditure Survey; SES = Socio-Economic Survey; TLSS/TLSLS = Timor-Leste Living Standards Survey/Timor-Leste Survey of Living Standards; VHLSS = Vietnam Household Living Standards Surveys.

China's National Bureau of Statistics has never given the World Bank access to the household-level data from its nationally representative large-scale household surveys.

The World Bank's poverty estimates for China are based on grouped data, which is information on mean per capita consumption levels for groups of the population equally spaced across the distribution. The 20-point grouped data are available for urban and rural areas separately.

The grouped data have been made available to the World Bank with a lag of three years. For example, the grouped data from 2013 household surveys were made available in the first quarter of 2016.

Grouped data for China are available every three years from early 2000s (2002, 2005, 2008) and each year since 2010 (2010, 2011, 2012, and 2013). A survey break occurred in 2013, so these estimates are not comparable with the previous ones.

Fiji

The Fiji Island Bureau of Statistics (FIBOS) conducted a nationwide Household Income and Expenditure Surveys (HIES) in 2002/03, 2008/09, and 2013/14.

The survey is nationally representative for urban and rural areas, divisions, and strata, and the sample was drawn from the 1996 and 2007 population censuses according to a two-stage, stratified, random sampling design. Data collection is continuous over a 12-month period.

The survey sample size was 5,245 households in 2002/03; 3,573 in 2008/09; and 6,020 in 2013/14.

Indonesia

Indonesia's National Socio-Economic Survey (SUSENAS) is carried out regularly by the Central Bureau of Statistics (BPS). The first SUSENAS was conducted in 1963. Since 1992, SUSENAS has been collecting two different types of data: core data and module data. Module data contain more detailed information.

In 2005–10, SUSENAS was conducted biannually—every February and July (2005–06) and then every March and July (2007–10).

From 2011 to 2014, SUSENAS was conducted quarterly: in March, June, September, and December. In 2011, the survey underwent major changes in the sampling methodology, level of representativeness, and weighting because of the availability of 2010 census data.

Beginning with 2015, the surveys have been conducted twice a year, in March and September. In 2015, BPS instituted several changes: (a) reducing the number of food items in the consumption module from 255 to 100; (b) changing the sample frame to stratify primary sampling units by wealth levels instead of by education levels; (c) dropping the quarterly approach and returning to biannual sampling (March and September); and (d) increasing the sample to 300,000 households.

Overall, SUSENAS uses a two-stage sampling method: selecting census blocks and selecting households within each designated census block. The Probability Proportional to Size (PPS) method is used when selecting census blocks from the Master Sampling Frame (MSF), which can be obtained from the population census.

SUSENAS is conducted in all areas in Indonesia, with a variety of sample sizes. For measuring poverty, the February (2002–07) or March (2008–15) rounds are used. The sample size is varied each year. In 2000 and 2001, the sample size was about 200,000 households; about 10,000 households from 2002 to 2006; between 66,000 and 72,000 from 2007 to 2014; and 286,000 in 2015.

Lao People's Democratic Republic

The Lao Statistics Bureau has conducted the Lao Expenditure and Consumption Surveys (LECS) at five-year intervals since 1992/93. The fifth and most recent round (LECS 5) was implemented between April 2012 and March 2013.

LECS 5 is a nationally representative survey designed to generate representative poverty estimates at national and provincial levels. The sizes of survey samples were 8,092 (2002); 8,296 (2007); and 8,226 (2012). All surveys are comparable.

Malaysia

The Household Income Survey (HIS) is carried out by the Departments of Statistics, Malaysia. Since 1973, the HIS has been carried out twice in five years, that is, two surveys within each Malaysia Development Plan period.

The main objectives of the HIS are to measure the economic well-being of the population; to collect information on income distribution patterns of households, classified by various socioeconomic characteristics; and to provide the base data for the calculation of the poverty line income.

Mongolia

The National Statistical Office of Mongolia conducted Household Socio-Economic Surveys (HSES) in 2010, 2011, 2012, and 2014.

All surveys are nationally representative and cover the whole of Mongolia. They aim to evaluate and monitor the income and expenditure of households, update the basket and weights for the consumer price index, and provide inputs to the national accounts. The HSES covers a 12-month period for analysis.

All available surveys (2010, 2011, 2012, and 2014) are comparable.

Papua New Guinea

The first Papua New Guinea Household Survey (PNGHS) was undertaken in 1996, with a total sample of 1,144 households. The fieldwork for PNGHS was staggered over the full calendar year to allow for any seasonality.

The samples were drawn from enumeration areas of the 1990 census, using stratified sampling (15 strata).

All poverty estimates from the 1996 survey took account of the clustered, stratified, and weighted nature of the sample.

The 2009/10 Household Income and Expenditure Survey (HIES) conducted by the National Statistical Office of Papua New Guinea ran from June 2009 until January 2011. One-third of interviews were in 2009, two-thirds in 2010, and less than 2 percent in January 2011.

The total sample of the 2009/10 HIES was 3,600 households from 10 strata, which covered rural and urban sectors in the four regions (Southern, Highlands, Momase, and Islands), along with the metro area.

The 1996 and 2009/10 surveys are not comparable.

The Philippines

The Family Income and Expenditure Survey (FIES) is a nationwide survey of households undertaken every three years by the National Statistics Office (NSO). It is the main source of data on family income and expenditure.

The FIES is designed to provide income and expenditure data that are nationally and regionally representative.

The survey used four replicates of the 2003 Master Sample (MS) created for household surveys on the basis of the 2000 Census of Population and Housing.

The 2003 MS was designed to produce the sample size needed for large surveys like the FIES. To facilitate subsampling, the 2003 MS was designed to readily produce four replicate samples from the full set of sampled primary sampling units.

The FIES enumeration is conducted twice. The first visit is done in July, covering the first semester (January to June) as the reference period; the second visit is made in January of the succeeding year, covering the second semester of the reference year (July to December). The same set of questions is asked in both visits.

The sample size for each FIES is about 40,000 households: 39,615 (2000); 42,094 (2003); 38,483 (2006); 38,400 (2009); 40,171 (2012); and 41,544 (2015).

All FIES results are comparable.

Thailand

The National Statistical Office (NSO) conducted its first survey on household income and expenditure, the Household Expenditure Survey, in 1957. In 1968/69, the title was changed to Socio-Economic Survey (SES), and that survey was conducted every five years until 1986.

In 1986, NSO was requested to conduct the SES every two years, to keep up with the country's economic circumstances and rapid expansion, as well as with data needs for policy planning and the formulation of poverty reduction strategies.

After the economic crisis in 1997, NSO conducted special rounds of the SES in 1999 and 2001 to measure the impact of the crisis on the Thai population.

Since 2006, the SES has been conducted annually. In even-numbered years, income, expenditure, and debt are surveyed, and in odd-numbered years, only expenditure is surveyed.

Timor-Leste

The first national Timor-Leste Living Standards Survey (TLSS) was undertaken in 2001 from August to November. The 2001 TLSS had a modest, though nationally representative, sample of 1,800 households covering 1 percent of the population.

The second national Timor-Leste Survey of Living Standards (TLSLS) took place from January 2007 to January 2008, with a sample of 4,500 households.

The 2001 and 2007 surveys are comparable.

The latest survey available is the TLSLS 2014, but the data had not been cleared for public use at the time of writing.

Vietnam

Vietnam carried out Living Standards Surveys (VLSS) in 1992/93 and 1997/98, with extensive technical support from international partners. Then the government financed a series of Vietnam Household Living Standards Surveys (VHLSS) every other year (2002, 2004, 2006, 2008) using an approach that was similar to the earlier VLSS. The main objective was to maintain comparability over time.

Strict comparability came at too high a cost, however. The 2010 VHLSS used a new master sample based on the 2009 Housing and Population Census, including a new set of communes and enumeration areas. The VHLSS household questionnaire was substantially revised (including revisions to the core consumption module) and shortened. In addition, an updated methodology was used to construct a more comprehensive consumption (welfare) aggregate. As a result, the 2010 VHLSS and related welfare aggregates represent a break with the 2002–08 VHLSS series.

Pacific Island Countries

Among Pacific Island countries, survey data are available from Kiribati, the Federated States of Micronesia, Samoa, the Solomon Islands, Tonga, Tuvalu, and Vanuatu.

The Federated States of Micronesia, the Solomon Islands, and Tonga have two data points, and the remaining countries have a single data point. The average gap between surveys is about eight years.

The two surveys in each country—the Federated States of Micronesia, the Solomon Islands, and Tonga—are not comparable.

Statistical Appendix: Methodology for the estimation of internationally comparable poverty estimates for East Asia

This appendix describes briefly the main element of the methodology adopted to measure poverty, namely, the use of welfare aggregates for the analysis and for the construction of internationally comparable annual data series.

With the exception of the application of different thresholds, the same methodological considerations apply to the measurement of economic classes.

Constructing internationally comparable welfare aggregates

Either consumption or income can be used as a measure of welfare. Most countries in developing East Asia and Pacific report their official poverty measures on the basis of consumption. Only Malaysia and the Philippines use income.

For monitoring poverty, the World Bank mostly employs the official welfare aggregates used by countries for calculating the national poverty rate. Official sources provide the consumption and income aggregates in either nominal (non–spatially deflated) terms or

spatially deflated terms, and occasionally in both forms. Methodologies vary by country. China, Indonesia, and Mongolia, for example, release data that are already spatially adjusted, whereas other countries do not. The more diverse and vast a country, the more the spatial adjustments will affect poverty estimates.

The East Asia and Pacific Poverty estimates, available from 2002 onward,[1] adopt as spatial deflators the ratio of location-specific poverty lines (urban/rural, regional, provincial) to the national poverty line. This deflation is applied to most East Asia and Pacific countries' nominal welfare aggregate, with the exception of Thailand's and the Solomon Islands' aggregates. Thailand produces household-level poverty lines that are adjusted for demographics and economies of scale. In the Solomon Islands, the food poverty line in the rural areas is underestimated compared with urban areas. Using a comparison between the two lines to construct a spatial deflator would significantly underestimate rural poverty incidence.

In addition to spatial deflation, adjustments are also sometimes performed over time, even within a given survey period.[2]

Producing regional poverty estimates

The welfare indicator obtained after the spatial and temporal adjustment previously described is expressed as per capita household consumption and income in annual terms. Those are then translated into purchasing power parity (PPP) terms to reflect purchasing power differences across countries and compared with the international poverty lines (or the relevant class thresholds).

The international poverty lines—originally proposed by the World Bank in 1990 to facilitate poverty comparisons across countries—in 2011 PPP stand at US$1.90 a day for extreme poverty. The East Asia and Pacific region of the World Bank has traditionally adopted a higher poverty line to capture moderate poverty. Such a line is currently estimated at US$3.10. These lines are the basis for poverty measurement across the region.

Regional poverty rates are obtained as population-weighted averages of country-specific poverty rates using the international poverty lines at 2011 PPP prices.

Constructing the internationally comparable annual series of poverty headcounts and number of poor people living in poverty

The annual series of poverty estimates presented in this report reflect a combination of

- Actual-year data for which the estimates are calculated on the basis of available survey data (table A.1) and
- Estimates for other years based on *interpolation* (that is, constructing estimates for years between those for which household survey data are available to directly estimate poverty) and *extrapolation* (that is, projecting beyond the most recent year for which survey data are available).

The interpolated and extrapolated estimates are obtained on the basis of available household survey estimates and the growth elasticity of poverty (GEP) to gross domestic product (GDP). The GEP is the percentage reduction in poverty rates associated with a percentage change in mean per capita income. It is estimated, as follows:

- For the interpolations, the GEP is estimated between the two closest available surveys before and after the missing year (the interpolation period). The GEP is then applied to the poverty estimate obtained from the last household survey before the missing year, using known changes in GDP per capita.
- For the extrapolations, two methods are used. In the first method, applied to countries for which at least two surveys are available, the GEP estimated from two previous surveys and annualized is applied to the latest available survey, using known changes in GDP per capita. If the projections relate to the future rather than to known GDP per capita changes, the second method uses projected GDP per capita. In the second method, a neutral shift in the distribution is assumed. This method is used in countries for which only one data point is available and in China. In the case of China, the extrapolation applies the distribution obtained from 20 grouped data points.

For the projections used in this report, GDP per capita for the years 2016 through 2018 is obtained from World Bank simulation models; for the years from 2019 through 2021, it is obtained from the World Economic Outlook of the International Monetary Fund (IMF). Longer-term projections through 2030 make the assumption that GDP growth from 2021 is constant.

Finally, the ratio of the number of poor to the total population in the region is used to obtain regional poverty numbers from the headcounts calculated based on the methodology just described. Total population estimates and projections are derived from the World Bank's Health Nutrition and Population Statistics database. Data are received from the World Bank's Development Data Group, which updates and publishes them twice a year, in April and July.

A note of caution: the regional estimates presented in this report may not compare with those published in PovcalNet (http://iresearch

.worldbank.org/PovcalNet/povOnDemand
.aspx) because of methodological differences
relating to spatial cost-of-living differences
and the ways estimates are interpolated.

Notes

1. Longer time series presented in this report
   are provided by PovcalNet, http://iresearch
   .worldbank.org/PovcalNet/povOnDemand
   .aspx.

2. *Nominal* in the context of this note refers
   to non–spatially adjusted. In addition,
   the concept of *over time* refers to the
   months during which a particular survey is
   undertaken, not the years in the macro-GDP
   sense of real GDP. Some national statistics
   offices not only make a spatial adjustment
   but also make a temporal adjustment of
   household incomes and consumption to a
   particular month of the year (or to a yearly
   average) for a given survey.

Statistical Appendix: Supplementary tables | C

TABLE C.1   **Growth rates in developing East Asia and Pacific, 1960–2015**

	1960–69 (%)	1970–79 (%)	1980–89 (%)	1990–99 (%)	2000–07 (%)	2008–15 (%)
East Asia and Pacific	8.9	5.0	5.3	3.7	4.6	4.0
Japan	10.4	4.1	4.4	1.5	1.5	0.2
NIEs	7.8	10.3	8.3	6.3	5.3	3.1
Hong Kong SAR, China	4.5	9.0	7.4	3.6	5.3	2.6
Korea, Rep.	8.3	10.5	8.6	6.7	5.4	3.1
Singapore	8.9	9.5	7.8	7.3	6.5	4.4
Taiwan, China	9.9	10.9	8.5	6.6	4.9	2.8
Developing EAP	3.9	7.3	7.7	8.2	9.1	7.8
Cambodia	…	…	…	7.2	9.6	6.1
China	3.0	7.4	9.8	10.0	10.5	8.6
Indonesia	3.7	7.8	6.4	4.8	5.1	5.6
Lao PDR	…	…	4.1	6.3	6.7	7.9
Malaysia	6.5	7.7	5.9	7.2	5.6	4.6
Mongolia	…	…	6.0	−0.3	6.6	8.2
Myanmar	3.0	4.4	1.9	6.1	12.9	7.9
Papua New Guinea	6.4	3.9	1.4	4.3	2.2	7.7
Philippines	5.1	5.8	2.0	2.8	4.9	5.3
Thailand	7.8	7.5	7.3	5.2	5.3	2.9
Vietnam	…	…	4.5	7.4	6.9	5.9
ECA	…	…	2.2	−0.4	6.1	2.8
LAC	6.1	6.9	2.5	2.7	3.5	2.9
MNA	9.5	5.5	1.5	4.2	4.8	2.3
SAR	4.1	3.0	5.6	5.4	6.7	6.5
SSA	4.6	4.0	1.7	1.9	5.1	4.1

Source: World Bank World Development Indicators (database), https://data.worldbank.org/data-catalog/world-development-indicators; IMF, World Economic Outlook Database, https://www.imf.org/external/pubs/ft/weo/2017/01/weodata/index.aspx.
Note: Values for regional aggregates denote GDP-weighted means. EAP = East Asia and Pacific; ECA = Europe and Central Asia; GDP = gross domestic product; LAC = Latin America and the Caribbean; MNA = Middle East and North Africa; NIE = newly industrialized economy; SAR = South Asia; SSA = Sub-Saharan Africa; … = missing.

TABLE C.2   Tax revenue in developing East Asia and Pacific, percentage of GDP, 2013

	Taxes	Taxes on income, profits, and capital gains (%)	Taxes on payroll and workforce (%)	Taxes on property (%)	Taxes on goods and services (%)	Taxes on international trade and transactions (%)	Other taxes (%)	GDP per capita (US$, 2011 PPP)
East Asia and Pacific	15.7	5.2	0.2	0.0	7.0	3.1	0.3	11,375
East Asia	14.2	5.6	0.0	0.0	7.5	1.6	0.3	11,130
Cambodia	13.6	2.9	0.0	0.0	7.9	2.8	0.0	2,955
China	10.6	2.9	0.0	0.0	7.2	0.5	0.0	11,805
Indonesia	13.0	5.6	0.0	0.0	5.4	0.5	1.5	9,675
Lao PDR	16.1	3.0	0.0	0.1	11.1	1.9	0.0	4,800
Malaysia	14.8	10.5	0.0	0.0	3.0	0.4	0.9	23,419
Mongolia	17.2	3.8	0.0	0.0	11.2	2.2	0.1	10,757
Myanmar	7.1	…	…	…	…	…	…	…
Philippines	13.6	6.4	0.0	0.0	4.5	2.7	0.0	6,365
Thailand	16.9	7.4	0.0	0.0	8.5	0.9	0.1	14,943
Timor-Leste	1.6	0.6	0.0	0.0	0.8	0.2	0.0	2,039
Vietnam	19.1	7.7	0.0	0.0	8.8	2.2	0.3	5,125
Pacific Island countries	18.7	5.8	0.3	0.1	7.3	5.0	0.3	4,997
Fiji	24.6	6.0	0.0	0.0	13.1	5.5	0.0	7,897
Kiribati	14.9	3.8	2.5	0.0	0.0	8.6	0.0	1,694
Marshall Islands	17.3	6.8	0.0	0.2	6.0	4.2	0.1	3,671
Micronesia, Fed. Sts.	5.2	2.5	0.0	0.0	1.5	1.2	0.1	3,300
Palau	18.9	3.3	0.5	0.0	7.9	4.6	2.7	13,152
Samoa	23.3	5.6	0.0	0.2	14.7	2.9	0.0	5,499
Solomon Islands	29.5	9.8	0.0	0.3	7.5	11.9	0.0	2,043
Tonga	17.0	3.1	0.0	0.0	12.0	1.9	0.0	4,888
Tuvalu	18.9	11.3	0.0	0.0	3.0	4.5	0.0	3,528
Vanuatu	17.2	…	…	…	…	…	…	2,890
ECA	18.3	4.4	0.0	0.0	12.0	1.6	0.2	13,501
LAC	17.5	5.4	0.0	0.2	9.2	2.3	0.3	13,731
MNA	14.2	4.3	0.0	0.6	7.8	1.1	0.4	11,574
SAR	12.9	4.4	0.0	0.0	5.8	2.3	0.4	5,067
SSA	21.7	7.9	0.1	0.1	7.1	6.2	0.3	3,324

Source: International Monetary Fund, Government Finance Statistics Yearbook and data files, http://data.imf.org/?sk=E86E9088-3830-4CA3-B240-1B0EC5E15221.
Note: Data refer to 2013, except for China (2011) and Indonesia (2007). ECA = Europe and Central Asia; GDP = gross domestic product; LAC = Latin America and the Caribbean; MNA = Middle East and North Africa; PPP = purchasing power parity; SAR = South Asia; SSA = Sub-Saharan Africa; … = missing.

TABLE C.3   **Access to basic services in developing East Asia and Pacific, 2015**

	Primary school enrollment[a]	Secondary school enrollment[a]	Access to sanitation[b] (%)	Access to improved water[c] (%)	Access to telecom[d]	Access to Internet[e]	GDP per capita[f]
East Asia and Pacific	100.5	83.1	74.8	93.6	13.4	44.9	12,308
Cambodia	97.4	38.2	42.4	75.5	1.6	19.0	3,278
China	103.9	94.3	76.5	95.5	16.5	50.3	13,572
Indonesia	89.7	75.0	60.8	87.4	8.8	22.0	10,385
Lao PDR	95.1	50.8	70.9	75.7	13.7	18.2	5,345
Malaysia	94.6	69.1	96.0	98.2	14.3	71.1	25,312
Mongolia	94.9	86.3	59.7	64.4	8.7	21.4	11,478
Myanmar	94.5	48.3	79.6	80.6	1.0	21.8	4,931
Philippines	96.0	67.4	73.9	91.8	3.0	40.7	6,938
Thailand	92.4	79.6	93.0	97.8	7.9	39.3	15,347
Vietnam	98.0	...	78.0	97.6	6.3	52.7	5,667
Fiji	95.1	83.4	91.1	95.7	8.1	46.3	8,756
Kiribati	96.4	69.1	39.7	66.9	1.4	13.0	1,873
Micronesia, Fed. Sts.	83.0	...	57.1	89.0	6.5	31.5	3,284
Palau	99.0	95.2	100.0	95.3	33.8	27.0	14,386
Papua New Guinea	86.0	...	18.9	40.0	2.0	7.9	2,723
Samoa	96.1	79.5	91.5	99.0	5.6	25.4	5,574
Solomon Islands	80.7	42.2	29.8	80.8	1.3	10.0	2,067
Timor-Leste	96.6	51.8	40.6	71.9	0.2	13.4	2,253
Tonga	87.2	75.4	91.0	99.6	12.4	45.0	5,198
Tuvalu	84.6	69.8	83.3	97.7	20.2	42.7	3,687
Vanuatu	98.9	51.6	57.9	94.5	1.8	22.4	2,806
ECA	92.4	86.7	94.1	94.8	21.4	42.9	13,224
LAC	91.8	73.7	81.0	93.8	17.8	42.6	13,938
MNA	95.6	71.5	88.0	89.7	16.1	31.2	11,728
SAR	89.6	51.4	29.6	64.6	1.3	14.7	3,259
SSA	77.1	33.2	39.8	91.2	2.6	11.6	4,635
World	89.1	65.5	63.6	89.3	16.7	35.6	13,682

Sources: World Bank World Development Indicators (database), https://data.worldbank.org/data-catalog/world-development-indicators; national statistical authorities.
Note: Data for EAP refer to 2015, with the following exceptions. Primary school enrollment refers to 2014, except Fiji (2013), Malaysia (2012), Papua New Guinea (2012), the Philippines (2013), Solomon Islands (2007), Vanuatu (2005), and Vietnam (2013). Secondary school enrollment refers to 2014, except Cambodia (2008), Fiji (2012), Kiribati (2005), Palau (2013), Solomon Islands (2012), the Philippines (2013), Thailand (2012), Vanuatu (2010), and South Asia (2008). Access to sanitation: Tuvalu (2013). Access to improved water: Palau (2011). Access to Internet: Palau (2004). GDP per capita: Papua New Guinea (2014). Data for all other regions and the world refer to 2012. Regional aggregates denote population-weighted means. ECA = Europe and Central Asia; GDP = gross domestic product; LAC = Latin America and the Caribbean; MNA = Middle East and North Africa; SAR = South Asia; SSA = Sub-Saharan Africa; . . . = missing.
a. Net enrollment, except gross enrollment for China.
b. Access to improved sanitation facilities refers to the percentage of the population using improved sanitation facilities. These include flush/pour flush (to piped sewer system, septic tank, pit latrine), ventilated improved pit (VIP) latrine, pit latrine with slab, and composting toilet.
c. Access to improved water is defined as the percentage of the population using improved drinking water sources. These include piped water on premises (piped household water connection located inside the user's dwelling, plot, or yard), and other improved drinking water sources (public taps or standpipes, tube wells or boreholes, protected dug wells, protected springs, and rainwater collection).
d. Access to telecom refers to the sum of active analog fixed telephone lines, voice-over-IP (VoIP) subscriptions, fixed wireless local loop (WLL) subscriptions, ISDN voice-channel equivalents, and fixed public payphones, per 100 people.
e. Access to Internet is defined as the number of individuals who have used the Internet (from any location) in the last 12 months per 100 people. Internet can be used via a computer, mobile phone, personal digital assistant, games machine, digital TV, and so on.
f. GDP per capita, purchasing power parity (PPP) in constant 2011 US$.

TABLE C.4   Access to sanitation and improved water in developing East Asia and Pacific, rural versus urban, 2012

	Access to sanitation[a] (%)		Access to improved water[b] (%)	
	Rural	Urban	Rural	Urban
East Asia and Pacific	57.8	75.9	84.5	97.3
Cambodia	26.4	79.9	62.9	91.9
China	60.9	84.4	88.5	97.5
Indonesia	45.5	71.4	77.2	93.6
Lao PDR	50.5	90.4	64.9	83.7
Malaysia	95.4	96.1	92.4	100.0
Mongolia	39.2	66.1	53.8	68.0
Myanmar	77.1	84.3	74.4	92.7
Philippines	67.8	76.8	88.7	93.4
Thailand	96.1	89.9	96.8	97.5
Vietnam	64.8	90.8	91.9	98.0
Fiji	88.4	93.4	91.2	99.5
Kiribati	30.6	51.2	50.6	87.4
Marshall Islands	55.5	84.2	97.5	93.4
Micronesia, Fed. Sts.	49.0	85.1	87.4	94.8
Palau	100.0	100.0	86.0	97.0
Papua New Guinea	13.3	56.4	32.8	88.0
Samoa	91.1	93.3	98.8	97.4
Solomon Islands	15.0	81.4	77.2	93.2
Timor-Leste	26.8	69.0	60.5	95.2
Tonga	89.4	97.6	99.5	99.2
Tuvalu	80.2	86.3	97.0	98.3
Vanuatu	55.4	65.1	88.4	98.3
ECA	90.9	96.8	88.9	98.6
LAC	62.3	86.1	82.3	97.1
MNA	80.2	93.5	82.7	94.6
SAR	22.6	40.7	52.6	85.8
SSA	29.9	61.1	89.2	95.4
World	46.5	79.3	81.5	96.5

Source: World Bank World Development Indicators (database), https://data.worldbank.org/data-catalog/world-development-indicators.
Note: All data refer to 2012, except for access to improved water in rural Palau (2011). Regional aggregates denote population-weighted means.
ECA = Europe and Central Asia; LAC = Latin America and the Caribbean; MNA = Middle East and North Africa; SAR = South Asia; SSA = Sub-Saharan Africa.
a. Access to sanitation is defined as the percentage of the population with access to improved sanitation facilities, including flush/pour flush (to piped sewer system, septic tank, pit latrine), ventilated improved pit latrine, pit latrine with slab, and composting toilet.
b. Access to improved water is defined as the percentage of the population with access to an improved drinking water source, including piped water and other improved drinking water sources (public taps, standpipes, tube wells, boreholes, protected dug wells, protected springs, and rainwater collection).

TABLE C.5 **Percentage of self-reported membership in different organizations, by economic security status**

Organization	PHL		THA		MYS		CHN	
	NS	S	NS	S	NS	S	NS	S
Religious	60	55	43	25	37	24	7	4
Sporting	34	24	34	23	23	13	11	9
Arts, music, education	24	21	32	17	20	9	9	7
Labor union	21	14	18	11	20	14	7	8
Political party	22	16	17	10	24	15	7	9
Environmental	29	21	24	14	16	7	3	2
Professional association	18	19	22	14	13	6	3	2
Humanitarian/charity	30	24	22	16	17	10	3	1
Consumer	20	13	22	12	15	9	4	1
Self-help or mutual aid	18	13	61	53	16	8	4	3
Other	20	20	16	10	9	5	1	1

Source: Wai Poi and others 2016 using World Values Survey data from Wave 6, 2010–14.
Note: Economic security is defined here on the basis of answers to the World Values Survey rather than on economic welfare as in the rest of the report. More specifically, the secure are those who never went without enough food in the past year, never or rarely went without medical treatment they needed in the past year, and did not deplete savings ("saved money" or "just got by") in the past year. For Thailand, only two of the criteria have to be met. This adjustment was made to ensure that the definition of security is roughly consistent with the economic definition obtained by household survey data. CHN = China; MYS = Malaysia; NS = nonsecure; PHL = Philippines; S = secure; THA = Thailand.

TABLE C.6 **Percentage of self-reported lack of confidence in public institutions, by economic security status**

Institution	PHL		THA		MYS		CHN	
	NS	S	NS	S	NS	S	NS	S
Churches	6	5	19	27	12	8	72	76
Army	28	36	21	32	20	20	10	6
Press	33	33	44	59	35	31	34	28
Television	26	24	39	50	32	29	30	26
Labor unions	48	57	50	56	28	21	37	33
Police	31	42	46	54	26	26	31	23
Courts	34	38	20	25	21	20	24	17
Government	41	50	41	48	23	25	10	7
Political parties	53	55	59	63	41	37	20	12
Parliament	42	43	46	55	37	30	18	10
Civil service	34	39	34	41	23	22	26	20
Universities	22	18	9	14	20	15	13	9
Major corporations	36	35	32	40	33	24	36	31
Banks	23	26	14	16	23	18	16	11

Sources: Wai Poi and others 2016 using World Values Survey data from Wave 6, 2010–14.
Note: Economic security is defined here on the basis of answers to the World Values Survey rather than on economic welfare as in the rest of the report. More specifically, the secure are those who never went without enough food in the past year, never or rarely went without medical treatment they needed in the past year, and did not deplete savings ("saved money" or "just got by") in the past year. For Thailand, only two of the criteria have to be met. This adjustment was made to ensure that the definition of security is roughly consistent with the economic definition obtained by household survey data. Respondents were asked how much confidence they had in each institution. They could choose "a great deal," "quite a lot," "not a lot," or "not at all." Lack of confidence as measured in the table reflects the last two answers combined. CHN = China; MYS = Malaysia; NS = nonsecure; PHL = Philippines; S = secure; THA = Thailand.

TABLE C.7   Indicators of financial inclusion, percentage of population age 15 and above, 2014

Country	Account in formal institution					Formal savings					Formal borrowing				
	All	Female	Rural	Poor	LE	All	Female	Rural	Poor	LE	All	Female	Rural	Poor	LE
Cambodia	12.6	10.7	11.4	8.8	10.5	3.6	2.6	3.0	2.7	3.1	27.7	29.4	28.5	25.8	29.3
China	78.9	76.4	74.3	72.0	72.8	41.1	41.2	37.5	30.5	37.1	9.6	8.7	7.5	5.9	7.1
Indonesia	35.9	37.2	28.5	21.9	15.8	26.6	26.8	21.3	13.8	11.0	13.1	11.2	11.4	11.3	9.5
Malaysia	80.7	78.1	73.7	75.6	58.6	33.8	32.3	32.6	25.6	22.3	19.5	16.6	17.0	15.2	9.5
Philippines	28.1	33.9	24.6	14.9	15.2	14.8	15.9	11.2	4.9	6.2	11.8	13.6	12.2	8.2	7.7
Thailand	78.1	75.4	78.2	72.0	73.2	40.6	37.9	35.8	31.3	38.1	15.4	13.7	16.7	16.2	14.7
Vietnam	30.9	31.9	27.0	18.7	15.3	14.6	13.7	11.9	9.1	9.0	18.4	21.3	20.7	19.9	24.8

Source: Global Findex 2014 database, http://www.worldbank.org/en/programs/globalfindex.
Note: All = all adults; Female = females; Rural = rural population; Poor = lowest 40 percent of income distribution; LE = least educated—primary only.

Reference

Wai-Poi, M., R. Purnamasari, T. Indrakesuma, I. Uochi, and L. Wijaya. 2016. "East Asia's Rising Middle Classes." Background paper for *Riding the Wave: An East Asian Miracle for the 21st Century*. Washington, DC: World Bank.

Statistical Appendix: A profile of economic class in developing East Asia and Pacific

D

TABLE D.1 Key socioeconomic characteristics of the various economic classes

	Extreme poor	Moderate poor	Economically vulnerable	Economically secure	Middle class	Rich
Population and consumption shares	Less than 3 percent of population	10 percent of population	about one quarter of the population	about half of population	about 17 percent of population	less than half a percentage point of population
Location	Predominantly rural—31 percent living in urban areas	Predominantly rural—35 percent living in urban areas	Mostly rural—39 percent living in urban areas	Slightly more urban than rural (51 percent) and about the same as the regional average	Predominantly urban—70 percent living in urban areas	Predominantly urban—78 percent living in urban areas
Transport	Almost no access to private modes of transport, such as motorcycles or cars	Limited access to private modes of transport	Less likely to have access to private modes of transport	More likely to have access to private modes of transport than lower economic classes; motorcycle ownership (72 percent) more common than car ownership (9 percent)	Car ownership (28 percent) much lower than motorcycle ownership (67 percent)	The only class for which car ownership (70 percent) is higher than motorcycle ownership (48 percent)
Education	Education level 4 years: among 3- to 4-year-olds, 14 percent are in school (about half the EAP average); after enrollment gap closes for 7- to 12-year-olds, it reemerges by adolescence—for those ages 13–15, 75 percent are in school (compared with the EAP average of 88 percent).	Education level 5.2 years: among 3- to 4-year-olds, 18 percent are in school; after enrollment gap closes by adolescence—for those ages 13–15, 83.6 percent are in school.	Education level 6 years: among 3- to 4-year-olds, 24 percent are in school (lower than the regional average of 28 percent); for ages 7–12, 98 percent (over the regional average) are in school; and in adolescence (ages 13–15), in contrast to the extreme and moderate poor, children of this group are no longer behind the average, with 90 percent in school.	Above-average human capital; education level 8 years: among 3- to 4-year-olds, 43 percent are in school; for ages 7–12, almost all children (97 percent) are enrolled; and in adolescence (ages 13–15), 94 percent of the economically secure are in school.	Education level 10 years; among 3- to 4-year-olds, 55 percent are in school; for ages 7–12, almost all children (97 percent) are enrolled; and in adolescence (ages 13–15), enrollment rates are virtually constant at 97 percent, in contrast to the lower classes.	Education level 13 years—almost twice the average for the region; in contrast to most other classes, enrollment rates are relatively constant over the life cycle; among 3- to 4-year-olds, 86 percent are enrolled; for ages 7–12, almost all are enrolled (99 percent); and in adolescence (ages 13–15), enrollment rates are almost constant (98 percent).

table continues on next page

STATISTICAL APPENDIX D 123

TABLE D.1 Key socioeconomic characteristics of the various economic classes *(continued)*

	Extreme poor	Moderate poor	Economically vulnerable	Economically secure	Middle class	Rich
Access to basic services	33 percent lack access to clean water; 36 percent lack access to improved sanitation (compared with 17 and 15 percent for EAP, respectively). 65 percent lack access to proper housing (33 percent EAP average). 78 percent have access to electricity (91 regional average).	24 percent of the moderate poor lack access to clean water; 27 percent lack access to improved sanitation. 54 percent lack access to proper housing. 87 percent of the moderate poor have access to electricity.	20 percent of the economically vulnerable lack access to clean water; 19 percent lack access to improved sanitation. 42 percent do not have access to proper housing. 91 percent have access to electricity.	16 percent lack access to clean water; 6 percent lack access to improved sanitation. 24 percent lack access to proper housing. 96 percent have access to electricity.	6 percent lack access to clean water; 0.9 percent lack access to improved sanitation. 10 percent lack access to proper housing. 98 percent have access to electricity.	4 percent lack access to clean water; 0.3 percent lack access to improved sanitation. 5 percent do not have access to proper housing. 99 percent have access to electricity.
Employment	For youth ages 15–24, 32 percent are neither in school nor gainfully employed (compared with the EAP average of 19 percent).	For youth ages 15–24, 29 percent are neither in school nor gainfully employed. The unemployment rate (for those ages 15–64 who are no longer in school) is 4 percent (4 percent of EAP on average).	For youth ages 15–24, 22 percent are neither in school nor gainfully employed. The unemployment rate (for those ages 15–64 who are no longer in school) is 3 percent. Self-employment rates among the extreme poor, the moderate poor, and the economically vulnerable are about 50–60 percent.	For youth ages 15–24, 15 percent are neither in school nor gainfully employed. The unemployment rate (for those ages 15–64 who are no longer in school) is 4 percent. Self-employment rates among the economically secure are equal to about one-third.	For youth ages 15–24, 9 percent are neither in school nor gainfully employed. The unemployment rate (for those ages 15–64 who are no longer in school) is 4 percent. Self-employment rates are about one-third.	For youth ages 15–24, 10 percent are neither in school nor gainfully employed. The unemployment rate (for those ages 15–64 who are no longer in school) is 3 percent. Self-employment rates equal about 15 percent.

Source: World Bank, East Asia and Pacific Team for Statistical Development.
Note: Data on the rich refer to the group living on more than US$50 2011 PPP a day. Given the overall small coverage of this group in household surveys, these data are presented for comparative purposes only. EAP = East Asia and Pacific.

www.ingramcontent.com/pod-product-compliance
Lightning Source LLC
Chambersburg PA
CBHW061151030426

42336CB00002B/17